HANDBOOK

OF THE

RUSSIAN ARMY.

1940

GENERAL STAFF, WAR OFFICE.

The Naval & Military Press Ltd

Published by

The Naval & Military Press Ltd
Unit 5 Riverside, Brambleside,
Bellbrook Industrial Estate,
Uckfield, East Sussex,
TN22 1QQ England

Tel: +44 (0) 1825 749494
Fax: +44 (0) 1825 765701

www.naval-military-press.com
www.nmarchive.com

In reprinting in facsimile from the original, any imperfections are inevitably reproduced and the quality may fall short of modern type and cartographic standards.

CONTENTS

Part I   Notes on the Red Army, 1940

Part II   New Notes on the Red Army
            No. 1: Tactics and Organization

Part III   New Notes on the Red Army
            No. 2: Uniforms and Insignia

INDEX

Chapter		Page
I.	**Historical sketch**	11
	1. Russia prior to 1914	11
	2. The War—August, 1914, to November, 1917	12
	3. Revolution, 1917–1921	15
	4. Reconstruction, 1921–1928	18
	5. Development, 1928–1935	19
	6. Setback—1936 onwards	21
	7. The rise of the Red Army	23
II.	**Military geography**	27
	1. Area and general description	27
	2. Communications	31
	3. Climate, meteorology and effect on health	35
III.	**Manpower and personnel**	37
	1. Population	37
	2. Law of military service	37
	3. Terms of service and general training ..	37
	4. Officers	39
	5. Non-commissioned officers	44
IV.	**General organization and strength**	45
	1. Functions, composition and organization in peace	45
	2. Peace strength and general distribution ..	46
	3. Composition and strength of an army ..	46
	4. Composition and strength of a corps ..	47
	5. Composition and strength of an infantry division	48
	6. Composition and strength of a cavalry division	49
	7. Composition and strength of an infantry brigade	49
	8. Composition and strength of a cavalry brigade	50
	9. Organization, composition and strength of air defence troops	50
	10. Organization, composition and strength of coast defence troops	50
	11. Armoured and mechanized formations and units	50
V.	**Administration, commands and staff**	51
	1. General notes on the higher administration of the armed forces	51
	2. Military councils	52

Chapter		Page
V. contd.	3. Administrative districts	54
	4. The general staff	55
	5. Administrative staff	55
	6. Organization of the higher command in peace and war	55
	7. Chain of command in the field	56
	8. Organization of an army staff	56
	9. Duties and organization of corps staff	58
	10. Duties and organization of divisional staffs	58
	11. Duties and organization of cavalry divisional staffs	59
	12. Duties and organization of brigade staffs	59
	13. Duties and organization of staffs of mechanized formations	59
	14. Chain of command for air and coast defences	59
VI.	**Infantry**	61
	1. General organization and strength	61
	2. Organization and strength of units	61
	3. Special units	67
	4. Designations of units and regimental colours	68
	5. Machine gun units	68
	6. Anti-aircraft machine gun units	68
	7. Anti-tank units	68
	8. Close support units (when manned by infantry personnel)	68
	9. Regimental specialists	68
	10. Regimental transport	69
	11. Ammunition supply	69
	12. Equipment	71
VII.	**Cavalry**	75
	1. General organization and strength	75
	2. Organization and strength of units	75
	3. Mechanized cavalry units	78
	4. Machine gun units	79
	5. Cavalry close support units	79
	6. Anti-tank units	79
	7. Anti-aircraft machine gun units	79
	8. Designation of units and regimental colours	79
	9. Cyclists with cavalry formations	79
	10. Motor machine gun units with cavalry formations	80
	11. Reconnaissance units	80
	12. Regimental specialists	80
	13. Regimental transport	80
	14. Ammunition supply	80
	15. Equipment	80
	16. The cavalry horse	81

Chapter		Page
VIII.	**Artillery**	83
	1. The arm	83
	2. Horse artillery	85
	3. Light and pack artillery	86
	4. Field artillery	87
	5. Medium artillery	90
	6. Heavy and super-heavy artillery	91
	7. Anti-aircraft artillery	93
	8. Coast defence (and fortress) artillery	95
	9. Anti-tank artillery	96
	10. Equipment	97
	11. Ammunition	98
IX.	**Engineers**	103
	1. Organization, administration and strength	103
	2. Engineer staffs	103
	3. Field units	104
	4. Field park units	106
	5. Bridging units	106
	6. Fortress units	108
	7. Electrical and searchlight units	108
	8. Camouflage units	109
	9. Water supply units	110
	10. Road construction units	110
	11. Railway construction units	110
	12. Quarrying units	110
	13. Boring units	111
	14. Mining units	111
	15. Searchlight units	111
	16. Engineer base workshops	111
	17. Engineer base store depots	111
	18. Workshop units	111
	19. Depots	111
	20. Regimental transport	111
	21. Armament and equipment of personnel	111
	22. Tools and miscellaneous equipment	111
	23. Explosives	112
	24. Portable bridging equipment	113
X.	**Chemical warfare**	115
	1. General policy	115
	2. Organization, administration and strength	115
	3. Defence	115
	4. Offence	120
	5. Research, and Research establishments	124
	6. Manufacturing establishments and depots	125
	7. Smoke	125
	8. Incendiary apparatus	126
	9. Bacteria	127

Chapter		Page
XI.	**Units equipped with armoured fighting vehicles**	129
	1. General organization, administration and strength	129
	2. Organization of independent formations and units	129
	3. Organization of divisional units	132
	4. Armoured car units	134
	5. Regimental specialists	134
	6. Regimental transport	134
	7. Maintenance in the field	135
XII.	**Signal service**	137
	1. Organization, administration and strength	137
	2. Signal units	137
	3. Experimental and research establishments	140
	4. Signal service in the field	140
	5. Wireless interception service and ground listening organization	140
	6. Cipher personnel	141
	7. Messenger dog units and dogs	141
	8. Carrier pigeon units and pigeons	141
	9. Despatch riders	142
	10. Telegraph codes	142
	11. Armament of personnel	142
	12. Equipment	142
	13. Regimental transport	147
XIII.	**Police, internal security troops and semi-military organizations**	149
	1. Introduction	149
	2. Functions and organization of the N.K.V.D.	150
	3. Central directorate of State security (G.U.G.B.)	151
	4. Internal security troops	152
	5. Frontier guards	153
	6. Escort troops	154
	7. The militia, or workers' and peasants' police forces	155
	9. Military settlers	156
	10. Red guard and partisan units	157
	11. Osoaviakhim	157
	12. Odr	160
	13. Women's organizations	160
	14. Juvenile organizations	161
XIV.	**Uniform**	163
	1. General notes	163
	2. Home service uniform	163
	3. Field service uniform	164

Chapter		Page
XIV contd.	4. Badges of rank	165
	5. Regimental crests and badges, distinguishing marks, etc.	165
	6. Staff distinctions	165
	7. Uniform worn by semi-military bodies	165
	8. Identity discs	166
	9. Distinguishing marks of specialists by arms	166
	10. Personal kit	166
	11. Orders, decorations and medals	167
XV.	**Forces in overseas possessions—not applicable.**	
XVI.	**The services**	169
	1. General organization	169
	2. Supply services	169
	3. Transport and transportation services	173
	4. Medical service	179
	5. Other services	181
XVII.	**Tactics and training**	185
	1. General principles	185
	2. Battle	185
	3. Information	186
	4. Protection	188
	5. Attack	190
	6. Defence	200
	7. Night operations	204
	8. Warfare under special conditions	205
	9. Combined operations	208
	10. Conventional signs used in map reading	209
XVIII.	**Military air forces**	211
	1. General organization, distribution and strength	211
	2. Distribution	212
	3. Air material	213
	4. Tactics and training	216
XIX.	**Naval**	219
	1. Policy	219
	2. Strength and distribution	219
	3. Marines	220

Appendix		Page
A.	Table of ranks of officers and N.C.O.s in the Red Army	221
B.	Minimum periods to be served in each rank in the Red Army in order to qualify for promotion..	225
C.	Characteristics of artillery weapons	227
	Coast defence	227
	Heavy and medium artillery	228
	Field, horse, mountain, and anti-tank ..	231
	Anti-aircraft..	235
D.	Tools and engineer stores carried in various units	239
E.	Equipment of unit chemical detachments ..	241
	1. Infantry regiment chemical platoon ..	241
	2. Cavalry chemical troop	241
	3. Artillery chemical detachment	241
	4. Sapper chemical section	241
F.	Characteristics of Soviet tank types	243
G.	System of communication. Ground to air, Army co-operation	247
H.	Conventional signs used on Soviet maps and signs used to denote units and formations [Short note on the Red Army, pp. 44 to 54 (and separate sheet)]	253
I.	Military and other abbreviations .. .. [Short note on the Red Army, pp. 57 to 87.]	265
J.	Glossary of certain Russian military terms .. [Separate pamphlet.]	297
K.	Russian weights and measures .. .. .. [Short note on Red Army, pp. 55, 56.]	309

PLATES

Plate
- I. 45-mm. anti-tank gun.
- II. 76-mm. field gun, short.
- III. 76-mm. field gun, long.
- IV. 122-mm. field howitzer.
- V. 107-mm. gun.
- VI. 152-mm. howitzer.
- VII. 203-mm. howitzer.
- VIII. 76-mm. anti-aircraft gun.
- IX. Light amphibian tank (T.37).
- X. Infantry divisional tank (T.26 light-medium).
- XI. B.T. cruiser tank.
- XII. T.28 heavy-medium tank.
- XIII. T.32 heavy tank.
- XIV. B.A.27 armoured car.
- XV. B.A. Broniford armoured car.
- XVI. B.A. amphibian armoured car.
- XVII. B.A. Ford armoured car.
- XVIII. General service uniform.
- XIX. Cap badges.
- XX. Distinguishing marks and specialist badges.
- XXI. Badges of rank.

CHAPTER I

HISTORICAL SKETCH

1. Russia prior to 1914

In order fully to appreciate the evolution of the present extraordinary spectacle of a Socialist Republic existing under the complete domination and dictatorship of one man it is well to probe into the history of the preceding ten centuries, for the Russian past has left unmistakable imprints on the character and ultimate outcome of the Bolshevik revolution.

Russia, more westernized than the countries of the East but always more eastern than the countries of Europe, was always a land of serfs; and during the period of the evolution, in European countries, of representative institutions and of democratic freedom, the bonds of serfdom in Russia continued to tighten, so that at the end of the eighteenth century 34,000,000 out of a total population of 36,000,000 were serfs, either of the state, or of private owners.

Russia was nearly always dominated by a complete autocrat in the person of the Tsar, whose authority was frequently being challenged by risings and revolutions of varying success all of which, at any rate until 1905, were eventually suppressed with an aftermath of extreme cruelty. Torture was employed more ruthlessly and more extensively than ever it was in Western Europe.

Ivan the Terrible (1533-84) originated a form of secret police with unlimited power over the lives and property of his subjects. The initiative of the individual was completely crushed beneath the omnipotent central state. Peter the Great (1689-1725) enforced westernization at a furious pace, but his beneficent actions were accomplished with repelling violence. Moreover, the execution of his reforms entailed vast expenditure and resulted in a still heavier load of taxation being laid on the peasants. Nicholas I (1825-55) perfected the espionage system and is reported to have written on a document containing the word progress, " This word must be deleted from official terminology." This attitude continued until 1905 when, with subterranean revolutionary activities always on the increase, open unrest and discontent, fanned by the disasters of the Russo-Japanese war, led the Tsar Nicholas II to institute the first Duma or parliament.

So for a period of many centuries the vast majority of the Russian population, of excellent type physically, showed an inexhaustible capacity for suffering and endurance, always crushed by the weight of the omnipotent central authority, accepting the trials and the miseries of the present rather than risk the still greater tribulations that might ensue from any effort to resist, or to evolve a brighter future.

During the latter part of the nineteenth, and the beginning of the twentieth centuries, subterranean revolutionary activity continued. Initiated by the revolutionary intelligentsia working largely from centres outside the country, it none the less continued actively among the workers and peasants at home, working in secret, each man distrustful of his neighbour, and ever watchful of the network of spies and secret police.

2. The War, August, 1914, to November, 1917

The outbreak of the Great War found Russia faced by many unsolved problems of vital consequence to the country. The struggle for political and civil rights, growing more intense every year, foreshadowed the inevitable conflict between Autocracy and Democracy. The Government classes saw no danger to themselves in a war and were convinced that such a conflict could have no disturbing effect on a community so essentially agricultural. This blind optimism, however, was not universal, for competent observers realised that Russia was not in general prepared for war. She was divided into two irreconcilable parties, official Russia, and the rest—the intelligentsia and the people.

From a military point of view, however, Russia was better prepared in 1914 than in 1904 or at the outbreak of any of her preceding wars. The peace strength of the Russian Army in April 1914 was 1,320,000, and the Army was organized in 37 Army Corps. The total number of Infantry Divisions was 70 and in addition there existed 18 Rifle Brigades. The number of Cavalry and Cossack Divisions was 24 and of independent Cavalry and Cossack Brigades 11. On mobilization (1st August, 1914) 35 reserve Infantry Divisions were formed by the detachment of cadres from a corresponding number of first line divisions. A number of additional Cossack Cavalry Divisions was also formed. Russia therefore commenced the War with the equivalent of 114 Infantry (1,596,000 rifles) and about 36 Cavalry Divisions.

So far as railway communications were concerned, those of Russia were, by Western European standards, inadequate. In the whole of Russia, there was only half a mile of railway to every 100 square miles of territory as compared with 20 miles of railway in a similar area in Great Britain. It was however as good a system as any in the world and was manned by a highly qualified personnel.

So far as road transport was concerned there were in Russia in 1914 only 679 Government motor-cars, of which 259 were passenger cars, 418 were lorries and 2 were ambulances. The most drastic requisitioning of civilian owned motor vehicles only succeeded in increasing this number by 475. Movement forward from railhead was therefore entirely dependent on horsed transport and very inferior roads.

With regard to concentration the Russian General Staff estimated that they would be in a position to assume the offensive on the 28th day after mobilization. In practice, however, in response to a French plea for speed, this time was quickened up to the fifteenth day. Naturally the full weight of the Russian Army could not be brought to bear so early as several divisions had to come from the Far East and other distant parts of the Empire. But in her initial operations, Russia deployed against both Germany and Austria-Hungary 73 Divisions, and 13 were held in reserve.

But although Russia was better prepared in 1914 than at the outset of previous wars, the enemy was correspondingly more formidable and this premature committal of the main Russian forces to battle before they were properly mobilized was to have far reaching results. The very first days brought defeats which by 1915 had become a catastrophic general retreat.

Meanwhile in the country at large things had also been going from bad to worse. Foreign trade was in great measure the foundation of the financial prosperity of the country. With the outbreak of war, those frontiers, through which the bulk of this trade passed, were closed, and those frontier stations which remained unaffected were ill-adapted to handle the extra burdens thrown upon them. As a result of this, Russia was almost completely blockaded. Her trade suffered severely and in consequence the exchange value of the rouble fell disastrously. The cost of living increased by leaps and bounds.

Discontent and alarm at the course events were taking grew on all sides and with it came the realization of the failure of the existing regime. The feelings prevailing so widely in the country spread inevitably to the Army where, by 1916, insubordination and desertion had reached formidable proportions.

Rumours of conspiracy filled the air. A number of secret organizations were active in Petrograd and were reported to include some of the Grand Dukes among their numbers. The murder of Rasputin on 30th December, 1916, showed how far these preparations had gone. By 1917 the Tsar and his Government were completely isolated and autocracy continued to function more by inertia than by its own authority and strength. An attempt to stifle the incipient revolution by police provocation failed. The Army could no longer be relied upon and began to take the side of the insurgents.

On the 14th March, 1917, the Tsar expressed his agreement with the appointment of a responsible Ministry, the choice and nomination of which was to be wholly in the hands of the President of the Duma.

By 15th March, the provisional Government with Prince Lvov as Premier was in power, and the same night in Pskov Nicholas II abdicated in favour of his brother the Grand Duke Michael. The latter, however, realising the hopelessness of any attempt to save the monarchy, refused to assume supreme power until such time as the will of the people should summon him to do so.

That the revolution was not the result of careful planning and conspiracy is apparent. It was the result of widespread dissatisfaction with the conditions prevailing in the country and with the inability of an autocratic government to deal with them.

The Provisional Government was no more able to deal effectively with the situation than its predecessor. None of the existing political parties had been able to gain experience in the art of governing. Confusion and uncertainty increased at an alarming rate. The power of the Soviets of workers and soldiers deputies—originally almost an accidental formation but one whose possibilities were quickly realised by the Bolshevik (Communist) Party—grew rapidly.

The re-organization of the Government on a Coalition basis took place in May, 1917, in an attempt to stem the current, and for a time it appeared that it would be successful. But already extremists of the Left and of the Right were organizing with a view to the establishment of a Dictatorship. In July of the same year a serious outbreak took place staged by the Bolsheviks. The preparations, however, had been insufficient and the Coalition Government were able to suppress it.

At the end of August occurred the Kornilov Rising, led by General Kornilov and organized by Alexeiev, the Commander-in-Chief. The intention appears to have been to establish a military dictatorship and to drag Russia back from the abyss towards which she was advancing. The rising failed, but its results were far reaching. It gave the Bolsheviks an excellent pretext for all manner of propaganda and it weakened the already sorely tried government.

The position of the Bolsheviks in Petrograd was now very strong. They had a predominating influence in the Petrograd Soviet and their party was spreading throughout the army and the country. They determined to act, and about 2nd November, 1917, they formed a special Military Revolutionary Committee to organize the *coup d'état*. On 7th November a proclamation was issued stating that " The provisional Government is deposed ; the powers of the State have passed into the hands of the organ of the Petrograd Soviet of the Workers and Soldiers Deputies, the Military Revolutionary Committee standing at the head of the Petrograd proletariat and garrison." On 8th November, 1917, a new Government was formed—the Soviet of the Peoples' Commissars with Lenin at its head, and the history of Russia entered on a new era.

From then onwards the history of Soviet Russia coincides with the history of the Russian Communist Party, for the small oligarchy of strong-willed, determined and fanatical men representing only 1½–2 per cent of the 170,000,000 inhabitants, has ruthlessly controlled this huge state which embraces nearly one-sixth of the world's surface.

The history of the Soviet Union since 1917 falls naturally into four periods :—

(a) November, 1917—March, 1921   Revolution.
(b) 1921–1928   ..   ..   ..   Reconstruction.
(c) 1929–1936   ..   ..   ..   Development.
(d) 1936   ..   ..   Setback.

3. Revolution, 1917–1921

The first two vital problems confronting Lenin were first of all the extension of his power throughout Russia and secondly the need for the immediate liquidation of the war with Germany : and to both he set his hand with the energy that was characteristic of this man who was to prove to be possibly the greatest genius cast up by the Great War. To convince Moscow of the blessings of revolution he found it necessary to call in the Army and to bombard the city; and from the very outset he realized the need for systematic terror to smother any counter-revolutionary movements. In that conception he was opposed by some of his closest adherents, but he gained his point and "terror" was organized methodically for the utter extermination of any relic of the bourgeois system. The peasants and work-people were encouraged to help in the work and to take possession of the property of the landowners and capitalists.

At the outset the Bolsheviks had offered peace to a people sick and tired of war and to the National Minorities, struggling for their independence, they had promised autonomy. Accordingly an attempt to start negotiations with Germany was made on 3rd December, 1917. No reply from Germany, was however, forthcoming. Four days later a further communication was made, this time to the Allies as well. This second note only evoked a protest from the Allies and remained ignored by the Germans. The Bolsheviks therefore ordered that the soldiers of the front should fraternise with the enemy and begin negotiations for peace on the spot. The inevitable outcome of this procedure was the final disintegration of the Russian Army.

In these conditions the Germans agreed on 14th December, 1917, to begin preliminary conversations. It is doubtful if the Russians could have been brought to accept the humiliating terms of the Treaty signed at Brest-Litovsk on 3rd March, 1918, but for the determination of Lenin to conclude peace at all costs and thus save the revolution. He was prepared to split the party rather than to jeopardise what had been gained.

By this Treaty the Soviet Government agreed to evacuate Finland, Poland, Latvia, Lithuania, Estonia, Ukraine and the South Eastern districts of Ardakhan, Kars and Batum, and to pay in addition a large indemnity as compensation for losses caused to Germany by Russian military measures.

From the very beginning the Bolshevik *coup d'état* had met with bitter opposition, but this opposition was hopelessly divided. For a time the Allies occupied certain strategically important points in Russia :—Murmansk, Archangel, Vladivostok. Between 1918 and 1920 a succession of campaigns was initiated chiefly in the South and East to overthrow the Soviet Government. Gradually the Red Army which had been completely re-organised by Trotsky defeated these attempts and put down ruthlessly various risings throughout the country.

The year 1920 saw the outbreak of the war with Poland in which the Poles at one time captured Kiev but were then forced to retire and for a time Warsaw itself was threatened. The Polish Army, however, was able eventually to drive back the Russians and the Treaty of Riga, signed on 18th March, 1921, put an end to hostilities.

By then the Soviet Government was firmly established, and it could feel itself free to develop its political and economic theories unhampered by the conduct of military operations.

The two main objects of the Russian Communist party when it came to power were :—

(a) At Home—The creation and development of a powerful classless proletarian state ; and (b) Abroad— The bringing about of world revolution and the violent overthrow of all existing Governments by civil war and their replacement by Communism.

In the early years the second object was regarded as the more important. It was held that, owing to the opposition that it would inevitably engender, one Communist state could not exist in a Capitalist world. Consequently the Third or Communist International (Comintern) was organized in opposition to the Second or Socialist International and charged with carrying out intensive Communist propaganda in foreign countries, particularly in those which were involved in the Great War.

Nevertheless, the first of the two objects had not been neglected ; from the outset a system of pure, or so-called militant, Communism was instituted and an economic system amounting practically to barter was attempted. At that time, however, the only real producer was the peasant because industry had been to all intents incapacitated as a result of the war. This led to a hopeless state of affairs economically as there were few or none of the necessaries of life, e.g. boots, clothes, etc., to give to the peasant in exchange for his grain ; in consequence he stopped producing more than was sufficient for his own individual needs. Food conditions grew steadily worse until, early in 1921, there occurred a terrible famine in which 5,000,000 to 10,000,000 persons perished.

Thus by the end of 1920 the Bolsheviks had successfully consolidated their position in Russia, but internally they were faced with the most serious economic problems, while externally their world revolution policy, although it had caused serious annoyance to many countries in the world, had failed to achieve any tangible results.

4. Reconstruction—1921-1928

Lenin quickly realised as a result of this famine that, if the Communist State were to survive, some private enterprise both for industry and agriculture would have to be tolerated. Accordingly in the face of considerable opposition from within the Party he instituted a new economic policy (called N.E.P.) which permitted some private enterprise under Government control. As a result an era of relative prosperity set in and enterprising individuals who were working farms, shops, factories and concessions began to make money.

This modification of Communist principles forced upon the Bolsheviks by circumstances which they were not strong enough to control was to have far-reaching results. It gave encouragement to those sections of the population who had accepted the Communist experiment because they were not in a position to refuse it; it restored an element of private trade; and led to that system of state socialism which is, in practice if not in theory, the same commercial system as exists in other and Capitalist countries, although under a strict Government control. The new economic policy therefore represented the defeat of the attempt to introduce pure Communism. This was naturally anathema to the pure Communist Left Wing of the Party, but Lenin realised that his policy was essential for the revival of trade and agriculture and remained adamant to all opposition.

On 21st January, 1924, he succumbed to paralysis and very soon afterwards there appeared an acute divergence of opinion as to future policy among the leaders, which was destined eventually to split the Party.

By the end of 1925 Stalin, who was merely Secretary-General of the Party, and whose position as the possible successor to Lenin was far from secure, was faced with a Left Wing opposition led by Trotsky clamouring for the blood of the bourgeois elements who had arisen under Lenin's policy, and at the same time with a moderate Right Wing opposition pressing for an extension of the benefits of N.E.P. Stalin then revealed the force and ability which have since made him Dictator of Russia.

He first persuaded the Party to continue N.E.P. as being the last wish of the great Lenin who was by now deified. Then he set about removing his political opponents by arraigning each opposition in turn before the Tribunal of the Party on a charge of " fractionism," or deviation from the Party creed of Lenin. The Left opposition under the redoubtable Trotsky was found guilty and liquidated. Trotsky himself being eventually banished from the country, The Right opposition publicly recanted and although outwardly forgiven lost most of its high positions which Stalin filled with his own supporters. By the end of 1927 he was master of the Party machine.

With the disappearance of Trotsky, essentially the international revolutionary, from the political stage, the first object of the Communist Party, namely, the development of the Soviet Union, began to take precedence over the second object, which was the bringing about of revolution throughout the world. Stalin now decided to adopt the internal policy of the defunct Left opposition by cancelling N.E.P. and reverting to pure state Communism, including the ruthless extermination of all the so-called bourgeois elements which had arisen under Lenin's liberal policy. This policy was to be carried out under the famous Five Year Plan, which marks the beginning of the third stage in the history of the Soviet Union.

5. Development, 1928-1935

The first Plan which began in October, 1928, had three main objects.

(a) *Industrial*.—To make the Soviet Union industrially self-supporting particularly in her backward heavy industries, and to develop her immense natural resources.

(b) *Agricultural*.—To develop large-scale agriculture by means of collective farms and thus ensure the Government's control not only of food supplies but over the still hostile peasant population.

(c) *Political*.—To exterminate the private traders, rich peasants and other class enemies who had arisen under N.E.P., and in general to move closer to a pure Communist organization of the country.

On the industrial side the most serious problem with which the Soviet State was confronted was the lack of capital, the normal methods whereby in a backward state a young industry is built up by foreign loans not being open to it. Consequently the leaders had to have recourse on the one hand to internal loans and heavy taxation amounting to approximately one-third of the total national revenue, and on the other to the export of primary commodities such as oil, timber and grain in order to raise credits abroad for the purchase of plant, machinery, etc., which could not be manufactured in Russia. It is significant of the lengths to which the rulers were prepared to go that they exported grain, butter and other food stuffs in large quantities while the home population was almost on starvation diet.

On the agricultural side, the problem confronting the Soviet Government was even more difficult; it was in fact a question of how to " kill the goose and yet have the golden eggs " since it was necessary both to eliminate the rich peasants who were the most efficient farmers, and to obtain the maximum amount of grain for export. The problem was only solved after the most serious opposition on the part of the peasants which took the form of passive resistance, the slaughter of horses and livestock, and even in some cases the resort to arson and murder. But the Government showed these recalcitrant elements no mercy and after a second great famine in the spring of 1933 in which 5,000,000 or more persons, mostly peasants, perished, the peasant population finally came to heel and accepted with what grace they could muster the collective farm system. After that their lot gradually improved, and having obtained a measure of relative prosperity they fell into line behind the Government.

On the political side the liquidation of private traders presented no difficulty although their disappearance, like that of the rich peasants, contributed in some degree to the general lowering of the standard of living of the people that occurred in the early years of the first Five Year Plan. But the further political object, viz. the reversion to pure classless Communism was to prove once again impossible of attainment.

It was soon found that the mere good of the State was not a sufficient incentive for those in positions of responsibility, especially in industry, to give of their best. That was not surprising when they saw that however hard they worked, or however much responsibility they took, neither they nor their families were any better off than the simple non-skilled workmen who worked under their direction. Furthermore in the early years of the Plans mere errors of judgment on the part of engineers in charge of plant, factory managers, and the like, led to charges of sabotage being laid and to frequent executions. In these circumstances the industrial development demanded under the Plans was seriously retarded and a change of social policy forced on the Soviet leaders. This took the form of payment according to ability and responsibility—a direct move away from the communist system. From an industrial point of view this was a highly successful move and progress became comparatively rapid; but from a social point of view it led at once to the division of the people into well-defined classes.

Side by side with these concessions to those engaged in industry, others were made to the now submissive peasantry. After delivering the required quotas of produce to the Government, collective farms were permitted to sell, in the open market, any surplus they might have over and above their own requirements, the proceeds being divided amongst all members. Peasants were permitted to own their own houses and gardens and to possess a limited amount of livestock including a cow, sheep and pigs; as a result their lot was considerably improved and their standard of life began to rise.

The first Five Year Plan had been completed in 1932, nearly a year ahead of schedule, and was followed immediately by the second Five Year Plan (1933–1937). Its objects were on lines similar to those of the first Plan with the exception that greater attention was to be paid to light industry and to the production of consumers' goods in order to accelerate the rise in the standard of life of the people. The Plan did in fact succeed in this process to a strictly limited extent although the system of distribution in the country was very seriously strained owing to the failure of the railway system to keep pace with the ever growing demands of industry upon it.

The movement towards a happier state of affairs reached its peak early in 1936. By that year the Soviet Union had come to be regarded by most foreign powers, with the exception perhaps of Germany and Japan, with a much more tolerant eye, and its relations with the outside world were closer than ever before. The " terror " of the early years of the Revolution seemed at long last to be a thing of the past, the standard of life of the people had certainly risen, and the people as a whole appeared to be happier and to be looking forward with confidence to a fuller life. It appeared, in general, that although the Soviet economic and social system was still fundamentally different from that of other countries, the Soviet Union was at last moving towards normality and becoming " respectable " again. Unfortunately from the point of view of the people of Russia this " respectability " was more apparent than real as the events of the second half of 1936 and of 1937 were to show.

6. Setback. 1936 onwards

Like the first Plan, the second Plan was completed a year ahead of schedule early in 1937, but the production figures of industry for 1936 were to prove the peak, for in 1937 a catastrophic decline set in. This setback may have been due to one of two causes or possibly to both— the severe political crisis which shook the Soviet Union in 1936 and to the " over-pushing " of men and machinery in a struggle to secure an ever increasing output from industry.

Reference was made in paragraph 3 to the acute divergence of opinion amongst Soviet leaders that followed Lenin's death and to the methods by which Stalin's views eventually prevailed. All those who opposed the latter, with the exception of Trotsky, remained in the Soviet Union and, after undergoing suitable penances, were eventually given minor appointments in the state machine. They thus remained in comparative obscurity until 1934, but after the assassination of Kirov, one of Stalin's closest associates, by a fellow communist in November of that year the more important of them, notably Zinoviev and Kamenev emerged into the limelight accused of complicity with Kirov's assassin. For this they received long sentences of imprisonment and nothing more was heard of them until 1936 when they and numerous other " old Bolsheviks " as Lenin's former associates had come to be known, were again put on trial charged this time with " anti-state activities under the direction of Trotsky." To this crime all pleaded guilty although there is considerable doubt whether they had, in fact, had any form of contact with him, as he had been banished from the Soviet Union several years before. In any case they were executed and their trial was followed early in 1937 by a virtual reign of terror which affected every walk in life in the Soviet Union, especially the Communist Party itself and not excepting even the Red Army. Industry suffered especially severely and large numbers of senior officials lost their appointments and even their lives. This must undoubtedly have been one of the causes of the setback in industry which ensued.

A phenomenal rise in the production figures of industry took place. Clearly these can only have been attained after so short a period of industrialization by the exploitation of machinery at its full capacity over long periods, insufficient time being left for essential maintenance. In these circumstances breakdowns were inevitable and they led equally inevitably under the Soviet system to charges of sabotage, " Trotskyism," etc., followed by the wholesale slaughter of engineers and managers. Thus Soviet industry became involved in a vicious circle.

The over driving of men arose from the so-called
"Stakhanov" movement designed to raise the low productivity of the Russian worker. It naturally received
the full support of the governmental propaganda machine;
in fact there are grounds for the belief that the Government
itself instigated Stakhanov to make the initial effort. On
the other hand although a limited number of the more
efficient workers benefited greatly from the movement,
the vast majority found their "norms" raised without
receiving any corresponding material benefit. This led
to a "go slow" movement in many industries and even,
in some cases, to the murder of prominent "Stakhanovites."

This widespread discontent among the industrial population probably led to the considerable increase in the rate
of wages which was decreed towards the end of 1937.

7. The rise of the Red Army

The re-organization of the Red Army by Trotsky during
the "intervention" period has already been mentioned.
The Treaty of Riga of 1921 put an end to the Polish War
and the hands of the military authorities were then free to
concentrate on the evolution of an army which, according
to their own statements, was to be not only the largest
and most powerful in the world, but also the equal of the
army of any capitalist state from the point of view of
material. The extent of the success with which they met
will be apparent from the table below showing the
progressive increase in size and from the succeeding
chapters :—

Year.	Army Corps.	Infantry Divisions.	Cavalry Divisions.	Mechanized Divisions.
1925	21	62	10	–
1926	22	67	11	–
1927	?	?	?	–
1928	21*	68	15	–
1929	17*	70	12*	–
1930	21	70	12*	–
1931	21	71	11*	–
1932	21	74	14*	–
1933	23	78	18	–
1934	21*	82	20	1
1935	23	83	19	2
1936	23	84	21	2
1937	21*	90	32	3
1938	32	104	33	5
1939	30	110	35	5

* These figures are open to some doubt.

Equally astonishing progress was made in the development in the design and manufacture of modern war material as the subjoined table of increases in armoured fighting vehicles in service shows:—

Year.	Number of A.F.Vs.
1930	Nil
1931	250
1932	500
1933	1,500
1934	2,400
1935	4,000
1936	6,000
1937	7,500
1938	9,000
1939	10,000

The above figures are estimates but are believed to be reasonably accurate.

It would serve no useful purpose to examine the various steps by which the present organization of the Army has been evolved. Except in one important respect that organization does not materially differ from those of other great continental armies. The "military commissar" system is, however, unique and some account of its evolution is necessary.

One of the greatest difficulties with which Trotsky met in his original organization of the Red Army out of the demoralized remnants of the Imperial Army was a great scarcity of officers. Large numbers of ex-Tsarist officers were available and, to save their lives, were willing to serve, but the question was, could they be trusted? Because the need was very great, ex-Tsarist officers were recruited in large numbers and drafted to the various fronts as a temporary measure while reliable officers of suitable parentage were being trained. In order, however, that the closest watch might be maintained on their activities, to each was attached a communist who was known as a military commissar. These men were entirely responsible for discipline, welfare, administration and interior economy in general, while the officers theoretically concentrated on actual operations. In practice their every order was subject to examination and even alteration by their military commissars.

This system was continued after the war when many of the ex-Tsarist officers, who had served the new regime faithfully, were allowed to remain in the service. In course of time, however, many of these men, especially those in high positions, became themselves full members of the Party with the result that army and party became more and more closely identified and the need for military commissars gradually ceased to exist. Party control was therefore slackened. Commissars continued to exist but merely as staff officers to the commanders to whom they were attached for political training and welfare, not as their co-equals, as was formerly the case.

This system endured until early in 1937 and there is little doubt that the slackening of political control over the armed forces contributed largely to the comparatively high standard of efficiency that was reached by then. But the efficiency of the Army was not the main consideration in the minds of the Soviet leaders; it was more important from their point of view that it should be absolutely reliable since the fate of their regime depended on it. Unfortunately for the Army, a doubt on this score appears to have arisen in Stalin's mind about the time of the notorious treason trials of 1936, with the result that a drastic " purge " was carried out early in 1937, eight of the most efficient and best known senior commanders being executed and a great number of others being removed from their appointments. The charges laid against these men included treason, violation of oath, preparation to hand over the Ukraine to Germany, etc.—all so fantastic on the face of it, as to be quite unbelievable. The truth of the matter was, possibly, a fear by Stalin that the army had become so independent of political control as to make it potentially dangerous to him. Discontent was rife in the country, industry was working badly and the standard of living was falling. A successful rising by the people alone was impossible but if the army were to take their side, Stalin himself would be lost. He determined, therefore, not only to remove the most prominent generals who might form the foci of any such rising, but also to bring the Army back under the close political control to which it had been subjected in the early years of the revolution. To that end the status of military commissars was restored to co-equality with commanders and the Red Army fell back in this respect to where it had been some 12 years before. Simultaneously even closer control of the commanders of military districts (commands) was ensured by the creation of military councils in all military districts to exercise functions which were formerly the personal responsibility of the commanders themselves. Full accounts, the duties, etc., of military councils and military commissars are given in Chapter V.

26

CHAPTER II

MILITARY GEOGRAPHY

Note.—This chapter requires some revision owing to the incorporation of Polish White Russia and the Polish Ukraine in the Soviet Union. Up-to-date, however, adequate data to carry this out has not been received so the chapter is published in its original form.

1. Area and general description

(a) *Area.*—The U.S.S.R., including Asiatic Russia, comprises some eight and a quarter million square miles, or over one-seventh of the world's land surface. Of this total roughly five million square miles are in Siberia.

(b) *Constituent Republics.*—The U.S.S.R. is composed of eleven republics within which are a number of smaller administrative sub-divisions known as Autonomous Republics, Regions, Territories, Districts, Areas, and Autonomous Towns. The eleven republics and their principal towns are as follows :—

  (i) Russian Soviet Federated Socialist Republic—Moscow.
  (ii) Ukrainian Soviet Socialist Republic—Kiev.
  (iii) White Russian Soviet Socialist Republic—Minsk.
  (iv) Azerbaidzhan Soviet Socialist Republic—Baku.
  (v) Georgian Soviet Socialist Republic—Tbilisi.
  (vi) Armenian Soviet Socialist Republic—Erivan.
  (vii) Turkmenian Soviet Socialist Republic—Ashkhabad.
  (viii) Uzbek Soviet Socialist Republic—Tashkent.
  (ix) Tadzhik Soviet Socialist Republic—Stalinabad.
  (x) Kazakh Soviet Socialist Republic—Alma Ata.
  (xi) Kirghiz Soviet Socialist Republic—Frunze.

(c) *General description.*—(i) *European Russia.*—European Russia forms a rough square measuring approximately 1,600 miles each way. The whole area from the White Sea to the Black Sea and from the Carpathians to the Urals, is the continuation of the great European plain which extends through Germany and Poland and is mainly a plateau some 800 ft. above sea level. Various rivers have split up the plain into valleys. Absolute plains are thus only found on the watersheds and in the broader parts of the river valleys. Where relief does exist, it is only a gentle rise above the general level, and takes the form of broad and gentle swellings, not of hills or mountains.

European Russia can be divided into five main zones :—

The tundra or frozen zone in the north is a treeless plain with many lakes and morasses. Over the latter movement is possible, as the ground is usually frozen many feet deep, except in summer when the thaw penetrates to a depth of rather more than one foot.

The forest zone which covers nearly one-third of European Russia. This zone starts with forests of small evergreens in the south ; then come the vast areas of pine forests, succeeded finally by forests of hardwood (oak and birch). In this area there are immense districts in which rivers are the sole means of communication.

The black soil zone which is the most fertile and densely populated portion of the U.S.S.R. This zone extends to a width of 200 to 300 miles and stretches from the Ukraine across the South of European Russia and far into Siberia.

The agricultural zone ; less fertile than the black soil zone but suitable for pastoral purposes. This zone is treeless.

The barren steppes, a dry and sandy belt destitute of vegetation, consisting of a sandy desert in its western parts which merges further East in the vicinity of the Aral and Caspian Seas, into the vast saline plain of the Kirghiz Steppes of Central Asia.

(ii) *Siberia.*—Siberia lies between the inhospitable waters of the Arctic Ocean on the north and the almost equally inhospitable mountains and deserts of Central Asia on the south. Its outlets are thus through European Russia on the west and across the formidable coastal ranges to the Bering and Okhotsk Seas on the east. Siberia's chief drawback is its inaccessibility ; another is its vast size. It is 5,000 miles from east to west and, in the west, about 2,300 miles from north to south.

Siberia may be divided primarily into Western, Central, and Eastern Siberia.

The five zones of European Russia apply in general to Western Siberia, in a lesser degree to Central Siberia, and not at all to Eastern Siberia. As the Yenisei River is approached, the black soil belt and the great plains give way to a mountainous and thickly wooded terrain which extends more or less continuously to the Pacific. In the extreme north the tundra zone persists until it meets the mountain and forest area mentioned above.

(iii) *Russian Central Asia.*—Russian Central Asia may be divided into :—

The Kirghiz Steppes.

Russian Turkestan proper—the Turanian Basin and its borders.

The Kirghiz Steppes.—South of the Black Earth belt is a wide tract of much drier and less fertile steppeland. This tract connects the southern end of the Urals on the one hand with the branches of the Altai and with Tien Shan on the other. It also connects the steppes of southern European Russia with the steppes of Mongolia. With a rolling topography, few water courses, and an absence of trees, it was a naturally cleared route along which journeyed the hordes of Mongolia under Gengis Khan in the Middle Ages.

Russian Turkestan Proper.—Russian Turkestan comprises the following :—

The plateau of Ust Urt, 500 to 600 ft. above sea level, lying between the Caspian and Aral Seas.

The desert of Kara Kum (black sand), lying south and south-east of the Ust Urt Plateau.

The Southern Borderland stretching along the frontiers of Persia and Afghanistan.

The Desert of Kizil Kum (red sand) between the Amu Darya and the Sir Darya, south-east of the sea of Aral. It includes small ranges of mountains and stretches of grassy steppes.

The Plain of Fergana is a small oval-shaped plain almost completely surrounded by mountains and watered by the Kara Darya and the Narin.

The Mountain Border occupies most of the remainder of Russian Turkestan. It includes the Tien Shan, the Pamir-Altai Group and the Balkan Mountains.

To sum up, deserts or very dry steppes occupy most of Turkestan ; the fertile areas, wherein most of the population is found, cover less than 15 per cent. of the surface.

Five belts of natural vegetation may be distinguished ; the desert belt, the steppe belt, the loess foothill belt, the mountain sparse-forest belt, and the Alpine zone.

(d) *Industrial areas.*—The following are the chief industrial areas in the U.S.S.R. :—

Leningrad area	Engineering and heavy industry.
Moscow area	General manufactures.
Gorki area (East of Moscow).	Chiefly steel and machine construction.
Ivanovo area (North of Gorki)	Textiles.
Ukraine	Mixed industry (but generally subsidiary to agriculture).
Don Basin (South Russia)	Coal-mining.

These areas have been industrial since the days before the revolution, but have been vastly developed under the Soviet regime.

In addition the following areas have been created since the war with the object of obtaining greater immunity from possible enemy attack and of making the Far Eastern areas more self-supporting :—

Ural Area	An immense area covering generally the southern half of the Ural range, and devoted almost exclusively to heavy industry.
Altai Mountains (Central Siberia).	Metal mining.
Komsomolsk-en-Amur (Far East).	General industry, and still in process of development.

(e) *Topographical features of certain frontiers.*—(i) *Finland.*—The northern half is mountainous country (750–1,000 ft.) much intersected by streams and lakes. The southern half runs through Lake Ladoga and thence in a generally south-west direction through flat and easy country to the Gulf of Finland opposite Kronstadt.

(ii) *Estonia.*—The frontier which has a total length of approximately 125 miles, runs for 85 miles through Lake Peipus. There are few obstacles to movement on the land portions of the frontier north and south of the lake. The lake is frozen and bears traffic for some months in the winter.

(iii) *Latvia.*—Length of frontier approximately 125 miles, all of which is through country offering comparatively few obstacles to movement.

(iv) *Poland.*—Although the frontier with Poland is some 500 miles long, nearly two-thirds of it are unsuitable, or even impossible, for military operations. These unsuitable areas are :—

The North-eastern corner of Poland	(110 miles).
The Nalibowska Forest	(30 miles).
The Area of the Pripet Marshes ..	(120–150 miles).
The Krzemieniec Forest	(15 miles).

The area traversed by the four main tributaries of the River Dniester which extends some 50 miles northwards from that river.

There are, therefore, four main areas suitable for military operations :—

North of the Pripet	{ The Molodeczno Gap. { The Baranowicze Gap.
South of the Pripet	{ The Rowne Gap. { The Tarnopol–Krzemieniec Gap.

(v) *Roumania.*—The River Dniester forms the frontier. It is believed that the only bridge in existence is the railway bridge at Tiraspol. The river is normally frozen over from January to March.

(vi) *Central Asia.*—The frontier everywhere runs through mountainous, rocky country.

(vii) *Manchukuo.*—The frontier is open for the first 50 miles and it is here that the railway from China crosses into Manchukuo territory by the frontier station of Manchuria. After this the frontier is formed by the rivers Argun, Amur and Ussuri. The River Ussuri rises near Lake Hanka and flows northwards. South of the lake the frontier runs southwards through broken and difficult country until it reaches the sea near Rashin.

Neither the Argun, the Amur, or the Ussuri are fordable, and the only bridge is the railway bridge which crosses the Argun in Manchukuo territory east of Manchuria.

2. Communications

(a) *Railways.*—In considering the railways it is important to remember that while the railways in Russia, Finland, Estonia, and the greater part of Latvia, are 5-ft. broad-gauge, those in Lithuania, East Prussia, Poland, Roumania and Manchukuo are 4 ft. 8½ in. standard-gauge.

All railways in U.S.S.R. are State-owned.

(i) *European Russia.*—Railways in European Russia may be broadly divided into those west of Moscow and those east of Moscow. The former are primarily of strategic importance, since they form the main lines of approach to the western frontier; while those east of Moscow are more of industrial importance and will form a vital connecting link between the Ural industrial area and the western frontier.

The western area is comparatively well served with railways, and in the Ukraine a high line density exists. Excluding the frontier with Finland there are altogether four double and eight single lines leading to the western frontier, and these would in theory be capable of maintaining 180 divisions. This figure, however, would be appreciably reduced in war time owing to factors such as enemy air action, requirements of essential railway maintenance traffic, and the probable inability of the Russians to operate the railway system to capacity over a period.

East of Moscow there are three main lines to the Urals, and a fourth line some 250 miles in length connects Moscow with the important Gorki industrial area. In the Ural area itself, line density would in all probability prove sufficient for requirements. Still further to the East all lines converge on Omsk, the starting point of the Trans-Siberian Railway, which is the only line to the Soviet Far East.

North of Moscow, the only lines of importance are those joining Moscow and Leningrad, with a continuation northwards to Murmansk; and the line from Moscow to Archangel. The former is a first-class double line as far as Leningrad, while the latter is at present single but is in process of being doubled.

South of Moscow there are two main lines joining the capital with the industrially important basin of the River Don.

It is important to note that work is now in hand to improve transit facilities in Moscow itself, and it is hoped that in the near future the acute congestion caused by north–south and east–west traffic meeting in Moscow will be relieved by a circular line round the capital.

(ii) *Trans-Siberian railway.*—The Trans-Siberian railway starts at Omsk, in Western Siberia, and continues via Krasnoyarsk, the south end of Lake Baikal and the north bank of the River Amur to Khabarovsk and thence to Vladivostok. The line is double throughout, with a maintenance capacity estimated at 34 divisions, and runs entirely through Russian territory. An alternative route to Vladivostok branches off from the main line at Kaimskaya, some 350 miles east of Lake Baikal, and runs to the Manchukuo frontier at Manchuria. Thence it continues in Manchukuo territory until the frontier close to Vladivostok. This line is the old Chinese Eastern Railway, and is the normal route for travellers in peace time.

The Trans-Siberian railway east of Lake Baikal runs for its entire length in close proximity to the Manchukuo frontier, and would be, therefore, very vulnerable in the event of war in the Far East. In order to overcome this disability, and acquire greater strategical freedom, a new line is being built which, branching off from the Trans-Siberian at a point west of Lake Baikal, will keep considerably north of the existing line. Few details of the progress and exact alignment of the new railway are available, but owing to the extreme difficulty of the country it is to traverse, it is definitely a project of a long-term nature. When completed, it will not increase the number of divisions which can be maintained in the Far East, as their number is limited by the capacity of the more westerly portions of the Trans-Siberian railway.

(iii) *Central Asian railways.*—There are three lines of railway connecting Central Asia and European Russia. These are the Tashkent, which affords direct rail communication with Moscow ; the Ashkhabad, which links up with the European system by a steamer service across the Caspian Sea from Krasnovodsk to Baku and Makhach Kala ; and the Turk-Sib which connects the Tashkent with the Trans-Siberian at Novosibirsk.

The Tashkent railway is a continuation of the Moscow–Orenburg line and runs from Orenburg to Aris and Tashkent at which place it joins the Ashkhabad railway. Another line from Uralsk to Iletsk (40 miles South of Orenburg) affords alternative communication from this point via Saratov with European Russia. Both lines are single track.

The Ashkhabad railway commences at Krasnovodsk on the eastern shore of the Caspian and runs east via Merv and Samarkand until it connects with the Tashkent railway at Tashkent. The track is single throughout.

The principal branches are :—
    Merv–Kushk (on the Afghan frontier).
    Kagan–Termez–Stalinabad (Termez is on the
        Afghan frontier).

The Turk-Sib railway, opened in 1931, connects the Siberian and the Tashkent systems and runs from Semipalatinsk to Lugovaya. The line is single and owing to the haste with which it was laid its capacity is very low. Its strategic importance lies in the fact that it affords an additional line of communication from European Russia to Central Asia. This importance, however, is considerably nullified by the existence of the bottle-neck from Aris onwards to the south, and the existence of the Turk-Sib does not at present increase the potential capacity of the railways to maintain troops on the Afghan frontier.

(iv) *Caucasian railways.*—The main railway line to the Caucasus runs from Rostov-on-Don to Makhach Kala and thence along the coast of the Caspian to Baku. It is double track as far as Prokhladnyenski and thence single. There are several single track branch lines, the more important being those to Novorossiisk and Tuapse on the Black Sea coast and that to Ordzhonikidze at the northern end of the Georgian Military Road. From Baku a line connects the Caspian and Black Seas, running via Tbilisi to Batumi. Portions of it are double and most of the single line track is electrified. From Tbilisi a branch runs south to Leninakan where it forks; a narrow gauge line crosses the Turkish frontier to Kars and a 5-ft. gauge line runs along the Turkish and Persian frontiers to Dzhulfa where it crosses into Persia and runs to Tabriz.

A line to connect Baku and Dzhulfa was commenced some years ago and was completed from Baku to within 50 miles of Dzhulfa. Work on the line is continuing.

A line along the Black Sea coast to connect Tuapse with Batumi is also being constructed. It is now complete except for a gap between Sukhumi and Adler.

(b) *Roads.*—With the exception of certain roads mentioned below and those in the immediate vicinity of large towns, the roads of the U.S.S.R. are in general few in number and of very poor quality.

The greater majority of roads are in reality no more than cart-tracks and resemble the dirt roads of the North American prairie. In many parts of Russia, however, movement by wheeled vehicles can take place independently of roads for about five months in the winter, when the ground is frozen solid. Chains must be carried. During the period of thaw, movement is virtually impossible except on metalled roads.

In European Russia, metalled roads are under construction between Moscow and Minsk and Moscow and Kiev.

The former is nearing completion. In the Caucasus a fair road known as the " Georgian Military Highway " runs from Ordzhonikidze to Tbilisi, and is continued to Leninakan. In Central Asia roads have been constructed between Osh and Khorog and between Ura Tyube and Stalinabad. The former is being continued to Frunze.

In the Far East, a good road known as " Stalin's Highway " runs between Khabarovsk and Vladivostok.

(c) *Canal and river transport.*—Rivers and canals are used as a means of communication in Russia during the navigation season, which seldom exceeds six months. Owing, however, to the present state of disorganization, this method of communication is unlikely to be of great military importance.

3. Climate, meteorology and effect on health

(a) *Climate.*—In a country so vast as the U.S.S.R., over half of which lies in Asia, climatic conditions vary very greatly. The only features general to most parts are that the climate is " continental," *i.e.*, the variations between mean summer and winter temperatures are great, and that January is the coldest and July the warmest month.

In winter, intense cold prevails in the north and south-east, while in the south-west mild winters are common. In summer, conditions of tropical heat exist in the south-eastern part of Central Asia.

In the Caucasus great extremes of climate are found in the hilly regions, but at sea level comparatively equable conditions are experienced throughout the year.

Except in the mild southern coastal areas, snow and ice conditions persist generally from December to March, and the majority of the rainfall occurs between April and July.

(b) *Meteorology.*—In winter, the " cold pole " of the earth is located in Eastern Siberia. The mean temperature of Vorkheyansk in January is $-59°$ F.; in February 1892 $-90°$ F. was recorded, this being the lowest reading ever taken on the surface of the earth. It is possible that these extremely low temperatures are found only in valleys in which the cold air collects, and neighbouring hills may be considerably warmer. From this " cold pole " there is a steady increase in temperature in all directions. The high pressure centre which is largely the result of the extreme cold lies further to the south, and a wedge of high pressure extends through Western Asia and Eastern Europe roughly along latitude 50° N. This wedge of pressure is a well-known wind divide. To the south of it, in Turkestan, the winds are north, north-east and east, very cold and dry. To the north of it the winds are west and south-west, and the ameliorating influences of the North Atlantic penetrate to the north-west of Siberia.

(c) *Effect on health.*—The U.S.S.R. covers a large part of the earth's surface and extends from Europe to the Pacific and from the Arctic to the borders of Persia, Afghanistan and the Himalayas. In such a large country climatic conditions vary greatly and, with the exception of tropical climates, the U.S.S.R. includes almost every known type. It is not possible, therefore, to generalise on the effect of the climate on health. The problem must be studied in relation to the particular area in which military operations are envisaged.

4. Population. *See* Chapter III, paragraph.1.

5. Coinage, Weights and Measures. *See* Appendix.

CHAPTER III

MANPOWER AND PERSONNEL

1. Population

The inhabitants of the U.S.S.R. consist of 180 different nationalities of which there are 19 with populations in excess of half a million. The total population of the country was reported in 1939 to be 170,467,186, a number which contained some 80,000,000 " Great Russians " and over 30,000,000 Ukrainians.

The population is mainly rural but the urban population is increasing rapidly as a result of industrialization and in 1939 had reached 32·8 of the total.

The average density of population per square mile is about three persons in the steppe lands, 15 in the forest areas, and 75 in the black soil areas. The small civil population in the Far East has been increased by settling on the land army reservists who are liable to recall on mobilization, and by rapid agricultural and industrial development in any suitable areas.

Note.—The population was increased by about 12,000,000 when the Polish Ukraine and Polish White Russia were incorporated in the Soviet Union.

2. Law of Military Service

Military service in the U.S.S.R. is regulated by the Law of Military Service dated 1st September, 1939. Military service is compulsory for all male citizens between the ages of 19 and 50. Women possessing certain technical qualifications may be called upon to attend courses of instruction in time of peace ; and those who have had this training may be called up for auxiliary and special service in time of war. A certain number of women are to be found in the combatant arms of the Red Army.

Exemption from military service is allowed in the following cases only :—

    (i) On medical grounds.
    (ii) For special family reasons.

3. Terms of service and general training

(a) *General.*—Male citizens are called up between the ages of 18 years and 8 months and 20 years and 8 months. except in the case of those who have passed five classes of a secondary school who are called up one year earlier. The annual class is generally called up between 15th September and 15th October.

(b) *Pre-enrolment training in civil schools.*—All male students must carry out preliminary military training for which five hours in each six-day period (the Russian week) are allotted :

(c) *Active service.*—The terms of service with the colours are :—

For rank and file of the land forces of the Army	2 years.
For Junior Commanding Personnel (N.C.O.s of the land forces of the Army)	3 years.
For other ranks and Junior Commanding Personnel of the Military Air Force	3 years.
For other ranks and Junior Commanding Personnel of Coast Defence Units	4 years.
For other ranks and Junior Commanding Personnel of the Navy	5 years.

Formerly some men of the annual class were allotted to territorial units, where they served for certain intermittent periods spread over five years. This system was abolished in 1939, but a considerable proportion of the reservists at present available was trained in this way.

Men who have been promoted into the Junior Commanding Personnel grade may, in certain circumstances, be permitted to re-engage for a further period of colour service.

(d) *Service in the Reserve.*—The Reserve is divided into two categories :—

1st Category ..	All men who have completed the statutory period of training with the colours.
2nd Category	Those who were surplus to requirements or were exempted from training on family or medical grounds.

The Reserve is also divided into three age groups.
    1st group up to 35 years.
    2nd group from 35 to 45 years.
    3rd group from 45 to 50 years.

Men between 40 and 50 will be allotted as far as possible to duties in the rear echelons of the Army.

(e) *Reserve training.*—Reservists may be called up for the following periods of training during their service in the various age groups:—

Category.	1st Group.	2nd Group.	3rd Group.	Total.
Privates, 1st category	Up to 6 periods of 2 months each.	Up to 5 periods of 1 month each.	One month	up to 18 months.
N.C.O.s, 1st category	Up to 6 periods of 3 months each.	Up to 5 periods of 1 month each.	One month	up to 2 years.
2nd category, all ..	Up to 9 periods of 2 months each.	Up to 5 periods of 1 month each.	One month	up to 2 years.

(f) *Outside the Army training.*—The object of this form of training is to provide a maximum of six months training to all men liable for military service who are surplus to the requirements of the Army and troops of the Commissariat for Internal Affairs and who have not obtained exemption from serving. The training, which must not exceed two months in any one year, is generally performed in short musters at various times of year, and is organized by the Osoviakhim, a patriotic society.

Formerly a considerable number of men were trained under this system, but with the growth of the Red Army the number has steadily declined.

(g) *Service in Labour Units.*—As many as are required of those men who are not allowed the honour of bearing arms may be called up for service for a period not exceeding three years in labour units, transport services, factories, etc. On the completion of their service they are placed in the Back Area Reserve and remain liable to recall up to the age of 41. Those who are not required to serve are transferred at once to the Back Area Reserve.

4. (a) Officers

(i) *General.*—Until 1935 no classification by ranks, such as is customary in most armies, existed in the Red Army. In 1935, however, the Government, apparently finding the existing system unworkable and incompatible with the proper exercise of command introduced a system of ranks details of which are given in Appendix " A."

In the same year the social classification of officers and N.C.O.s was estimated to be :—

Workmen	45 per cent.
Peasants	27 per cent.
Others	28 per cent.

The last category contained a certain number who received their military education in the Imperial Russian Army, but the number of these has been gradually decreasing, a process which was hastened considerably by the " purge " of 1937–38.

Although the large majority of officers are members of the Communist party, the commanders of formations and units are assisted by a Military Commissar or Political Assistant. Further details of these political officers are given in paragraph 4 (b).

(ii) *Recruitment*.—The normal method of recruiting combatant officers is through the Military Colleges. The essential condition for admission to these institutions is that candidates should have completed a primary national school, *i.e.*, an elementary school where children up to 14 years of age are taught reading, writing and arithmetic. Provided they have this educational qualification, candidates are accepted either from among serving N.C.O.s, or from workmen and peasants between the ages of 17 and 22 who have not yet commenced their military service. The latter may be either volunteers or men selected by the recruiting commissariats. All candidates have to undergo a competitive examination at the end of their course in the Military College. Generally about one-third of the successful candidates in the examination are men drawn originally from the ranks of N.C.O.s, slightly less than one-third from volunteers, and the remainder from the men specially selected by the recruiting commissiariats.

The course of instruction at these colleges lasts two years for infantry and cavalry and three years for artillery and technical troops and includes periods of summer or autumn training camp. On completion of the course N.C.O.s at once become junior officers. Those who have done no military training with the active army serve for nine months with a unit on probation before they are finally accepted as officers.

Under a regulation dated May, 1934, selected N.C.O.s may now, after a minimum of 6 months' satisfactory service as such and subject to passing an examination, be appointed direct as junior officers.

(iii) *Promotion.*—Provided he has the necessary qualifications, any officer will be promoted after serving the minimum period in his rank as shown in Appendix " B." Before being promoted to the rank of Major, officers must have completed a special course at the school of the arm of the service to which they belong. To qualify for the rank of Brigade Commander, officers must have shown marked ability and have graduated at a Military Academy or passed one of the courses for higher commanders.

The Commissar for Defence is empowered in exceptional cases to promote officers over the head of others of the same date or to lessen the period to be served by an officer in a particular rank. Staff officers and officers on the Staff of Departments or of Military Educational Establishments may receive in this way accelerated promotion, with the proviso that, if the promotion is from Major to Colonel, the officer in question must at some time or other have actually commanded a battalion, artillery group or corresponding unit for at least a year. Similarly, before an officer can be promoted in this way to Brigade Commander, he must have actually commanded a Regiment or held a similar independent command for at least two years.

Promotion to Divisional Commander and above, is not governed by length of service in the previous rank, but will be made at the pleasure of the People's Commissar.

The promotions up to the rank of Captain are made by the O.C. Military District, who is also reponsible for the promotion of administrative and political officers up to Major. Promotions to the higher ranks are made by the Commissariat for Defence.

In the event of an officer, whether combatant or otherwise who is qualified by length of service for promotion, receiving an unsatisfactory report he may be allowed to remain for not longer than two years in the rank he holds, and, if at the end of that period he is still unfit for promotion, he will be transferred to some other duty or relegated to the Reserve.

Relegation to a lower rank will only be permitted in exceptional cases and then only by the order of the People's Commissar, or, in the case of officers holding the rank of Brigade Commander or its equivalent, by order of the Government of the U.S.S.R.

(iv) *Retirement.*—Officers normally serve part of their service on the active list and part in the Reserve.

Officers may be relegated to the Reserve as surplus to establishment, in order to take up employment in civil life or on reaching the age limit.

The age limits are :—

Junior Lieutenants and equivalents	30 years
Senior Lieutenants and equivalents	35 years
Captains, Majors and equivalents	40 years
Lieutenant Colonels, Colonels and equivalents	45 years
Brigade Commanders and equivalents	55 years
Divisional Commanders or Senior and equivalents	60 years

The Commissar for Defence may, however, retain the services of any officer for a further period of 10 years if he considers such action necessary in the interests of the army.

(v) *Statistics.*—The total number of officers serving in the active army is estimated at 62,000. The average number passing through Military Colleges is about 6,000 each year. It is anticipated that, with the object of attaining an eventual annual output to the reserve of 15,000 officers, the numbers of students at Military Colleges will gradually be increased.

(b) Technical and Specialist Officers.—(i) *General.*—Administrative, medical, veterinary and political officers are ranked, as shown at Appendix " A ," in a similar way to combatant officers. They are recruited either by promotion from non-commissioned officers ; from officers of other arms unfit for regimental duties ; or from officers transferring voluntarily.

(ii) *Military Commissars.*—Military commissars constitute a corps of their own and are a branch of the Communist Party in the Army. They are allotted to each unit and formation, and their object is principally to ensure loyalty of military personnel to the Communist regime not only during their service in the Army but on their return to civil life.

The part played by political officers in the Military Councils of Military Districts is described in Chapter V, paragraph 2.

Before being appointed to the Army, the majority of military commissars are passed through military political academies, which exist in most military districts. They are recruited either direct from civil life or from the ranks (including officers) of the army. Combatant officers who undergo the course pass out as commissars and do not remain combatant officers.

The output of military political academies is at present being supplemented by the appointment of a certain number of so-called " junior political leaders " direct from the ranks of the army. They appear to be employed in units below the battalion or its equivalent.

The above applies to the new entry. Most of the present senior commissars of the Red Army served as such or as combatant officers during the civil war.

When ranks were introduced for officers, equivalent ranks (with different titles) were also introduced for commissars, but only from the equivalent rank of Major upwards ; the smallest unit to which a fully fledged military commissar (as opposed to junior political leader) is attached is the battalion or its equivalent, commanded by a Major. Promotion of military commissars is carried out on a time scale up to the equivalent rank of Colonel and above, and is then by selection as in the case of combatant officers.

The duties of military commissars are of an all-embracing nature, as they include taking an active part in every form of military training in addition to the performance of their primary role of the political training of the troops. Together with the Commanding Officer, they bear full responsibility for the state of preparedness of the unit for war and for its administration ; also for the state of its armament, discipline, political reliability and training. In certain cases they appear to take command of the unit in the absence or on the disablement of the Commanding Officer.

The military commissar is solely responsible for the carrying out of all orders relating to the preservation of military secrets, and has himself to set an example in this respect. His political work includes the leadership of the party organizations within the army, the direction of propaganda in units and the maintenance of continuous connection with local party organizations.

(c) Reserve Officers.—The Reserve of Officers is divided into three sections. Army officers serve in the various categories up to the ages specified below.

	1st Section.	2nd Section.	3rd Section.
Junior Lieutenants and equivalents	40	50	55
Senior Lieutenants and equivalents	45	55	60
Captains, Majors and equivalents..	50	55	60
Lieutenant-Colonels, Colonels and equivalents.	50	55	60
Divisional Commanders or Senior and equivalents.	60	—	65

During their service in various categories officers may be called up for the following periods of training :—

>In 1st section .. Up to 3 months in each year.
>In 2nd section .. Twice, for periods of not more than 3 months each.
>In 3rd section .. Once, for not more than 2 months.

In order to obtain additional officers the following may be appointed as officers of the Reserve :—

(a) N.C.O.s who have completed their colour service and passed certain schools and classes.

(b) Students at higher educational establishments who have attained a certain standard of military preparation.

5. Non-commissioned officers

(a) *Recruitment.*—N.C.O.s are recruited from men in the ranks who have distinguished themselves by good service or have attained a satisfactory standard of education and completed at least one year's service, which includes a period of training at the special courses in the regimental schools. All conscripts who are members of the Communist Party or Komsomol* must attend the regimental school; others can do so if they volunteer and are accepted. Men who have passed through only five forms of a State " gymnasium" are detailed to the school for section commanders; those who have completed seven forms, to the school for platoon commanders.

Administrative N.C.O.s are drawn from personnel who have received training in administrative duties during their service and from N.C.O.s of other arms unable to continue in their duties owing to ill-health.

(b) *Terms of service.*—N.C.O.s serve under the same regulations as the rank and file, both in the active army and in the reserve. On completion of their service, they may be either sent on extended leave or allowed to re-engage for periods of one year at a time as volunteers up to the age of 45.

Promotion procedure is similar to that for officers, vacancies being filled within the regiment or, if there is no one qualified in the regiment, from the divisional qualification list.

---

* Communist League of Youth.

CHAPTER IV

GENERAL ORGANIZATION AND STRENGTH

1. Functions, composition and organization in peace.

(a) *Functions.*—The Red Army, in addition to fulfilling the normal functions of a national conscript army in peace, *i.e.*, training the youth of the nation for war, maintaining internal security and providing for the defence of the frontiers, is the principal agency on which the Soviet Government relies to maintain the stability of the present régime.

The Government attempts through the Army to popularise the communist doctrine among the peoples of the U.S.S.R. The conscript, during his service, is well looked after materially, given a rudimentary education and submitted to a continuous and intensive course of communist propaganda, with the object that he shall become a convinced supporter of the régime and, on his return to civil life, exert himself amongst his fellows to spread the Communist doctrine.

(b) *Composition.*—The Red Army comprises regular and territorial troops, though the territorial element is rapidly disappearing *vide* Chapter III 3 (d).

Regular units include a permanent cadre of officers and N.C.O.s except of the most junior grades : the remainder are conscripts who serve the first two years of their military training continuously and are then transferred to the Reserve.

Territorial units contain strong permanent cadres of regular personnel, who train the territorial " changeable personnel " when they come up for their annual period of training. The numbers of changeable personnel are, however, falling as no more are being recruited, and territorial units are gradually being converted to a regular basis.

Certain, if not the majority, of regular divisions have additional cadres over and above the normal peace strength of the division, which train the reservists who will form second line divisions on mobilization.

Divisions containing some territorial and some regular units are classified as " mixed divisions." Such divisions are usually in a transitional state between the territorial and regular organizations.

(c) *Organization.* In peace, where the highest fighting formation existing is the Corps, the Red Army is distributed in Military Districts and Commissariats, the headquarters of which are responsible for the administration and training of the formations and units located therein, performing in fact very much the same functions as a Command Headquarters in the U.K. In certain special cases armies may be formed, as has occurred in the Far East.

There are at the present time 15 Military Districts and 2 Military Commissariats in the U.S.S.R.

2. Peace strength and general distribution

(a) *Strength.*—It is estimated that, at the present time, the peace strength of the regular army, including the air arm and the permanent cadre of territorial formations, is about 2,000,000 which includes some 115 infantry divisions, 35 cavalry divisions, and 5 mechanized corps (each roughly equivalent to a light armoured division).

The total number of " changeable personnel " undergoing training with territorial formations in any one year is difficult to assess, as it is not known how long the various divisions have been in process of conversion to a regular basis.

(b) *Distribution.*—The peace-time distribution of the army depends partly on the density of the population and partly on considerations of internal security and strategy. The great bulk of the army is located in peace in the frontier districts.

3. Composition and strength of an Army

The highest formation headquarters existing in peace is that of a corps with the exception of armies formed for a special purpose such as the 1st and 2nd Independent Red Banner Armies in the Far East. During the wars in Poland and Finland the N.K.O. appears to have performed the functions of a G.H.Q., but it is uncertain whether it would do so in a war of the first magnitude ; Front Headquarters and Army Headquarters were formed to direct operations in the various sectors. No definite information is available as to how the transformation to a war organization is effected ; but the following is an estimate of what would occur should the Soviet Union become engaged in a war of the first magnitude.

As regards G.H.Q., it is probable that either :—
  (a) The Commissariat for Defence (N.K.O.) will act as G.H.Q.;
      or
  (b) A separate G.H.Q. will be formed;
      or
  (c) In the event of hostilities on more than one front, a G.H.Q. will be formed for each theatre, subordinate either to the N.K.O. or to supreme G.H.Q.

The composition of an Army is not known, but in the event of war on a large scale, it is believed that Armies would each consist of 3–6 Infantry Corps, plus cavalry, army troops, etc.

4. Composition and strength of a Corps

(a) *The Infantry Corps* contains in peace from two to three infantry divisions. Its normal composition in war is as follows :—

  Corps Headquarters.
  Three Infantry Divisions.
  One or two Regiments of Corps Artillery.
  One Corps A.A. Artillery Group.
  One Corps Sapper Battalion.
  One Corps Signal Battalion.
  Administrative troops.
  One Corps Reconnaissance ⎫
  Squadron of two flights   ⎬ (attached).

(*Note.*—Chemical battalions have been formed on a scale roughly sufficient to provide one per infantry corps. It is probable, however, that these battalions will be retained at G.H.Q. or Army Troops and not permanently allocated to infantry corps.)

The war establishment of an infantry corps is approximately 62,000 all ranks.

(b) The Cavalry Corps contains both in peace and war two or three cavalry divisions. Its normal composition in war is as follows :—

  Corps Headquarters.
  Two Cavalry Divisions.
  One Corps Signal Squadron or Group.
  Administrative Troops.

The war establishment of a cavalry corps of two divisions is approximately 17,000 all ranks.

5. Composition and strength of the infantry division

Infantry divisions are of two types, normal establishment and mountain divisions.

(a) *Infantry divisions on normal establishments.*—The basis of the organization of all infantry divisions, except mountain divisions, is as follows :—

    Divisional Headquarters.
    Three Infantry Regiments.
    One or two Divisional Field Artillery Regiments.
    One Divisional Sapper Battalion.
    One Divisional Signal Battalion.
    One Divisional Reconnaissance Battalion.
    One Divisional Tank Battalion.
    Administrative Troops.

An independent Anti-Tank Group (O.P.T.D.) is generally attached to each Infantry Division in war-time. For composition and strength, *vide* Chapter VIII, 9.

Chemical warfare companies have also been identified in some divisions.

Many regular infantry divisions, if not all, also contain a special cadre of about 3,000 all ranks which is detached on mobilization to form the nucleus of a second line division.

The war strength of an infantry division is about 18,000. The peace strengths of various types are believed to be as follows :—

    Regular divisions in Far East and certain ones in western frontier districts .. .. About 16,000
    Other regular divisions .. .. About 13,500

(b) *Mountain divisions.*—These divisions are located in the Central Asian and Trans-Caucasian military districts.

They have a special peace organization as follows :—

    Divisional Headquarters.
    Three Regiments (believed to be on a low establishment).
    Field Artillery Regiment (H.Q. and possibly only two groups).
    Sapper Battalion.
    Signal Battalion.
    Reconnaissance Group.
    Administrative Troops.

It has also been reported that these divisions each contain either a tank company or a tank battalion.

The transport of these divisions is largely on a pack basis.

6. Composition and strength of the cavalry division.

Cavalry divisions may be either normal establishment or mountain divisions.

(a) *Cavalry division on normal establishment.*—These divisions contain permanent cadres of regular personnel and regular or territorial conscripts in the same way as infantry divisions, although the territorial element is disappearing. Five of these divisions are "cossack divisions," and contain exclusively cossack personnel.

All are organized as follows :—

>Divisional Headquarters.
>Four (Horsed) Cavalry Regiments.
>One Mechanized Cavalry Regiment.
>One Horse Artillery Regiment.
>One Sapper Squadron.
>One Signal Group.
>Administrative Troops.

Chemical warfare troops have been identified in some cavalry divisions.

The war establishment of a cavalry division is believed to be between 6,000 and 7,000.

(b) *Mountain cavalry divisions* are located in the C.A.M.D. and are regular formations.

They have a special peace organization which is as follows :—

>Divisional Headquarters.
>Four Cavalry Regiments.
>One Horse Artillery Group.
>One Sapper Squadron.
>One Signal Squadron.
>One Mechanized Group.
>Administrative Troops.

Chemical warfare troops have also been reported in mountain cavalry divisions.

Mountain cavalry divisions are believed to be equipped largely on a pack basis.

7. Composition and strength of an infantry brigade

No brigade organization exists in the infantry. The organization of the regiment is given in Chapter VI, paragraph 2.

8. Composition and strength of a cavalry brigade

There are only two cavalry brigades; one in the North Caucasus and one in the Trans-Baikal military District. They are reported to consist of three cavalry regiments and a horse artillery group.

9. Organization, composition and strength of air defence troops

These consist of :—

(i) Air defence divisions and anti-aircraft defence brigades, forming a part of the Army Artillery (A.R.G.K.), the organization of which is described in Chapter VIII, G.1 (*a*).

(ii) Independent anti-aircraft defence troops, the function of which is to protect those parts of the country outside the zone of active operations. These troops are controlled by the Air Defence Department of the N.K.O. Details of their organization are given in Chapter VIII, G.1 (*b*).

10. Organization, composition and strength of coast defence troops

These troops are the responsibility of the Naval Department of the Commissariat of Defence. They consist of mobile and non-mobile brigades of heavy artillery.

11. Armoured and mechanized formations and units

These consist of :—

Mechanized Corps—corresponding in size to armoured divisions.

Mechanized Brigades—at the disposal of the higher command.

Mechanized Brigades—permanently allotted to definite cavalry corps.

Independent Tank Brigades and occasionally battalions.

Mechanized Cavalry Regiments.

Divisional Units.

Their organization is given in Chapter XI.

CHAPTER V

ADMINISTRATION, COMMANDS AND STAFFS

1. General notes on the higher administration of the armed forces

The supreme authority in the U.S.S.R. responsible for the organisation of the armed forces, including the passing of the Military Budget, etc., is in theory the Supreme Council of the U.S.S.R., or, if that body is not sitting, the Presidium. In practice, however, the supreme executive and administrative body in the government is the Council of People's Commissars (Sovnarkom), which corresponds to the Cabinet in Great Britain.

Directly responsible to the Sovnarkom is the body known as the Council of Labour and Defence (S.T.O.). Working in conjunction with the S.T.O. is the Commissariat for Defence Industry. The delimitation of responsibility between it and the Commissariat of Heavy Industry on the one hand and the S.T.O. on the other is not yet clear, as no decrees have been published, and no opportunity for judging the working of the organization has yet occurred since the Commissariat for Defence Industry was only created in the latter part of 1936.

The supreme "military organ" for the control of the armed forces was, up to 1934, the Revolutionary Military Council. In that year the Soviet Government, recognising apparently the need for eliminating collective control and strengthening the element of personal command, abolished this council, changed the title of the then Commissariat for Military and Naval Affairs to Commissariat for Defence (N.K.O.), and made its chief responsible directly to the Sovnarkom. Thus, although no Commander-in-Chief is actually appointed in peace-time, the supreme command of the Red armed forces is, in fact, vested in the Commissar for Defence. In 1939 the formation of a General Military Council containing many of the most influential members of the Government was announced. Though this body is nominally of a more or less advisory nature, it is probable that in practice it also enjoys executive control over the Army; and is in effect the equivalent of the Committee of Imperial Defence.

The Commissariat for Defence is responsible for the organization, training and administration of all the armed forces of the U.S.S.R., with the exception of the Navy, and of the troops of the Commissariat for Internal Affairs (N.K.V.D., ex-O.G.P.U.) particulars of which are contained in Chapter XIII.

The N.K.O. has recently undergone considerable re-organization, full details of which have proved impossible to obtain. It appears to consist of the following six main elements :—

> The People's Commissar for Defence, his three deputies, and certain senior officers who are attached for special duties.
> The Secretariat of the N.K.O.
> The General Staff and Inspectors.
> Independent Departments, of which there are 19.
> Independent Sections of which there are four.
> The Military Council of the Supreme Court.

2. Military Councils

(a) *The General Military Council.*—No detailed information about the functions or composition of this Council is available.

(b) *The Military Council.*—On the abolition of the Revolutionary War Council in 1934, this Council was instituted : but whereas the former had executive power (which then became vested in the newly-constituted N.K.O.), the latter is a purely advisory body. The Commissar for Defence appoints its members, subject to the approval of the Sovnarkom, determines when it shall meet and what subjects it shall discuss, and has to confirm its decisions before they can be put into effect. The members number approximately 80, and represent Departments of the N.K.O. and the staffs of Military Districts and of higher formations. The Council appears, in fact, to be designed to fulfil the same role of discussion and investigation as the annual Staff Conferences held in this country.

(c) *District Military Councils.*—In May, 1937, a decree of the Central Executive Committee of the U.S.S.R. announced the establishment of a Military Council in each Military District.

The Commander of the Military District is ex officio President of the Council which has two other members and sometimes apparently more. These members appear to include a senior army officer such as the Deputy O.C., a senior Political Officer of the Red Army who may be the Chief or ex-Chief of the Political Department, or a highly placed official of the party organization in the district. The object of the organization is almost certainly to tighten up political control in the Red Army, for simultaneously with the publication of the decree the reinstitution of Military Commissars into all units was announced. It is probable that this dual system of control is having an adverse effect on the military efficiency of the Red Army.

The regulations for the guidance of District Military Councils are :—

(i) At the head of a military district (or army) is a Military Council, comprising the commander of the forces and two members.

(ii) The commander of the forces of the district (or army) presides over the meetings of the Military Council.

(iii) The Military Council of district (or army) is the highest representative of military authority in the district (or army). All military units and military institutions located in the territory of the district (or army) are subordinate to the Military Council.

(iv) The Military Council of a district (or army) has full responsibility for the political and moral condition, and for the fighting and mobilization readiness of the military units and military institutions located in the territory of the district.

(v) The Military Council of a district (or army) is subordinated directly to the People's Commissar of Defence of the U.S.S.R.

(vi) The Military Council of a district (or army) is charged with :—

Directing the military and political training of the forces of the district (or army). Preparing the forces of the district, the means of transport and the means of communication in the territory of the district for mobilization.

Studying and selecting commanding cadres of the units and institutions of the district (or army). Educating the Red Army men and all commanders in the spirit of selfless devotion to the fatherland and Soviet power, in the spirit of a merciless struggle against the enemies of the people, against spies, diversionists and wreckers.

Directing the supply of the units and institutions of the district (or army) with all forms of technical and material equipment.

Organizing anti-aircraft defence of the territory of the district, controlling and inspecting the work of anti-aircraft defence of all civil institutions and public organizations.

Directing the enrolment of citizens of the U.S.S.R. for active military service and periodic training.

Directing defence and non-defence construction in the territory of the district (or army).

Taking an active part in the work of the civil organizations in strengthening the rear.

(vii) All orders for the district (or army) are signed by the commander of the forces, by one of the members of the Military Council, and by the chief of the Staff of the District.

(viii) In view of the fact that the commander of the forces of the military district (or army) is the supreme chief of all the forces and military institutions located in the territory of the district (or army), orders for the district (or army) are given in the name of the commander of the forces (" I order........ ").

3. Administrative districts

For purposes of military administration, the U.S.S.R. is normally divided into the following 15 Military Districts, 2 Independent Armies; and 2 Military Commissariats:—

Moscow (M.M.D.).
Leningrad (L.M.D.).
Kalinin (Ka.M.D.).
White Russian (W.R.M.D.) recently organized into the White Russian front.
Orel (O.M.D.).
Kharkov (Kh.M.D.).
Odessa (Od.M.D.).
Kiev (K.M.D.) recently organized into the Ukrainian Front.
North Caucasus (N.C.M.D.).
Trans-Caucasian (T.C.M.D.).
Pri-Volga (P.V.M.D.).
Ural (Ur. M.D.).
Central Asian (C.A.M.D.).
Siberian (S.M.D.)
Trans-Baikal (T.B.M.D.).
The 1st and 2nd (Red Banner) Armies.
In the Far East the Northern Military Commissariat (N.M.C.) and the Kazakh Military Commissariat (K.M.C.).

4. The General Staff

The General Staff of the N.K.O. is responsible for all questions concerning the preparation of the armed forces for war and the study of potential theatres of operations. At the head of this department is the Chief of Staff who is responsible directly to the Commissar for Defence. It is organized in sections and inspectorates directly subordinate to the Chief of the General Staff which are shown below :—

Sections	*Inspectors*
Operations.	Infantry.
Training.	Cavalry.
Military communications.	Artillery.
Intelligence.	P.T. and sports.
L. of C.	Military bands.
Mobilization.	

5. Administrative staffs

The administrative branch of the N.K.O. is organized in independent departments, which include the following :—

Personal services.
Higher training establishments.
Military educational establishments.
Artillery.
Engineers.
Signals.
Chemical warfare.
Mechanization and armoured forces.
Anti-aircraft defence.
Political.
Supplies.
Stud farms.
Transport, supplies and equipment.
Medical.
Veterinary.
Military works and barracks.
Air force.
Technical department.
Remounts.

6. Organization of the Higher Command in peace and war

(i) *Peace.*—The Commissar for Defence fulfils the function of Commander-in-Chief in peace. No formation headquarters higher than that of Corps exists in peace except in special circumstances in frontier districts. The orders of the Commissar for Defence are issued to the Commanders of Military Districts, who together with the other members of District Military Councils, are responsible for the training and administration of all troops, military schools and institutions in their districts, and for the organization of the defences of any frontier which these districts may include.

Technical branches are allowed to issue instructions on purely technical subjects to the corresponding branch in the next lower formation.

(ii) *War*.—The possibility that, in war, a G.H.Q. might be formed for each front in addition to the formation of armies is referred to in greater detail in Chapter IV, 3.

It is understood that the peace-time system of command through the headquarters of military districts will continue to function in war in those parts of the country which are outside the zone of hostilities.

7. Chain of command in the field

A Commander-in-Chief, selected by the Sovnarkom, would be appointed in war either for the whole of the military forces of the U.S.S.R., or for one theatre, should active operations be thus limited. Under the Commander-in-Chief would be various fronts or armies according to the extent of the operations and the size of the forces involved. Thus armies would contain a varying number of infantry corps, and either cavalry corps or separate cavalry divisions.

Special formations, such as mechanised formations and the heavier natures of artillery, are " at the disposal of the Higher Command ". In peace time this means that they are under the Commanders of Military Districts, and in war they would presumably come either under G.H.Q. or under Army Commanders.

8. Organization of an Army Staff

The only formation in peace approximating to an army, of which any details are at present known, is the Primorskaya Group in the Far East which has become the 1st Primorskaya (Red Banner) Army and which previously possessed :—

> Commander.
> Possibly a deputy O.C.
> Commissar.
> Chief of Political Department.
> Chief of Staff.
> Chief of Engineers.
> Chief of Signals.
> Chief of Mechanized Forces.
> Assistant for Ordnance and Supplies.
> Assistant for Air Forces.

The Staff of an army may, however, be based on that of a military district in peace. The Commander of the district is also President of the Military Council and is assisted by :—
    Members of Military Council (usually two members).
    Deputy Commander.
    Chief of Staff (and sometimes also a Deputy Chief of Staff).
    Chief of Political Department (and sometimes a deputy).
    Assistant for Ordnance and Supplies.
    Assistant for Air Forces.
    Army Inspector (in certain cases).

The Headquarters are organized as follows :—

(a) *Department of Chief of Staff* with sections dealing with :—
    (i) Operations.
    (ii) Training.
    (iii) Communications.
    (iv) Intelligence.
    (v) Organization and mobilization.
    (vi) Air defence.
    (vii) Remounts.
    (viii) Administration and supply of headquarters.

(b) *Chiefs of Arms and Services* :—
    Chief of Artillery.
    Chief of Tank and Mechanized Units.
    Inspector of Air Defence.
    Chief Engineer.
    Chief Signal Officer.
    Chief of Chemical Troops.
    Chief of Medical Services.
    Chief of Veterinary Services and in L.M.D., M.M.D., and P.V.M.D. only.
    Chief of Military Schools.

(c) *Department of Ordnance and Supply.*—The Assistant for Ordnance and Supplies is responsible for ordnance, supply, barrack and accountant services, etc., of all formations, etc., in the military district.

His department is sub-divided into sections with :—
    Ammunition supply.
    Technical stores (explosives, mechanical transport, etc.).
    Food and clothing supply.
    Military contracts and barracks.
    Finance.
    Etc., etc.

(d) *Political Department.*
(e) *Co-operative Department.*
(f) *Military Tribunal.*
(g) *Air Force Department.*

9. Duties and organization of corps staffs

(a) *The headquarters of an infantry corps,* with an approximate war establishment of 46 officers (including 9 political) and 156 other ranks, is organized as follows :—
    (i) Command—Corps Commander.
    (ii) General Staff—Under the Chief of Staff are the following sections :—
        (a) Operations and training.
        (b) Organization (equivalent to our "A" branch).
        (c) Communications.
        (d) Intelligence.
        (e) Back Areas (equivalent to our " Q " branch),
        (f) Commandant's.
        (g) Mobilization.*
    (iii) Corps Artillery Headquarters.
    (iv) Corps Engineer Headquarters.
    (v) Corps Signals.
    (vi) Medical Branch.
    (vii) Veterinary Branch.
    (viii) Chemical Warfare Branch.
    (ix) Chief of Supply Branch.
    (x) Commissar.
    (xi) Political Branch (under Chief of Political Department).
    (xii) Military Tribunal.

(b) The headquarters of a cavalry corps with an approximate war establishment of 52 officers (including 13 political) and 183 other ranks, is organized in the same way as that of an infantry corps.

10. Duties and organization of divisional staffs.

The headquarters of the infantry division, with an approximate war establishment of 41 officers and 291 other ranks, is organized on similar lines to that of a corps (*see* paragraph 9).

Its organization is as follows :—
    (i) Command—Divisional Commander ;
        Assistant Divisional Commander.

---

* It is understood that the Mobilization Section would, in the event of war, remain in the Corps Administrative District when the corps itself moves to the front.

(ii) General. Under the Chief of Staff and organized in the Staff and following sections :—
    (a) Operations and Training.
    (b) Organization.
    (c) Communications.
    (d) Intelligence.
    (e) Back Areas.
    (f) Commandant's.
(iii) Chief of Divisional Artillery.
(iv) Chief Engineer.
(v) Chemical Warfare Branch.
(vi) Medical Branch.
(vii) Veterinary Branch.
(viii) Chief of Supply Branch.
(ix) Political Branch—under the Chief Political Officer.

11. Duties and organization of Cavalry Divisional Staffs

The headquarters of the cavalry division has an approximate war establishment of 58 officers (including 21 political) and 177 other ranks, and has the same organization as that of an infantry division.

12. Duties and organization of Brigade Staffs

There is no brigade organization in the Red Army.

13. Duties and organization of staffs of mechanized formations

No details of these staffs are known. It is probable, however, that the staff of a mechanized " Corps " is similar to that of an infantry division.

14. Chain of command for air and coast defences

(a) *Air defences.*—The system of command of air defence troops underwent a change with the formation of an independent air defence department of the N.K.O. in 1935. It appears that the new department is responsible not only for the co-ordination of protective measures for the home country as a whole and for the training of the civilian population in defence measures but also, in theory, for the " command " of the independent anti-aircraft defence troops, *i.e.*, all air defence troops except the anti-aircraft brigades of the A.R.G.K. and anti-aircraft units in active formations of the Red Army. It is probable, however, that, while the department will issue orders as to the organization, equipment and location of these units it will exercise its power of command through the commanders of the military districts.

It is not known where the dividing line defining the areas of responsibility of the department and of the commanders of front or armies will be drawn in war.

(b) *Coast defence.*—Coast defence is the responsibility of the Naval department of the N.K.O., and coast defence units are subordinate to the local Naval Commander.

CHAPTER VI

INFANTRY

1. General organization and strength

The infantry of the Red Army consists of :—

(a) *Regular and occasionally mixed divisions.*—Normally these each comprise three regiments, the number of which run in sequence, the highest being the divisional number multiplied by three ; but since mobilization a large number of regiments have been renumbered or transferred to other formations so this rule no longer holds good.

(b) *Mountain divisions.*—These are regular divisions each consisting of four regiments, the numbers of which are not necessarily consecutive. In peace, regiments in mountain divisions contain only one battalion and one battery.

(c) *Local infantry units.*—These consist of battalions and companies stationed in various localities for guard and defence purposes.

2. Organization and strength of units

(a) *The Regiment.* (*For mountain regiments,* see *paragraph* 3 (d)). (i) *General.*—The infantry regiment consists of :—
    Regimental Headquarters.
    Three battalions.
    One Group Regimental Artillery.
    One Anti-Aircraft Platoon (four A.A. M.G.s).
    One Platoon of Mounted Scouts.
    One Detachment of Snipers.
    One Signal Company.
    One Sapper and Camouflage Platoon.
    One Chemical Platoon.
    One Medical Detachment.
    One Veterinary Detachment.
    One Supply Company (includes Ammunition Supply).
    N.C.O.s' Training Cadre.
    Political Section and Club.

The war establishment of an infantry regiment is about : 3,400 men, 800 horses, 330 vehicles. Its fighting strength is reported as 1,100–1,500 rifles, 82 light automatics, 81 grenade throwers, 70 machine-guns, six 76-mm. guns, ten 37-mm. or 45-mm. guns, six mortars and four A.A. M.G.s.

(ii) *Regimental Headquarters.*—Regimental headquarters is organized as follows :—

    Staff, divided into sections for :
      Operations.
      Personnel.
      Intelligence.
      Signals.
      Supply.
    Band.
    Provost Platoon.
    Meteorological Section.

The war strength of regimental headquarters is approximately : Staff 48 men, Band 26 men, Provost Section 49 men.

(iii) *The Battalion.*—*See* paragraph 2 (b) below.

(iv) *The Regimental Artillery Group.*—The regimental artillery group is organized as follows :—

    Group Headquarters.
    H.Q. Platoon (includes signal and reconnaissance party).
    Supply Platoon and Transport.
    Ammunition Platoon and Transport.
    Two batteries each of three 76-mm. 1927 pattern guns.
    One anti-tank battery of six 37-mm. or 45-mm. guns.

The war establishment of the group is about 311 men, 210 horses, 10 guns and 14 vehicles.

(v) *The Anti-Aircraft Platoon.*—The anti-aircraft platoon is equipped with four anti-aircraft machine guns. At present carts are used for transport but it is believed that M.T. vehicles will soon be provided with M.G.s mounted on them in pairs.

The present war establishment of the platoon is reported to be : 33 men, 16 horses, 8 vehicles, 4 M.G.s.

(vi) *The Platoon of Mounted Scouts.*—The platoon of mounted scouts is reported to have a war strength of 42 men, 42 horses, two vehicles, and one light automatic.

(vii) *The Regimental Detachment of Snipers.*—Snipers are trained in the regimental detachment and on service are attached to companies in accordance with tactical requirements.

It is reported that the strength is four pairs of snipers per company.

(viii) *The Signal Company.*—The signal company is organized as follows :—

    Headquarters.
    Headquarter Platoon :—
        Platoon H.Q.
        One section for communication with aircraft.
        One despatch rider section.
        One dog section.
    Telephone Platoon :—
        Platoon H.Q.
        Four sections.
    Wireless Platoon.

Transport is considered to be platoon rather than company transport.

The war establishment of the company is about 132 men, 27 horses, 11 vehicles and three motor-cycles.

For details of technical equipment, *see* paragraph 12 (*d*).

(ix) *The Sapper and Camouflage Platoon.*—The war strength of the sapper and camouflage platoon is about 23 men, 25 horses, and 12 vehicles.

Reports have recently been received that the platoon may be expanded into a company. It is reported to carry 500 anti-tank mines, camouflage netting, smoke candles, one standard bridging set sufficient for building a footbridge 56 metres long, and three rubber boats.

(x) *The Chemical Platoon.*—The chemical platoon is primarily equipped for defensive purposes but has a small quantity of offensive equipment.

It is organized as follows :—

    Headquarters.
    Three Chemical Warfare Sections.
    One Transport Section.

The chemical platoon carries the following stores :—

    10 per cent. reserve gas masks for the regiment.
    Four decontamination sprayer outfits.
    Fifteen sirens for gas alarm.
    Chloride of lime.
    Toxic smoke candles.
    Smoke producing apparatus.
    Forty gasproof suits (war establishment).

The war strength of the platoon is about 45 men, 16 horses and eight vehicles.

(xi) *The Medical Detachment.*—The medical detachment is organized as follows :—
>   Headquarters.
>   Medical Sections in each company.
>   Dressing Station.
>   Bath and Laundry Detachment.
>   Transport.

The war strength of the detachment is about 69 men (including three or four doctors) 46 horses and 23 vehicles.

(xii) *The Veterinary Detachment.*—The veterinary detachment consists of the veterinary surgeon and his assistants, together with the farriers of the regiment.

The war establishment of the detachment is about 15 men, 3 horses, 2 vehicles.

(xiii) *The Supply Company.*—The supply company is organized as follows :—
>   Headquarters.
>   Supply Section.
>   Ammunition Supply Section.
>   Equipment and Material Store.
>   Workshops.

The war strength of the supply company is about 192 men, 137 horses, 82 H.T. vehicles, 1 motor car and 4 lorries.

(xiv) *The N.C.O.s Training Cadre.*—In peace, every regiment has a school for the purpose of training N.C.O.s. Each school is organized in a headquarters and a varying number of rifle and machine gun platoons.

In addition, in regular regiments, training battalions are formed to train new recruits during their first year of service. These battalions are organized in a headquarters and a varying number of rifle and machine gun companies ; the most efficient officers are supposed to be allotted to them.

(xv) *The Political Section and Club.*—The political section and club (or regimental institute), are under the command of the political assistant or commissar. The personnel includes one political officer per company, who is directly subordinate to the political assistant. A propaganda instructor is appointed to each regiment as instructor of political personnel, officers and permanent staff ; he must have passed the Military Political Academy.

The political branch largely deals with instruction in such subjects as discipline, morale, esprit de corps, hygiene, anti-gas defence, etc.

(b) *The Battalion.*—(i) *General.*—The organization of the battalion is as follows :—

>Battalion Headquarters.
>Signal Platoon.
>Three Rifle Companies.
>One M.G. Company.
>Battalion Artillery Platoon.

The war strength of the battalion is about eight hundred and thirty-one men, ninety-three horses, fifty-seven vehicles, twenty-seven light automatics, twenty-seven grenade throwers, eighteen to twenty-two machine guns, two 37-mm. or 45-mm. guns, and two mortars.

(ii) *Battalion Headquarters.* — Battalion headquarters consists of :—

>Battalion Commander.
>Adjutant and two ⎱ Operations
>Assistant Adjutants ⎰ Intelligence.
>Chief of Supply Services.
>Signal Officer (who is also O.C. signal platoon).

(iii) *The Signal Platoon.*—The signal platoon includes telephone operators, personnel for visual signal communication, orderlies and dogs.

The war strength of the platoon is twenty-eight men, three horses, three vehicles.

(iv) *The Rifle Company.*—*See* paragraph 2(c) below.

(v) *The M.G. Company.*—*See* paragraph 2(d) below.

(vi) *The Battalion Artillery Platoon.*—The battalion artillery platoon is organized in two platoons. One has two 37-mm. or 45-mm. guns, and the other contains two 58-mm. or 81-mm. mortars.

(c) *The Rifle Company.*—(i) *General.*—The organization of the rifle company is as follows :—

>Company Headquarters.
>H.Q. Platoon.
>Three Rifle Platoons.
>One M.G. Platoon.

The war strength of the rifle company is about one hundred and ninety-two men, eleven horses, seven vehicles, nine light automatics, nine grenade throwers, two machine guns.

(ii) *Company Headquarters.* — Company headquarters consists of :—
> Company Commander.
> Political Officer.
> Second-in-Command.
> Sergeant-Major.

(iii) *The Headquarter Platoon.*—The headquarter platoon consists of :—
> Signal and Observation Section.
> Medical and Stretcher-bearer Section.
> Supply Section.
> S.A.A. Section.

(iv) *The Rifle Platoon.*—The rifle platoon is organized as follows :—
> Platoon Headquarters.
> Three Rifle and Light Automatic Sections.
> One Grenade Thrower Section.

Platoon headquarters consist of the platoon commander, the platoon sergeant, one orderly and two S.A.A. carriers.

Each rifle and light automatic section consists of nine to twelve men and one light automatic. Each grenade thrower section consists of seven men and three Dyakonov grenade throwers.

(v) *The Machine Gun Platoon.*—The machine gun platoon is organized as follows :—
> Platoon Headquarters.
> Two Sections (each with one machine gun).

(d) *The Machine Gun Company.*—(i) *General.*—The organization of the machine gun company is as follows :—
> Company Headquarters.
> H.Q. Platoon.
> Three or four M.G. Platoons, each of four guns.

The war strength of the machine gun company is about 186 men, 43 horses, 27 vehicles and 12–16 machine guns.

(ii) *The Headquarter Platoon.*—The headquarter platoon is organized as follows :—
> Signal Section.
> Medical Section.
> Supply Section.
> Ammunition Section.

(iii) *The Machine Gun Platoon.*—The machine gun platoon consists of four sections, each equipped with one machine gun.

3. Special Units.

(*a*) *Local infantry units.*—Local infantry units are of two kinds :—

(i) Infantry units employed in guarding important military depôts and stores, etc.

(ii) Machine gun units employed in anti-aircraft defence.

Units are organized in battalions and companies of varying strength according to the task allotted to them.

Terms of service are similar to those of the regular infantry and men are obtained from the annual contingents.

(*b*) *Independent units.*—(i) Independent rifle battalions are composed of two, three or four companies.

(ii) Independent rifle companies are composed of two, three or four platoons.

(iii) Independent rifle platoons are composed of three, four, five or six sections.

These units are directly subordinate to the commanders of the nearest rifle divisions and the latter are responsible for their training and readiness for war. No information regarding their role is available.

(*c*) *Mechanization.*—A motorised brigade, which contains three motorised " infantry and M.G. " battalions forms an integral part of each motor-mechanised corps, and is described in Chapter XI. Every existing infantry divisional reconnaissance battalion is believed to include a motorised infantry company, which is organized in the same way as the units described in paragraph 2 above.

Motorised infantry units have also been identified in other formations such as certain individual mechanised brigades, and they have undoubtedly been so used during training, but so far as is known they do not, at present, form a permanent part of all such formations, though one motorised infantry battalion is possibly included in most independent mechanised brigades.

(*d*) *Mountain regiments.*—The infantry regiments of mountain divisions contain in peace only one strong battalion, and have only one battery of regimental artillery. Transport is largely on a pack basis. Details of their organization are not known.

(*e*) *Air-landing units.*—The Red Army has for some time been experimenting with parachute units. These appear to belong to " Heavy Air Corps " and normally to consist of air-landing groups each of three or more battalions and certain ancillary units.

4. Designations of units and regimental colours

Many formations and units have a special designation or title in addition to their serial number.

These titles are mainly of a territorial nature but are sometimes derived from the names of prominent people or revolutionary organizations. Units which have specially distinguished themselves are given the further title " Krasnoznamenni "—Order of the Red Banner. Designations also on occasions include the Order of Lenin and the Labour Red Decoration. Examples of titles are :—

    4th Leningradskaya Cavalry Division,
  im. Voroshilova.
    29th Vyatskaya Division, im. Finlandskovo Proletariata.

5. Machine-gun units

Each mechanised corps (*see* Chapter XI) in the Red Army has one mechanised brigade containing three battalions each of three M.G. companies and one rifle company. Each battalion is reported to be armed with about 36 machine guns.

6. Anti-aircraft machine gun units

Certain local infantry units are organized for anti-aircraft defence as stated in paragraph 3 (*a*). No details of the organization of these units are known.

7. Anti-tank units

There are no infantry anti-tank units in the Red Army other than those forming part of regimental artillery groups, described in paragraph 2 (*a*) (iv).

8. Close support units (when manned by infantry personnel)

There are no close support units in the Red Army other than regimental artillery groups described in paragraph 2 (*a*) (iv) above.

9. Regimental specialists

All specialist personnel for the various sub-units and branches of the infantry regiment, that is, gunners, signallers, sappers, etc., and tradesmen such as artificers, cooks, etc., are drawn from the annual contingent and receive special training. Men with civil qualifications are allotted to suitable branches, sub-units and trades as far as possible.

N.C.O.s of regimental signal companies are trained in the divisional signal battalion. Signallers are trained in the regimental signal company.

N.C.O.s of regimental artillery groups are trained in the divisional field artillery regiment. Regimental artillerymen are trained in the regimental artillery group.

N.C.O.s of regimental sapper and camouflage platoons are trained in the divisional sapper company.

N.C.O.s of regimental chemical platoons are reported to be trained at certain centres under extra-unit instructors.

Snipers are trained in the regimental sniper detachment. (*See* also paragraph 2 (*a*) vi).)

10. Regimental transport

(*a*) *General.*—An infantry regiment contains about 801 horses and 333 vehicles of which 279 horses and 171 vehicles are in the three battalions and 210 horses and 14 vehicles (exclusive of guns) are in the regimental artillery group.

It is probable that a large proportion of the transport, carts, harness, animals, etc., will be called up from civil sources on mobilization. The disadvantages of this system have, however, probably been considerably reduced by the present policy of standardization of all civilian carts and harness in types identical with or similar to those used in the army.

(*b*) *Sub-division of regimental transport.*—In the field the transport of the regiment will normally be divided into two parts :—

(i) Transport of the 1st category, comprising the ammunition carts, essential supply carts and signal carts of the regiment, under the command of the chief of Ammunition Supply of the regiment.

(ii) Transport of the 2nd category, consisting of the remaining transport, under the command of the O.C. Supply Company of the regiment.

The transport of the chemical and medical detachments will accompany either of the above categories as required.

11. Ammunition supply

(*a*) *System of supply.*—(i) *S.A.A.*—The system of supply of S.A.A. and other ammunition from railhead to the infantry unit is dealt with in Chapter VIII. The Officer in Charge Ammunition Supply controls the regimental S.A.A. reserve. A regimental ammunition point is opened by the transport platoon about 6–8 km. in rear of the front line.

The regimental ammunition point refills the battalion ammunition point which is situated about 4 km. in rear of the first line. Within the battalion, ammunition supply is carried out by the ammunition supply section which is part of the battalion supply platoon.

Company ammunition points, under senior N.C.O.s are established by rifle and M.G. companies about 2 km. in rear of the front line and comprise two or three 2-wheeled carts per company. They may throw out advanced company ammunition points each consisting of 3–5 ammunition carriers. Transport of ammunition forward to platoons is made by carriers, dogs, handbarrows, rollers or sleighs.

A platoon ammunition point is established in rear of the firing line. Sections send back men to the platoon ammunition point to fetch ammunition as necessary.

S.A.A. is issued packed in wooden cases with rope handles. Each case contains about 600 rounds.

The capacities of the various methods of transport are as follows :—

	Rounds
Dog	120
Dog harness to sleigh	600
Carrier	600
Handcart or barrow	1,800–2,400
1-horse wagon	6,000
1-horse 2-wheeled cart	7,200
2-horse 2-wheeled cart	14,000
2-horse wagon	15,500

(ii) *Ammunition supply of the regimental artillery group.*— The ammunition supply platoon of the artillery group is organized in sections corresponding to the numbers of batteries in the group. It is situated 3–4 km. in rear of the battery positions and supplies ammunition direct to battery areas. The ammunition supply platoon replenishes its ammunition by sending convoys of vehicles back to refill from the advanced platoon of the artillery park. (*See* Chapter VIII).

(iii) *Ammunition supply of the battalion artillery.*—The battalion artillery is supplied direct from the battalion ammunition point.

(b) *Scale of S.A.A. carried.* — The amounts carried per rifle are :—

	Rounds
On the man	120
In company and regimental reserve	80
In divisional artillery park	100
In corps artillery transport	100

(c) *Scale of grenades carried.*—Grenades are carried on the following scale :—

(i) *Hand grenades* :—
>With the regiment .. .. .. 4 per man
>In divisional and corps reserve .. 4 per man

(ii) *Rifle grenades* :—
>With the regiment   8–10 per grenade thrower
>In divisional and corps reserve ..   .. 8–10 per grenade thrower

(d) *Light automatics and machine guns.*

(e) *Guns.*—The scale of ammunition carried is laid down in Chapter VIII.

(f) *Armour piercing and tracer ammunition.*—Armour piercing and tracer ammunition is carried by N.C.O.s armed with rifles and by snipers.

The scale of ammunition carried is not known.

12. Equipment

(a) *Personal.*—The personal equipment of the Red Army soldier includes :—
>Web equipment with leather belt and ammunition pouches.
>Knapsack (*i.e.*, a pack of " rucksack " type).
>Greatcoat.
>Haversack.
>Water bottle.
>Mess tin.
>Ground sheet.
>Entrenching tool.
>Gas mask.
>Emergency ration (two days).

The pack contains a change of under-linen, first-aid outfit and emergency ration. The haversack is used to carry rations. All infantry are equipped with a rifle and bayonet, except officers and certain men in each light automatic, grenade thrower or machine gun section, who are equipped with a pistol.

Each man carries 120 rounds S.A.A. and 3 grenades.

The total weight is about 65 lb.

(b) *Steel helmet.*—Steel helmets have been reported of a type similar to the French pattern and having a red star in front. They do not appear to be a general peace issue.

(c) *Gas mask.*—The type of gas mask now being issued to the troops consists of a rubber facepiece which leaves the ears, the crown of the head and part of the forehead uncovered, and is fixed to the head by five bands, each adjusted by a sliding buckle. The eyepieces give a wider field of vision than with the earlier types. An anti-dimming pencil is carried in the gas mask haversack. The exhalation valve is of an improved type in which resistance to exhalation is reduced. It is situated in the connecting piece at the top of the corrugated tube where there is less danger of its freezing when the mask is used under winter conditions.

(d) *Signalling, W/T and R/T equipment.*—(i) The signal equipment of an infantry regiment consists of :—

	Per Regt.*	Per Bn.
W/T sets (radius six miles)	2	1
Telephones	27	6
Exchanges	1 (20 line) 1 (12 line)	1 (6 line)
Cable	25 miles	5 miles
Flags	—	—
Lamps	—	—
Ground sheets	—	—

(ii) Motor cycles, bicycles and dogs are employed by the despatch rider section.

---

* Includes all sub-units except battalions.

(e) *Tools.*—In addition to the entrenching tool carried by all men, it is reported that other tools are carried as follows :—

	Infantry Coy.	Infantry Bn.	Infantry Regt.	Infantry Regt. Artillery.	Sapper and Camouflage Platoon.
Spades	14	54	300	47	150
Hatchets	20	70	—	38	—
Light axes	2	20	150	11	75
Heavy axes	—	—	—	12	75
Light picks	20	60	200	—	20
Heavy picks	2	7	50	8	20
Crowbars	—	2	20	2	15
Chisels	—	—	—	—	5
Cross-saws	—	1	14	2	20
Wire-cutters	—	—	50	—	50

(f) *Rangefinders.*

(g) *Tents and bivouacs.*—The ground sheet measures approximately 5 ft. by 5 ft. and can be used as a bivouac tent.

(h) *Vehicles.*—The chief vehicles in use in the infantry regiment are as follows :—

    1-horse, 2-wheeled cart.
    2-horse, 2-wheeled cart.
    1-horse wagon.
    2-horse wagon.

CHAPTER VII

CAVALRY

1. General organization and strengths

The cavalry of the R.K.K.A. comprises :—
  Regular cavalry regiments.
  Cavalry squadrons of divisional reconnaissance battalions.

The cavalry formations consist of :—
  Nine cavalry corps.
  Thirty cavalry divisions.
  Five mountain cavalry divisions.

The remainder of the cavalry is organized in independent brigades and infantry divisional cavalry squadrons.

Cavalry squadrons of divisional reconnaissance battalions.— All normal infantry divisions and probably also the mountain divisions have a divisional reconnaissance unit which contains a squadron of cavalry organized on similar lines to squadrons of cavalry regiments but having in addition a troop of machine guns. They contain :—
  Headquarters.
  Four Troops, each of two sections.
  One M.G. Troop of two sections (each of 1 M.G.).
  Administrative Troop.

The transport of a divisional cavalry squadron consists of :—
  Six 2-horsed carts for supplies and baggage.
  One 2-horsed cart for S.A.A.
  Two 2-horsed carts for M.Gs.
  One 2-horsed cart for sick.
  One field kitchen.

The war establishment of these squadrons is slightly higher than that of a normal squadron.

Reserve cavalry squadrons appear to be employed under Military District H.Q. for the reception and training of cavalry regiments. No details of their organization are, however, known.

2. Organization and strength of units

(*a*) *Organization and strength of the regiment.*—Cavalry regiments, other than mountain cavalry regiments, consist of :—
  Regimental Headquarters.
  Four Sabre Squadrons.

One M.G. Squadron.
One Regimental Horse Artillery Battery.
Signal Half-Squadron.
Anti-aircraft M.G. Troop.
Chemical Troop.
Sapper Troop.
Medical Section.
Veterinary Section.
Headquarters Employed and Supply Section.
Regimental Transport.
Political Section and Club.

The war establishment of the regiment is approximately : 1,200 men, 1,300 horses, 124 H.D. vehicles, 6 M.T. vehicles, 40 light automatics, 40 grenade throwers, 20 machine guns, three anti-aircraft machine guns, two 37-mm. A.T. guns, four 76-mm. guns.

Regimental headquarters has recently been re-organized in five sections :—

(i) Operations, Personnel.
(ii) Organization.
(iii) Communications.
(iv) Intelligence.
(v) Rear Services.

(b) *The organization and strength of the sabre squadron.*— The sabre squadron consists of :—

Headquarters, including signal section.
Four Troops, each of two sections.
Administrative Troop.

Each section is sub-divided into two sub-sections, one armed with a light automatic (Degtyarev type) and the other with a grenade thrower (Dyakonov type).

The war establishment of a sabre squadron is approximately 169 men, 187 horses, 5 vehicles, 8 light automatics, 8 grenade throwers.

(c) *The organization and strength of the machine gun squadron.*—The machine gun squadron consists of :—

Headquarters, including signal section.
Five machine gun Troops, each of four sections of one machine gun.
One anti-tank Troop of two sections, each having one 37-mm. gun.
Administrative Troop.

The war establishment of a machine gun squadron is approximately 240 men, 300 horses, 32 vehicles, 20 machine guns (Maxim type), two 37-mm. guns.

(d) *The organization and strength of the regimental artillery battery.*—The battery consists of four 76-mm. guns (1927 pattern) and is organized on similar lines to a Horse Artillery Battery (*see* Chapter VIII).

(e) *The organization and strength of the signal half-squadron.*—The half-squadron consists of :—
> Headquarters.
> Two Telephone Sections.
> One W/T Section.
> One Air Liaison and Observation Section.
> One Despatch Rider Section.

War establishment is approximately 46 men, 57 horses and four vehicles.

(f) *The organization and strength of the A.A. machine gun troop.*—The troop consists of four anti-aircraft machine guns mounted in pairs on lorries or M.T. vans.

(g) *The organization and strength of the chemical troop.*—The chemical troop consists in peace of O.C., one chemical instructor and five other ranks.

The war establishment is reported to be 17 men, 19 horses and two carts.

(h) *The organization and strength of the sapper troop.*—The sapper troop is organized in headquarters and two sections.

The war establishment is reported to be 15 men, 20 horses and one cart.

(i) *The organization and strength of the medical section.*—The medical section consists of :—
> 26 men (of whom two or more are doctors).
> 25 horses.
> 7 vehicles (including 5 ambulances).

(j) *The organization and strength of the veterinary section.*—The veterinary section consists of :—
> 11 men (of whom two are veterinary surgeons).
> 8 horses.
> 1 vehicle.

The section is responsible for the care of sick and wounded horses and for the shoeing of all animals.

(k) *The organization and strength of the supply section.*—The supply section includes the regimental transport and is under the Chief of Rear Services of the regiment. This officer is responsible not only for food supplies and transport, but also for the supply of ammunition.

It is organized in sub-sections as under :—
   (i) Office.
   (ii) Supply of Equipment, Rations and Forage.
   (iii) Ammunition Supply.

The strength of the supply section is estimated to be 80 men, 90 horses and 44 vehicles.

(*l*) *The organization and strength of the regimental transport.*—Regimental transport is included in the supply section and contains the following :—

	"A" Echelon.	"B" Echelon.	Total.
Pack horses	45	—	45
Two-horsed carts	27	51	78
One-horsed carts	6	19	25
Machine gun carts (two-horsed)	23	—	23
Guns and limbers	5	—	5
Ammunition limbers	8	—	8

(*m*) *Political section and club.*—The political assistant of the O.C. is the head of the political section.

(*n*) *Mountain cavalry regiments.*—The organization of mountain cavalry regiments of mountain cavalry divisions differs from that of normal cavalry regiments in that there are only three sabre squadrons, and the machine gun squadron has only three troops. Squadron transport is on a pack basis but regimental transport includes carts.

3. Mechanised cavalry units

There appear at present to be two forms of mechanised units for use with cavalry. These are mechanised cavalry regiments within the organization of cavalry divisions, and independent mechanised brigades permanently allotted in war to, but not part of, the organization of cavalry corps.

(*a*) *Mechanised cavalry regiments.*—Each cavalry division contains a mechanised cavalry regiment which is reported to contain :—

   Regimental Headquarters.
   B.O. (literally "battle security," consisting of auxiliary and protective units) squadron, containing :—
      Reconnaissance platoon or squadron of amphibian tanks ;
      Signal Platoon ;
      Chemical Platoon ;
      Sapper Platoon ;
      Traffic Control Platoon.

One armoured car squadron of 10 armoured cars and possibly 4 M/Cs. (with M.G.).
Two squadrons each of 10 B.T. tanks, and possibly :
One battery of four 76-mm. guns.
One troop of anti-aircraft machine guns.

Until sufficient B.T. tanks are available to meet all requirements it is probable that certain mechanised cavalry regiments will continue to be armed with T.26 tanks.

(b) *Mechanised brigades allotted to cavalry corps.*—It appears to be the intention to place permanently at the disposal of each cavalry corps in war one independent mechanised brigade. This is an ordinary armoured formation and not a special cavalry formation and details of its organization are given in Chapter XI, 3 (b).

4. Machine gun units

There are no cavalry machine gun units other than the machine gun squadron included in each cavalry regiment.

5. Cavalry close support units

There are no cavalry close support units other than the regimental artillery battery included in each cavalry regiment.

6. Anti-tank units

There are no cavalry anti-tank units other than the anti-tank troops included in the M.G. squadrons of cavalry regiments.

7. Anti-aircraft machine gun units

There are no cavalry anti-aircraft machine gun units other than the anti-aircraft machine gun troops included in cavalry regiments.

8. Designation of units and regimental colours

In addition to numbers, most cavalry regiments and cavalry formations have designations or titles ; the majority of these are territorial, though some units, etc., have their national titles, and others are named after a prominent revolutionary organization or individual, *e.g.* :—

    .... th Pyatigorsky Cavalry Regiment.
    .... th Armenian National Cavalry Regiment.
    .... th Terski Cavalry Regiment, im. Angliskovo Proletariata.
    .... th Samarsky Cavalry Regiment, im. Frunze.

9. Cyclists with cavalry formations

10. Motor machine gun units with cavalry formations

11. Reconnaissance units

12. Regimental specialists

Regimental specialists, except doctors and veterinary surgeons, are trained under unit arrangements.

In peace there is a school in each regiment for training junior commanding personnel.

Higher formations also arrange courses for more advanced training.

13. Regimental transport

The transport of a cavalry regiment is given in paragraph 2 (1). It is probable that a considerable amount of civilian transport will have to be brought into use on mobilization.

14. Ammunition supply

The method of supply of S.A.A. and other ammunition from railhead to the cavalry unit is as described in Chapter VIII, Section J.

The amounts of S.A.A. carried per rifle are :—

	Rounds
On the man	80
In company and regimental reserve	40
In cavalry divisional artillery park	60
In corps artillery transport	60

Rifle grenades are carried on the following scale :—

With the regiment	7 per grenade thrower.
In divisional and corps reserve ..	7 per grenade thrower.

15. Equipment

(a) *Personnel.*—The cavalryman is armed with a carbine, bayonet and sabre, the last named, however, being left attached to the saddle when fighting dismounted. The lance appears to have been completely abolished.

Officers, N.C.O.s and machine gunners are armed with a pistol.

The sabre " universal pattern 27 " has a wooden scabbard covered with leather or canvas.

The carbine is a 1924–1927 model made at the Tula or Ijevski works.

The revolver carried by cavalry is of the Nagan type.

The equipment of the cavalry soldier is similar to that of the infantry soldier (*see* Chapter VI).

The average weight carried on the horse is estimated at nineteen stone.

(b) *Saddlery and horse furniture.*—Saddles are of the Russian " Dragoon " type made of leather, with light stirrups and girths made of strong webbing, except those of officers which are of the former officer's type (KOCH pattern). Saddles are fitted with numnahs.

Bits are of the port-mouthed type.

The following equipment, etc., is carried on the saddle (the items marked * being carried in the saddle bags) :—

    Pair saddle bags.
    Rations* and forage for man and horse.
    Canvas bucket.
    Hoof trimmer.*
    Pair spare horse shoes.
    Personal small kit.*
    Gas mask and protective sheet for horse.
    Greatcoat when not worn.

(c) *Steel helmet.*—As for other arms.

(d) *Gas mask.*—As for other arms.

(e) *Signalling equipment.*
    Two 6-line central exchanges.
    12 telephones.
    40 miles of telephone cable.

(f) *Tools*—
    For Squadrons :
      60 small spades.
      15 picks.
      40 axes.
      6 saws.
      4 jemmies.
      45 wire-cutting shears.

(g) *Range-finders.*

(h) *Tents and bivouacs.*

(i) *Vehicles.*

16. The cavalry horse

The standard cavalry horse is a cross between a thoroughbred or half-bred and a farm horse of good quality. The minimum height for army purposes is 14·2 hands.

Many military districts have remount depôts and breeding establishments. The depôts do not hold horses to meet cavalry requirements in case of war, but registration of horses suitable for military service is carried out in each district with a view to impressment on mobilization. The quality of horses available for impressment is not high.

The gravity of the horse supply situation has caused the N.K.O. of the U.S.S.R. to take steps to encourage and improve horse breeding throughout the country, but the results achieved have not yet affected the question of remounts for cavalry. The whole situation was most adversely affected by the wholesale destruction of livestock during the period of compulsory collectivization of farmers.

CHAPTER VIII
ARTILLERY
1. The Arm

(a) *General organization.*—The organization of the artillery of the Red Army is still the subject of experiment and no uniform organization appears to have been adopted up to the present (1939). The organizations given in this chapter are those which appear to be most common at the present time.

In the Red Army the proportion of artillery weapons to infantry soldiers has always been a low one when judged by Western European standards, but on the other hand the scale of distribution and decentralization of artillery is wide, nearly every unit or formation from an infantry battalion to a corps having its own quota of artillery weapons.

The organization of horse, pack, divisional and corps artillery is discussed in the appropriate paragraphs, and special mention will only be made here of artillery of special natures and organization.

Every infantry or cavalry regiment possesses its own regimental artillery group for close-support and anti-tank purposes. In addition each infantry battalion has its own artillery platoon of anti-tank guns and mortars. The guns are manned by regimental personnel who receive training as artillerymen. Details of the organization of these groups are given in Chapters VI and VII.

Army artillery is known as A.R.G.K., that is artillery at the disposal of the Higher Command. This consists of artillery regiments and groups, largely of a medium or heavy nature. The organization of the A.R.G.K. has recently undergone many changes and details of what is considered to be the present organization are given in paragraph 6. In addition there is a certain amount of artillery, mostly mobile, which is not A.R.G.K. but which is permanently allotted for the defence of certain fortified areas.

Coast defence artillery comes under the Commissariat for Naval Defence and is not therefore part of the Red Army. It is organized in mobile and non-mobile brigades, groups and batteries. The composition and armament of the non-mobile units obviously varies in accordance with the importance of the areas which they are called upon to defend.

There has been a considerable increase in recent years in anti-aircraft artillery. While previously it consisted almost entirely of Anti-Aircraft defence troops of military districts and of special localities, each infantry corps has now been given its own corps Anti-Aircraft group and it is believed that the 45-mm. guns now being issued to infantry battalions and regimental artillery groups are dual purpose weapons that can be used either for anti-tank or anti-aircraft purposes. Details of the organization of anti-aircraft artillery are given in paragraph 7.

Up to the beginning of 1938 anti-tank gun units existed solely as part of infantry cavalry or mechanized units. A start has now been made with the provision of divisional units armed with the dual purpose weapon referred to above. Some further details on these units are given in paragraph 8.

(b) *General notes for armament and technical tendencies.*—
(i) *Armament.*—Except for anti-aircraft and anti-tank guns there has been little sign of the introduction of many new weapons, but many old patterns have been modernised so as to obtain a better performance, by such measures as the adoption of muzzle brakes, the fitting of rubber and pneumatic tyres, and the provision of improved methods of traction. The increase in anti-aircraft artillery has been referred to above, and in addition certain field artillery units have been equipped with new mountings which enable them to be used for anti-aircraft fire.

Details of the various equipments are given in Appendix C.

(ii) *Mechanization.*—The great progress in mechanization generally and in the tractor industry in particular, coupled with the decrease in the number of horses available, has had considerable repercussions on artillery traction.

All army artillery and most of the corps artillery now appears to be mechanized. These are both tractor drawn. Certain field artillery regiments which have also been mechanized are either carried on lorries as "Artillerie portee" or are drawn by lorries on which the gun-teams ride.

The allotment and organization of artillery of mechanized and motorized formations is still in the experimental stage. The tendency was to allot "Artillerie portee" to the motorized formations and artillery on self propelled mountings to mechanized formations, but no finality has been reached, and there are some indications that no artillery is to be definitely allotted to mechanized formations.

(c) *Artillery staffs.*—Questions of training, organization, establishments, mobilization and inspection of artillery units come under the Department of the Chief of Artillery, a department which is also responsible for the study of information concerning artillery matters in foreign countries.

Each military district has a Chief of Artillery who in addition to being responsible for these questions within his own district also deals with artillery supplies.

The Corps Artillery Commanders of Infantry and Cavalry Corps are responsible to their respective corps commanders and district chiefs of artillery for the administration and training of the artillery in the Corps. They are also responsible for all artillery supplies which they receive from the Artillery Department of the N.K.O. through the district chiefs of artillery.

The commander of the divisional artillery regiment of an infantry or cavalry corps acts as C.R.A. of his formation.

(d) *Regimental specialists.*—Specialists include scouts, observers, signallers, and medical or veterinary personnel, besides tradesmen such as mechanics and artificers.

(e) *Survey units.*—Reconnaissance sections, forming part of the Headquarter platoons of batteries and groups perform normal artillery reconnaissance duties within the unit. In addition there are survey batteries included in the headquarters of artillery regiments and survey groups in the special service groups of A.R.G.K. formations. Sections of the latter can be detached to accompany army artillery units which have been sub-allotted to corps.

Survey batteries of the divisional artillery contain an aerometric station for providing meteorological information, while those of corps artillery also contain flash-spotting and sound-ranging units.

2. Horse Artillery

(a) *General.*—Each cavalry division contains one horse artillery regiment, formerly armed with 76-mm. guns and 122-mm. howitzers., but now in process of re-equipment with 122-mm. howitzers only. Mountain cavalry divisions contain one horse artillery group only. In addition every horsed cavalry regiment has its own regimental battery armed with 76-mm. guns.

(b) *The horse artillery regiment.*—The horse artillery of cavalry divisions consists of a regiment of two groups. In addition there are medical, veterinary, S. & T. and political detachments. The regimental headquarters contains signal, survey and chemical sections together with an anti-aircraft M.G. platoon of four guns.

It is possible that the regiment may also contain an anti-aircraft or anti-tank battery.

The approximate war strength of the regiment is 1,170 men, 1,350 horses and 16 76·2-mm. guns and 122-mm. howitzers.

(c) *The horse artillery group.*—Horse artillery groups of mountain cavalry divisions are dealt with in paragraph 4.

The horse artillery group of horse artillery regiments each contain two batteries, an administrative and a supply platoon, the headquarters containing the survey and signals.

Some groups are said to contain three four-gun batteries, and it is possible that this will be the normal organization when sufficient equipment is available.

(d) *The horse artillery battery.*—The battery contains a headquarters' platoon with signal and liaison personnel, four 122-mm. howitzers and one or two machine-guns.

(e) *Armament.*—The horse artillery howitzer is the 122-mm. 1910/30 model, the details of which are given in Appendix C. The regimental battery contains 76-mm. 1927 pattern guns, or possibly in some cases still the 76-mm. 1902/30 pattern.

Traction may be by horse, tractor or lorry. When towed by M.T. guns or howitzers, are fitted with rubber-tyred wheels.

(f) *Ammunition.*—The gun fires shrapnel or high explosive, but the howitzer fires high explosive only, though gas, smoke, and propaganda shell are issued in war.

3. Light and Pack Artillery

(a) *Organization, administration and strength.*—(i) Light artillery is included in the organization of infantry regiments and battalions, details of which are given in Chapter VI.

(ii) Mountain artillery regiments and mountain horse artillery groups form part of the artillery of mountain infantry and mountain cavalry divisions respectively. Organization is on similar lines to corresponding field and horse artillery units (*see* Sections B. and D.) with the exception of transport.

(b) *Armament.*—(i) Light artillery consists of :—

37-mm. guns ⎫ Main armament of battalion artillery.
or   ⎬ Anti-tank batteries of regimental
45-mm. guns ⎭ artillery groups.
47-mm. guns   Old pattern, details given in Appendix C.

(ii) Mountain artillery consists of :—
76-mm. (1909 model) gun.
122-mm. howitzer.

Details are given in Appendix C.

(c) *Close support artillery.*—This is not at present manned by artillery personnel but by regimental personnel in infantry divisions (*see* Chapter VI).

(d) *Regimental transport.*—Mountain artillery. It is believed that transport is largely on a pack basis and that the guns themselves, but not howitzers, can be transported on pack.

4. Field Artillery

(a) *Organization, administration and strength.*—Field artillery is organized in :—

    (i) Artillery regiments of infantry divisions.

    (ii) Artillery groups of infantry regiments (*see* Chapter VI).

    (iii) Field artillery groups, etc., of A.R.G.K. artillery regiments.

(i) The field artillery regiment is organized as follows :—

H.Q. Signals Survey Chemical A.A.M.G.s (4 Med. M.G.s)	Medical detachment	Veterinary detachment	S. & T. detachment	Political detachment	Group	Group	Group

Armament :—

    Twelve 76-mm. guns.
    Twenty-four 122-mm. howitzers.
    Four medium anti-aircraft machine-guns.
    Eighteen light machine-guns.

(Some regiments have 24 guns and 12 howitzers, probably because sufficient howitzers are not yet available to equip all regiments on these lines.)

War establishment is about :—

    2,000 officers and men.
    1,260 horses.
    160 vehicles.
    72 ammunition wagons.
    4 medium machine-guns.
    18 light machine-guns.
    36 guns and howitzers.

Note.—In some field artillery regiments a medium group (12 medium guns and howitzers) has been identified, but it is not considered that such groups exist in the majority of regiments.

(ii) Organization of the field artillery group. The group is organized in :—

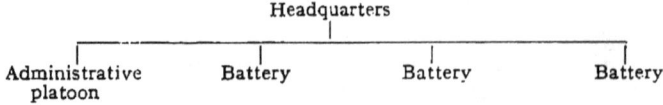

Armament :—
Four 76-mm. guns.
Eight 122-mm. howitzers.
Six light machine-guns.

Note.—At present (1939) owing to shortage of howitzers, some groups are armed with eight 76-mm. guns and four 122-mm. howitzers.

(iii) Organization of the field artillery battery. The field artillery battery is organized as follows :—

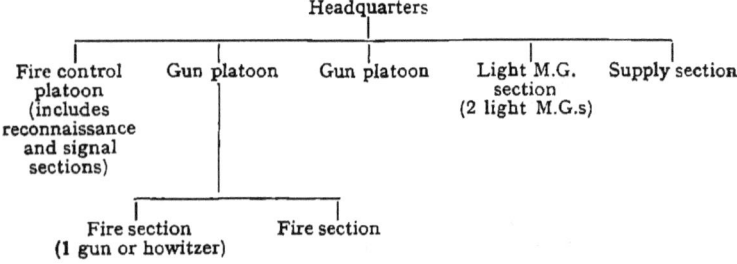

The war establishment is about :—
130 officers and men.
100 horses.
4 guns or howitzers.
2 light machine-guns.
8 ammunition wagons.
2 spare vehicles.

Details of artillery equipments are given in Appendix " C."

(iv) *Non-divisional field artillery units.*—Non-divisional field artillery exists in the shape of field artillery regiments of the A.R.G.K. and independent groups and batteries in a few isolated stations.

Their organization is believed to conform generally to that of divisional field artillery regiments, except that those in the A.R.G.K. are either mechanized or in process of mechanization.

(b) *Armament.* (i) *Field artillery guns and howitzers.*—
Guns : 76-mm. 1902/30 type.
Howitzers : 122-mm. 1909/10 and 1910/30 models.
Details of these weapons are given in Appendix C.

(ii) *Ammunition.*—Shrapnel and high explosive are normally used by the 76-mm. gun and 122-mm. howitzer. In addition gas, smoke, propaganda and incendiary shells can also be used.

The proportions of the various natures carried are given in paragraph 2 (c) of Section J.

(iii) *Mechanization.*—Mechanized batteries exist in various forms, some portee, some tractor-drawn and some lorry-drawn. It is probable that some form of self-propelled mounting is being introduced for most mechanised formations.

(c) *Regimental transport.*—*Regimental headquarters* :—
Headquarters transport :—
Two telephone carts.
Nine two-horsed carts.

Survey battery :—
Four carts.

Anti-aircraft machine-gun platoon :—
Four carts or two lorries.

Supply detachment :—
One carriage.
Sixty two-horsed carts.
Two one-horsed carts.
Eleven field kitchens.
Eleven boilers on wheels.

Medical section :—
One two-horsed cart.
Eleven one-horsed carts.

Veterinary section :—
One one-horsed cart.

Club :—
One two-horsed cart.

Group headquarters (each) :—
Two telephone carts.
One workshop cart.
Five two-horsed carts.

Battery transport (each) :—
Six ammunition wagons.
One telephone cart.
One two-horsed cart.

5. Medium Artillery

(a) *Organization, administration and strength.*—Medium artillery is included in both :—
>Corps artillery regiments.
>Army artillery (A.R.G.K.) regiments or groups (*see* section F.)

A corps artillery regiment forms part of all infantry corps. Corps artillery regiments are all now mechanized or in process of mechanization

(i) *Organization of the corps artillery regiment.*—Corps artillery regiments are organized in :

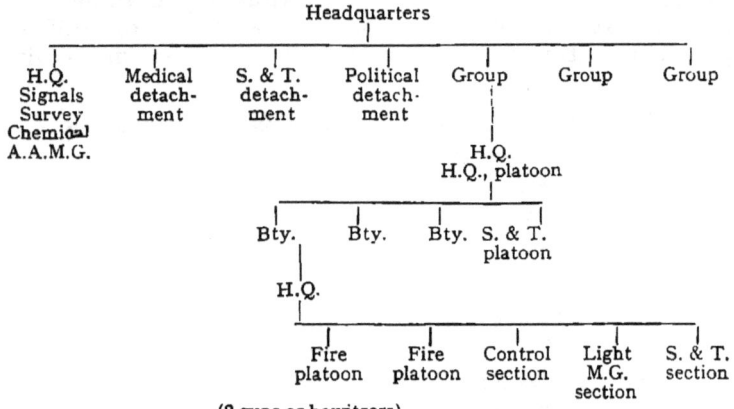

Armament :—
> Twenty-four 107-mm. guns.
> Twelve 152-mm. howitzers.
> Four anti-aircraft machine-guns.
> Nine light machine-guns.

It is probable that the proportion of howitzers to guns is being gradually increased.

Regimental headquarters consist of the staff and political personnel.

Headquarters platoon consists of signals and a scout detachment.

Anti-aircraft machine-gun platoon consists of four anti-aircraft machine guns.

(ii) *Organization of the medium artillery group.*—Medium artillery groups are organized in :—
> Headquarters.
> Headquarters Platoon.
> Three Batteries of 107-mm. guns or 152-mm. howitzers.
> Supply and Transport Platoon.

(iii) *Organization of the medium artillery battery.*—Medium artillery batteries are organized in :—
>Headquarters.
>Administrative Platoon.
>Two Gun Platoons.
>Light Machine-gun Section.
>Traction Platoon.

Administrative platoons include sections for reconnaissance and signals.
>Gun Platoons are organised in :—
>Headquarters.
>Two Sections of one gun or howitzer.
>One Machine-gun Detachment.

Traction platoons include all transport and tractors or horses.

(b) *Armament.*—(i) *Medium artillery guns and howitzers.*—
>Medium artillery guns are : 107-mm. 1910/30 model.
>Medium artillery howitzers are : 152-mm. 1910 model.

Details of the above weapons are given in Appendix C.

(ii) *Ammunition.*—Medium artillery guns fire both shrapnel and high explosive shells ; the proportion of each carried is not known definitely, but the amount of shrapnel is comparatively small.

Medium artillery howitzer carry a high proportion of high explosive shell. Smoke, gas and incendiary shells are also carried.

(c) *Regimental transport.*

6. Heavy and super-heavy artillery. (A.R.G.K.)

(a) *Organization, administration and strength.*—All heavy artillery in the R.K.K.A. forms part of the artillery reserve of the higher command (A.R.G.K.).

The A.R.G.K. is organized in :—
>A.R.G.K. regiments.
>A.R.G.K. groups.
>A.R.G.K. batteries.
>A.R.G.K. armoured train units.

Some of these form part of the next larger unit and formation, while others appear to be independent.

The armament of A.R.G.K. units consists of railway-mounted, super-heavy, heavy, medium field guns and howitzers and anti-aircraft guns.

Reorganization and expansion, however, appears to be still continuing and the information in this section is therefore issued under reserve.

(i) *Organization of A.R.G.K. regiments and groups.*—
Medium, field and A.A. artillery regiments of the A.R.G.K.
are organized on the lines laid down in Sections E, D and G
respectively of this chapter, with the exception that they
probably each possess their own ammunition park.

Heavy regiments are organized in :—
    Headquarters.
    Administrative Detachment.
    Medical Detachment.
    Supply and Transport Detachment.
    Political Section and Club.
    Reconnaissance Battery.
    Two to three Groups, each of two to three batteries
    Ammunition Park.

Heavy artillery groups are organized in :—
    Headquarters.
    Administrative Section.
    Two to three Batteries of guns or howitzers of
    varying calibre.

(ii) *Organization of A.R.G.K. Batteries.*—*Medium, field
and anti-aircraft batteries* are organized as shown in
sections E, D, and G, respectively.

Heavy batteries are organized in :—
    Headquarters.
    Administrative Platoon.
    Gun Platoon.

A gun platoon consists of :—
    Headquarters.
    Administrative Section.
    Two Sections of one gun or howitzer each.

The actual establishment of batteries varies according
the calibre of the gun or howitzer.

(b) *Armament.*—(i) *Heavy artillery guns and howitzers.*—
The armament of the A.R.G.K. comprises mainly guns of
a calibre of over 122-mm. and all howitzers of a calibre
of over 152-mm.

Many new types of improved guns have appeared on
recent anniversary parades and this appears to indicate
that efforts are being made to re-arm the A.R.G.K. with
modern equipment.

The following are, however, the three main types on which the Red Army appears to be concentrating :—
 152-mm. gun (1904 type).
 203-mm. howitzer (Vickers type).
 203-mm. howitzer (new type).
 280 ? mm. howitzer (new type).

Details of these weapons are given in Appendix " C."

Medium guns and howitzers and anti-aircraft guns of A.R.G.K. units are of normal types.

(ii) *Ammunition.*—High explosive shells are chiefly used with heavy artillery guns and howitzers. Gas shell is also carried and smoke shell for certain calibres. Shrapnel is not used.

(c) *Regimental transport.*—No details as regards regimental transport are available but it appears that all mobile heavy batteries are either mechanised or in process of mechanization.

It is reported that there are four systems :—

(i) Tractor-drawn ordnance on wheels	107-mm. gun.
(ii) Tractor-drawn ordnance on caterpillars	203-mm. howitzers.
(iii) Tractor drawn in parts, *i.e.*, gun-carriage and piece separately	152-mm. gun.
(iv) Vickers armoured vehicle carrying the detachment and towing the gun .. .. · ..	76-mm. gun.

7. Anti-aircraft artillery

(a) *Organization, administration and strength.*—Anti-aircraft artillery is organized as follows :—

 In the zone of the armies, anti-aircraft divisions, brigades and regiments of the A.R.G.K.

 Anti-aircraft groups of corps.

 Home defence independent anti-aircraft regiments, groups and batteries allotted permanently to the defence of certain localities. Many of these have non-mobile armament.

The organization of the various anti-aircraft units is as follows :—

(i) *Organization of the anti-aircraft division.*—Anti-aircraft divisions are composed of :—

>Headquarters.
>Three to five anti-aircraft Regiments.
>One anti-aircraft M.G. Regiment or Battalion.
>One Electro-Technical (Searchlight) Regiment.
>One Signal Battalion.

(ii) *Organization of the anti-aircraft brigade.*—Anti-aircraft brigades are composed of :—

>Headquarters.
>Two Artillery Regiments.
>One anti-aircraft M.G. Battalion.
>One Electro-Technical Battalion (searchlights—*see* Chapter IX).
>One Training Battalion (peace only).

(iii) *Organization of the anti-aircraft regiment.*—An anti-aircraft regiment is organized in :—

>Headquarters :—
>>Staff.
>>Signal Group.
>>Reconnaissance Group.
>>Despatch rider Group.
>
>Administrative Detachment.
>Supply Detachment.
>Medical Detachment.
>Political Section.
>Three to five Groups, each of three batteries.
>Anti-aircraft M.G. Company.
>Electro-Technical Company (searchlights).
>Signal Company.

Brigades or regiments may include batteries of fixed anti-aircraft defences or batteries mounted on railway trucks, lorries or trailers.

(iv) *Organization of the anti-aircraft battery.*—Anti-aircraft batteries normally consist of :—

>Headquarters.
>Headquarter Platoon.
>Two to three gun platoons of two guns each.

It is accepted as a general rule that each battery must be served by a searchlight platoon and have a M.G. platoon for local defence.

(v) *Corps anti-aircraft groups.*—A group of mechanised anti-aircraft artillery is now allotted to each corps. It is reported that these groups consist of three anti-aircraft batteries, but that expansion is envisaged eventually into corps anti-aircraft artillery regiments of two groups each.

(vi) *An independent A.A. group consists of* :—
  Headquarters.
  Headquarters Platoon.
  Three batteries.
  A.A. M.G. Platoon.
  Ammunition Column.
  Searchlight Company (*see* Chapter IX).

(b) *Special small arm anti-aircraft units.*—(i) *In the zone of the armies.*—*Anti-aircraft machine gun battalions* are included in anti-aircraft divisions and brigades of the A.R.G.K. and are organized in :—
  Headquarters.
  Four companies each of three to four Platoons.
  Each Platoon has two to four guns.

Anti-aircraft machine guns are normally used in fours on coupled mountings. Double and treble and quadruple mountings are also in use.

(ii) *Home defence.*—No details are available other than as in 2(*a*) above.

(c) *Armament.*—(i) *Anti-aircraft guns and machine guns.*—Details of all anti-aircraft guns, other than field guns used for anti-aircraft purposes by means of special mountings, are given in Appendix " C."

Recent indications show that the U.S.S.R. intends to equip all anti-aircraft units with modern anti-aircraft guns.

Anti-aircraft machine guns are of the normal type but on special mountings.

(ii) *Ammunition.*—Shrapnel and high explosive are both used. Details of fuzes are not known.

(d) *Regimental transport.*—No details are known as regards regimental transport, but it appears that all mobile anti-aircraft artillery units are now mechanised or in process of mechanisation.

Guns are mounted on lorries, trailers or railway trucks.

8. Coast defence (and fortress) artillery

(a) *Organization, administration and strength.*—Coast defence artillery forms part of the naval forces. It is organized in mobile and non-mobile brigades, the former forming part of the A.R.G.K.

The mobile units of coast defence artillery consist of :—
  (i) Heavy railway batteries.
  (ii) Tractor drawn batteries.

(1) *Organization of the coast defence brigade.*—Coast defence brigades are organized in :—
  Headquarters
  Sapper Company
  Signal Company
  Administration Detachment
  Varying number of Groups

and are responsible for the defence of a particular port or section of the coast.

(2) *Organization of the battery.*—Coast defence batteries are organized in :—
  Headquarters.
  Varying numbers of sections according to the size of the guns.

(b) *Armament.*—Guns and howitzers employed in coast defence are of many and various types and sizes. Details of all types known are shown in Appendix " C."

It is understood that steps have recently been taken to replace by modern guns many of the older types.

9. Anti-Tank Artillery

Organization, composition and strength of independent anti-tank group (O.P.T.D.).—One such group is normally attached to each infantry division, as part of its full mobilization establishment. Comprises :

  Three batteries each of four 45-mm. anti-tank guns. 60 men per battery.
  Technical unit—twenty-five men.
  Ammunition supply platoon—thirty men.
  The group is mechanised.
  There are thirty " Komsomol " tractors in the group : eight per battery and the remainder in the ammunition supply platoon.
  N.C.O.s and O.R.s carry rifles, 20 rounds S.A.A. and two grenades.
  There are about ten supply lorries in the group.
  Staff of the group is :
    Commander.
    Commissar.
    Chief of Staff.
    Finance officer.
    Administrative officer.
    Three clerks.

They carry as armament :
One light machine gun.
Several rifles.
Revolvers.
Fifty grenades.
There are no horses.

10. Equipment

(a) *Personal.*—Personnel carry rifles or revolvers in the approximate proportion of 1 : 2. Bayonets are not carried.

(b) *Technical equipment.*—The technical equipment used includes :—

(i) *Aerometric and meteorological stations* :—
Aneriod barometers.
Hygrometers.
Anemometers—Fuss pattern.
Field wind-gauges—Arkadev pattern.
Small captive balloons.
Theodolites.
Thermometers.

(ii) *Topographical batteries, platoons and sections* :—
Theodolites.
Kiprigeli (? Indian clinometer).
Bussoli (directors) with compass magnetic error accurately determined.
Instruments for map making.

(iii) *Photometrical service* :—
Photo-theodolite.
Stereo-Komparator—prepares maps from air photo data.

(iv) *Optical batteries, platoons and sections* :—

Per section
{
One Mobile W/T Station.
One R.F. (Goertz 2 metre base).
One " Steroetruba " (double prismatic periscope measuring angles).
Plane table, celluloid and brass protractors and " Khorduglomer " (for measuring angles).
One Field telephone.
Three Bicycles.
}

(v) *Sound-ranging batteries and platoons.*
Sound ranging instrument (Sperry type).
Artillery sound direction finding instruments (pelengatori).
Warners (preduprediteli).
Directors (bussoli with compass error accurately determined).
Field telephones.

The smallest independent sub-unit appears to be the platoon.

(c) *Anti-aircraft artillery—technical equipment.*—Few details are available as regards technical equipment, but it appears to include the following :—

(i) *Predictors.*
A large number of Sperry predictors have been bought abroad but it is doubtful if the number approaches in any way the total required to equip all Anti-aircraft units.
Predictors, it is understood, are not at present made in the U.S.S.R.

(ii) *Range-finders :—*
Zeiss.

(iii) *Sound-ranging instrument :—*
Ivanov.

(d) *General.*—In general the tendency is to adopt modern technical instruments which can be manufactured in the country.

11. Ammunition

(a) *General system of ammunition supply in the field.*— The ammunition supply in the Red Army conforms to the general lines of ammunition supply in other armies. On the man and with each gun there is the minimum quantity for immediate requirements, which is replenished from the regimental reserve (*see* paragraph 2 (*a*) below). In rear of the regiment there is the Divisional Artillery Park which carries a further supply of S.A.A. and grenades and gun ammunition for the whole division (*see* paragraph 2(*b*)(i)). In rear of the Divisional Artillery Park is the Corps Transport which contains a further reserve of ammunition of all natures, and delivers from railhead to the Divisional Artillery Park (*see* paragraph 2 (*b*)(ii)).

The total maximum normal radius of supply of the above echelons is about 25 miles. In the event of the distance to railhead being in excess of this, the maximum which can be delivered has to be reduced, or army transport units have to be used to provide the additional link or links required.

In the unit the total ammunition of all natures carried is based on what is estimated to be the expenditure in one day's fighting and is called the " battle complement " or " full field complement." Divisional artillery parks and corps transport each carry the equivalent of half the " battle complement."

The totals represented by the " battle complements " are given in paragraph 2(c).

The basis of the ammunition supply is from rear to front ; rear units being responsible for replenishing echelons in front of them.

(b) *Details of ammunition supply affecting various branches.*
—(i) *Artillery* (other than infantry and cavalry regimental artillery). The transport for ammunition in the artillery regiment is provided by either regimental or battery transport.

All ammunition wagons other than the artillery limbers form :—

    (I) Regimental artillery posts.
    (II) " Group " ammunition sections.

Ammunition is normally brought forward by carts as far as " group " ammunition sections, where it is unboxed and sorted and sent forward to batteries in the battery ammunition wagons.

(ii) *Ammunition supply units.*
    (I) *Divisional artillery park.*

A divisional artillery park forms part of each division and is organized in :—

    Headquarters.
    Two platoons each of four sections.
    Medical detachment.
    Supply detachment.
    Veterinary detachment.

It carries half the " battle complement " for the division and has about 260–300 two-horse carts carrying ammunition as follows :—

S.A.A. for rifles and machine guns	110–112 carts.
Fireworks and grenades	4–5 carts.
58 mm. T.M. and 37 mm. ..	10 carts.
76 mm.	70–75 carts.
122 mm.	90 carts.

Each platoon includes an infantry platoon with 3 L.As. for local protection.

The maximum radius of action of the divisional artillery park, working in a single echelon, is 10 miles.

The park normally, however, operates in two echelons with a forward and a rear platoon, each carrying a quarter of the " battle complement." By this method the radius of action can be increased to 20 miles, but the maximum delivery in a day is reduced to a quarter of the " battle complement."

It is understood that as soon as M.T. becomes available half the above complement of two-horse carts is to be replaced by 3-ton lorries on a scale sufficient (estimated 36 lorries) to allow a half of the " battle complement " of ammunition to be transported over a distance of 60 Km. per day, leaving a quarter as a reserve on horsed transport.

(II) *Corps artillery park.*

Corps artillery parks form part of each corps and are organized into a varying number of sections corresponding to the number for formations, etc., in the corps.

They can be H.T. or M.T. and, in the former case, can carry the equivalent of half the " battle complement " and in the latter the whole.

Their organization is similar to that of division artillery parks.

(iii) *Scale of ammunition carried.*—The scale of ammunition carried in the case of gun ammunition is as follows:—

	Battle Complement.		Divisional Artillery Park.	Corps Artillery Park.	Total.
	Battery and Group.	Regiment.			
76-mm. divisional artillery.	212	96	150	150	608
122-mm. divisional artillery.	112	36	74	74	296
107-mm. corps artillery.	47	47	—	100	194
152-mm. corps artillery.	40	20	—	60	120

The above figures cannot be definitely accepted. It has recently been reported that the total battle complement for 76-mm. divisional artillery is only 212 rounds per gun. Again, if as stated in (*b*) (ii) (I), a quarter of the battle complement is to be held as a reserve in horsed transport in addition to the half battle complement carried in lorries, the total amount carried by the divisional artillery park will be increased by 50 per cent. over the pre-mechanization figures.

The approximate proportion of various natures of ammunition carried by divisional artillery is as follows :—

	76 mm. %	122-mm. %	Remarks.
H.E.	30	60	—
Shrapnel	30	10	—
Gas	30	20	—
Incendiary	5	5	Thermite filling.
Propaganda	?	?	Not known.
Star	5	5	

(iv) *Ammunition reserves in the field.*—Ammunition depôts in military districts form the ammunition reserves of the front or armies to which they are allotted.

Ammunition requirements are either despatched to the railhead of the corps or army concerned or to forward dumps formed in the vicinity of railhead from which it can be drawn as required.

(v) *Ammunition transport and loads carried.*—Ammunition transport consists of tractors and trailers, lorries and/or trailers, horse transport and pack animals.

The quantities which can be carried in the various forms of transport are shown below :—

	Gun limber.	Ammunition wagon.	One-horse cart.	Two-horse cart.	Lorry.	
					30 cwt.	3 ton.
76-mm. gun	36	88	24	48	120	240
122-mm. howitzer	12	50	8–9	16–18	40	80
107-mm. gun	—	49	8–10	16–20	40	80
152-mm. howitzer	—	22	4–5	8–10	25	50

(c) *Types and markings.*—(1) *Body of shell.*—The main colour of the body indicates the nature of the projectile :—

Grey	H.E.
Yellow	Shrapnel.
Green	Toxic substances
Dark blue	Incendiary.
White	Illuminating.
Red	Propaganda.

(ii) *Bands on shell.*—The colour of the shoulder indicates the explosive with which the shell is filled :—

Grey ..	.. Trotyl.
Yellow..	.. Melinite.
Green ..	.. Schneiderite.
Light Blue	.. Xylol.
White ..	.. Amatol.
Red ..	.. Piroxilin.
Brown ..	.. Ammonai.
Violet ..	.. " Ammiachnaya," saltpetre and " sol. venil."
Black ..	Black powder..

Mixed explosives are denoted by a shell-head of the colour of the main explosive and a ring of the colour of another explosive, *e.g.* :—

Trotyl with xylol : grey with a light blue ring.
Schneiderite with trotyl : red with a grey ring.

The head of armour piercing shell filled with trotyl is marked grey with a yellow band.

(iii) In peace time practice black powder shell is used in addition to the other types mentioned above.

Peace time practice shells are marked " **Prakt.**" " **D.P.**" specimens are marked with the letters " **UCHEB.**"

CHAPTER IX

ENGINEERS

1. Organization, administration and strength

Engineer field units are permanently allotted to formations as follows :—

    Corps   ..   ..   { Corps Sapper Battalion.
                                   { Corps Engineer Park.
    Motor Mechanized   Corps Sapper Battalion.
      Corps.
                               { Divisional Sapper Battalion (or
    Infantry Division {   Company).
                               { Divisional Engineer Park.
    Cavalry Division..   Divisional Sapper Squadron.

In addition, a sapper and camouflage platoon is included in each infantry regiment, a sapper troop in each cavalry regiment (*see* paragraph 3 (*c*)), and a sapper company in each mechanised brigade.

Engineer troops not permanently allotted to formations include the following :—

    Land fortress sapper units.
    Pontoon regiments and battalions.
    Electro-technical (searchlight) battalions and companies.
    Camouflage battalions and companies.
    Water supply companies.
    Railway units.
    Coast defence engineer companies.

There are also a large number of labour units which work under the Military Works Directorate and are not, properly speaking, engineer troops.

2. Engineer staffs.

The Commissariat for Defence (N.K.O.) includes the Department of the Chief Engineer, which is responsible for the direction of policy in all engineer matters, except works and buildings, and whose chief is responsible for the equipment and training of all engineer units of the Red Army, except coast defence and railway units. Works and buildings come under the Military Works Department of the N.K.O.

Coast Defence Engineer Companies are subordinate to the Department of the Chief Engineer in technical matters only; for all other purposes they are under the Naval Department of the N.K.O.

Railway units are under the Department of the Chief Engineer for technical questions only. For operative working instructions they are under the Department of Military Communications.

The headquarters staff of each military district includes a Chief of Engineers, who is subordinate to the Chief of Ordnance of the district.

Each corps has a Chief of Corps Engineers, who is in executive command of all troops engineer units.

Each division has a Divisional Engineer, who advises the Divisional Commander on engineer matters, but who is not in actual command of the divisional engineer unit.

3. Field units

(a) *Non-divisional sapper units.*—(i) *The Corps or Independent Sapper Battalion.*—Both these types of units are organised on the same basis, and comprise:—

    Battalion Headquarters.
    Three Sapper Companies.
    One Bridging and Road-building Company.
    Chemical Warfare Section.
    Medical Detachment.
    Supply Unit.
    Battalion Transport.
    Political Section and Club.

The war establishment of a sapper battalion is approximately 1,000 men, 250 horses and 125 vehicles.

In peace the battalion has two or three companies, each with a strength of about 170 men, and includes the cadre of the corps engineer park.

(ii) *The bridging and road-building company.*—The bridging and road-building company consists of company headquarters, three bridging platoons, and one road-building platoon. It has an approximate war strength of 218 men, 39 horses and 20 vehicles, the working strength of each platoon being about 40.

(iii) *The sapper company.*—Each sapper company consists of company headquarters, and four platoons, each organised in four sections.

Each member of a sapper company receives training in entrenching, wiring, field fortifications, road-building, building and ferrying, as general subjects; and in any one specialist subject, *e.g.* camouflage, demolitions, tunnelling, concrete work, carpentry work, etc. Personnel specially trained in demolition work is distributed among the various platoons and sections. There is no special demolitions section or platoon.

(iv) *Equipment*.—The equipment of a sapper battalion includes a mechanised mobile saw-mill, special road building machinery, and floating bridge equipment, which is carried in the corps engineer park in the case of corps battalions.

(b) *Divisional sapper units*.—(i) *The sapper squadron*.— Every cavalry division includes a sapper squadron which is organised in Headquarters and three troops.

Each troop consists of one demolition and one bridging section, and has a strength in peace of 25–30 men, in war of approximately 50 men. The total war establishment of the squadron is approximately 230 men, 250 horses and 25 vehicles.

Tools and equipment are shown in Appendix D.

In peace the squadron includes a N.C.O.s' training cadre, with an establishment of 25–30 ; this includes 3 men from each cavalry regiment in the division, the remaining personnel being taken from the sapper squadron itself.

(ii) *The divisional sapper battalion*.—All infantry divisions are reported to contain a Divisional Sapper Battalion composed as follows :—

Headquarters.
Two Sapper Companies.
One Technical Company.

In addition the Divisional Engineer Park is under the O.C. Sapper Battalion.

Details of the technical company are not known.

(iii) *The sapper company*.—Each sapper company in a divisional sapper battalion is organized in company headquarters, three sapper platoons, one bridging and road-building platoon, and transport platoon.

The peace strength of the company is approximately 185 ; the war establishment is about 260 men, 59 horses, and 32 vehicles, each platoon having a working strength of approximately 50 men.

Tools and equipment are shown in Appendix " D."

(c) *Sapper and camouflage platoon*.—A sapper and camouflage platoon forms part of every infantry regiment (*see* Chapter VI). Its personnel is supplied by the infantry regiment concerned, but N.C.O.s are training in divisional sapper companies. Officers are either graduates from an engineering college or have passed an engineering course.

The war establishment of the sapper and camouflage platoon is 23 men, 25 horses, 12 vehicles.

The platoon carries enough T.Z.1. (*see* paragraph 25(*b*)) rope, transoms and roadway to build a footbridge 56 metres long. Other engineer tools and equipment carried in an infantry regiment are shown in Appendix " D."

(*d*) *Sapper troops.*—Every cavalry regiment contains a sapper troop, whose duties and organization correspond to those of the sapper and camouflage platoon of an infantry regiment. The same bridging equipment is also carried.

4. Field park units

(*a*) Engineer parks are included in the war organization of corps and divisions. In peace, however, they do not exist as units, but only in cadre form in corps and divisional engineer units.

(*b*) *Divisional engineer parks.*—The divisional engineer park carries a reserve of engineer tools and bridging material, which it brings forward to the divisional sapper battalion or company as required (*see* Appendix D). The park is organized in :—

> Headquarters.
> One Platoon, road-building and bridging material (includes mechanized road-building column).
> Three Platoons, trench and construction stores.
> Workshop.

The park carries sufficient pontoon and trestle bridging equipment to build 120 metres of light bridge, or 85 metres of medium bridge, or 70 metres of heavy bridge. This material is carried in a column of 22 tractors (20–35 H.P.) with 65 trailers (64 of which carry bridging material).

The mechanized road-building column for employment by the bridging and road-building platoon of the divisional sapper company is equipped with 10 tractor-drawn road building machines.

(*c*) *Corps engineer parks.*—Corps engineer parks carry a reserve of engineer tools, stores and bridging material with which to replenish the divisional engineer parks and to supply the corps sapper battalions.

The organization of a corps engineer park is believed to correspond to that of a divisional engineer park.

5. Bridging units

(*a*) *General.*—Field bridging and the ferrying of forward fighting troops is normally the duty of corps and divisional engineer units, and is accomplished with the aid of bridging and ferrying equipment contained within the corps or division.

The Red Army also includes a number of special non-divisional bridging units, termed pontoon battalions, to supplement the engineers of forward formations when they encounter broad rivers, for the crossing of which the equipment carried with the corps or division is insufficient.

The duties of these pontoon battalions also include the construction of bridges in the rear of forward fighting troops and the improvement of rear road communications by constructing heavy bridges over broad rivers.

(b) *The Pontoon battalion.*—The pontoon battalion is organized in :—

>Battalion Headquarters.
>Two Pontoon Companies.
>One Motor Pontoon Company (does not exist in all battalions).
>Bridging Park (with mobile repair shop).
>Medical Detachment.
>Supply and Transport Detachment.
>Chemical Personnel.

and in peace-time includes an N.C.O.s training centre. It has a strength of about 1,000 men, and its transport is now completely mechanized.

Two pontoon regiments, each containing two battalions, are known to exist, but appear to be primarily peace-time units, formed to facilitate training, administration and the supply of technical equipment.

(c) A pontoon company is organized in a headquarters and four platoons with a peace strength of 134 all ranks.

(d) A motor pontoon company is similarly organized and is equipped with eight 8-ton motor pontoons.

Motor pontoons can be used for towing convoys of vessels, for ferrying heavy loads up to 20 tons on a raft made up of two pontoons for landing operations.

(e) The bridging park of a pontoon battalion is organized into two or three platoons. The pontoon and trestle equipment is carried on trailers pulled by Kommunar tractors equipped with folding cranes, and includes motor-tugs and outboard motors for ferrying purposes. The equipment carried in a park of three platoons is sufficient to construct the following bridges :—

>Normal bridge, loads up to 11 tons, single stream of traffic 177 metres, double stream 101 metres.

>Strengthened bridge, loads up to 20 tons, single stream of traffic 127 metres, double stream 76 metres.

The equipment can also be used to form rafts for ferrying loads up to 11, 20, 30 and 50 tons.

The equipment in the park is sufficient for five 11-ton and six 20-ton ferries, or eight 11-ton and three 30-ton ferries.

(*f*) *Bridging in armoured formations.*—Armoured and mechanized units carry bridging and ferrying equipment of their own for the transportation of tanks, armoured cars, etc. This includes short lengths of heavy bridge and heavy road bearers which are laid over narrow gaps and channels by tanks fitted with cranes; it also includes road bearers, which are laid by lorries fitted with cranes and derricks, and short girder bridges (in sections), which can be used to cross gaps up to 20 metres in width.

6. Fortress units

Land fortress sapper units exist in various fortified areas. They are organized in companies of four platoons. The strength of companies varies according to the importance of the locality in which they are stationed.

Coast defence sapper units are under the Naval Directorate. No details of their organizations are known.

7. Electrical and Searchlight units

(*a*) *General.*—The organization of the so-called electro-technical units, either battalions or companies, which appear to carry out both anti-aircraft and ground electric light duties, is not known precisely.

(*b*) *Electro-technical battalions.*—Anti-aircraft artillery brigades include electro-technical battalions, which until recently consisted of one electro-technical company and two to three searchlight companies. The electro-technical company consisted of four platoons, each equipped with a mobile power station. The searchlight company was organized in three platoons, each containing four searchlights and two sound locators. It has been reported recently, however, that battalions are to contain six to eight homogeneous companies, each being either a searchlight or a sound locator company.

(*c*) *Independent searchlight units.*—Independent anti-aircraft artillery regiments include electro-technical companies, organized similarly to the searchlight company of an electro-technical battalion but containing also an electro-technical platoon.

Independent anti-aircraft groups and batteries include special anti-aircraft searchlight units, allotted normally on the basis of one company to each anti-aircraft group of nine to twelve guns.

(*d*) *Independent electro-technical units.*— Independent electro-technical units (normally companies) are attached to headquarters of armies in the field and to headquarters of Defended Areas (*e.g.*, Leningrad, Karelian frontier, etc.).

Their duties include anti-aircraft work, electrification of wire obstacles, searching of approaches by searchlight, illumination of routes and special points, lighting of formation headquarters.

(*e*) *Equipment.*—The searchlight reflectors in normal use are of 120 cm. diameter. 60 cm. diameter projectors are still used in horse-drawn searchlight companies, but they are being replaced by larger mechanized projectors. A certain number of 150 cm. projectors have also been reported.

The sound locator is of the SPERRY type.

(*f*) *Transport.*—The transport of all electro-technical units will probably be mechanized in war, with the possible exception of units attached to Defended Areas.

8. Camouflage units

(*a*) *General.*—The value of camouflage is fully appreciated by the Red Army authorities and considerable attention is paid to training in camouflage by units.

Corps and divisional sapper units carry out camouflage work in the corps and divisional areas respectively, and supervise the work done by the regimental sapper and camouflage platoons. Camouflage material and technical equipment for the above work is carried in unit transport. Reserve camouflage stores are carried in the corps and divisional engineer parks.

(*b*) *Specialist units.*—Purely camouflage units exist in the Red Army in the form of camouflage battalions, each of two to three companies, and of independent camouflage companies. They appear to be on the scale of one battalion or company to each Military District.

In peace the strength of a company is about 155 men and includes an N.C.O.s training cadre.

No details of the war strength are known, nor of the quantity or types of camouflage equipment carried.

9. Water supply units

Specialist officers, who are responsible for the preparation and supervision of water-supply projects, are included in the staffs of army and corps headquarters.

Water supply work in forward areas is carried out by the sapper units in corps and divisions, and purification of local drinking water supply is carried out by the medical personnel of lower formations and units.

The main water supply system of the field armies is provided by water companies, of which at least six exist in peace time. No information is available as to their organization or transport, but their equipment includes :

> Endless chains for raising water from wells.
> Hand pumps with piping and filter (Norton tubewell type).
> One-man pack filters.
> Filters carried on pack-horses. (With a purification capacity of 250 litres per hour.)
> Filter carts (with a purification capacity of 400 litres per hour).
> Filter lorries (with a purification capacity of 10,000 litres per hour).
> Canvas tanks.

10. Road construction units

No special units for road construction exist, but corps and divisional sapper battalions and companies, and labour units, are trained in this work. Particular attention is paid to the rapid construction of roads fit for mechanical transport by treating earth roads with a special road oil.

11. Railway construction units

It is believed that railway construction units may no longer form part of the Red Army peace-time organization.

A percentage of railway troops is in the railway construction " brigades " which have been reported in W.R.M.D., M.M.D., and the Far East. The bulk of the personnel of these brigades is drawn, however, from penal settlements or from conscripted labour reserves, and they work under the Commissariat for Ways and Communications. They may, therefore, be considered as essentially labour organizations and not as units of the Red Army.

12. Quarrying units

No information available.

13. Boring units
No information available.

14. Mining units
Mining units were previously organized in fortress mining detachments and independent mining companies, but such units no longer appear to exist in the Red Army.

15. Searchlight units
See paragraph 6. Electrical units.

16. Engineer base workshops
No information available.

17. Engineer base store depôts
Engineer stores and workshops come under the Ordnance Department.

18. Workshop units
Engineer workshop units are known to form part of engineer parks, mechanised units, etc.
No details of their organization are available.

19. Depôts
No information available.

20. Regimental transport
It is probably the intention to mechanise the transport of all technical engineer units. Pontoon battalions, corps engineer parks, bridging parks and electrical units have already been mechanised or are in process of mechanization.

21. Armament and equipment of personnel
All engineer and pioneer units are classified as fighting troops. The personnel is armed and equipped as in the Infantry (*see* Chapter VI), except in the case of sapper squadrons. Mounted sappers are armed in the same way as cavalry personnel (*see* Chapter VII). Each mounted sapper carries, in addition, an entrenching or workshop tool in a special leather or tarpaulin cover.

22. Tools and miscellaneous equipment
(*a*) *Entrenching and workshop tools.*—Engineer units carry a reserve of tools of all kinds, the quantity varying according to the unit concerned. Details are given in

Appendix D. In addition to these tools, certain units hold special sets of carpenter's, joiner's, blacksmith's, fitter's tools, etc.

(b) *Roadbuilding equipment.*—Roadbuilding equipment includes barrows, gradient measuring apparatus, metal parts of pile-drivers, etc.

The road-building columns which move in corps and divisional engineer parks include tractor-drawn ditch-ploughs, rippers, rollers, planers, shovels, heavy graders and tree stump removers.

(c) *Bridging and ferrying equipment.*—The quantities of bridging and ferrying equipment carried in corps and divisions are given in paragraphs 3, 4 and 5.

(d) *Field-works stores.*

23. Explosives

(a) The chief explosives in use are piroxilin, trinitrotoluene and melinite, which are made up in slabs and sticks of various weights.

The quantities of explosives carried in various units are as follows:—

Corps engineer park	1,000 kilos.
Divisional engineer park	400 kilos.
Sapper companies—each	900 kilos.
Sapper squadrons—each	500 kilos.

(b) *Detonators.*—Detonators of various types are in use, and, in addition, units are supplied with standard "ignition tubes," consisting of detonators already attached to varying lengths of fuse.

(c) *Anti-tank mines.*—The Red Army employs anti-tank type "T—IV," whose dimensions are 21·5 by 21·5 by 10 cms. The weight of the mine, including the charge, is 4·2 kilograms. The weight of the charge alone is 2·6 kilograms (five large and three small sticks of T.N.T.).

(d) *Fuzes.*—Time fuzes of three types are used. They are:

(i) Alarum clock type, which can be set with an accuracy of 15 minutes between limits of half an hour and 10 hours.

(ii) "35 days" type, which can be set with an accuracy of 12 hours between limits of 12 hours and 35 days.

(iii) Chemical type, which can be set between limits of a few days and three months.

24. Portable bridging equipment

(a) *The A-3 pneumatic rubber boat.*—This consists of an oblong all-round pneumatic air container, with rounded ends and of circular section, made of rubber-coated tarpaulin, saturated with a special chemical solution. It weighs 170 kg. and has a maximum carrying capacity of $3\frac{1}{2}$ tons, or 25 armed men in addition to her crew. The boats can be made into a foot-bridge or into rafts for ferrying purposes.

(b) *T.Z.1 floats.*—These consist of a covering of rubber-impregnated tarpaulin, stuffed with unsinkable material. Each float has a buoyancy of 350 kgs. The floats can be made into a footbridge or into rafts which will carry a 76-mm. gun.

(c) *The small pneumatic boat.*—This also consists of an all-round air-container. Each boat carries four men with full equipment and one machine gun.

Each sapper and camouflage platoon and sapper troop carries three of these boats.

(d) *Polyanski floats.*—A Polyanski float consists of an outer tarpaulin skin and an inner air-container of rubber-treated material. It can be blown up by mouth in six to seven minutes, weighs 2 kilograms and carries one armoured man.

(e) *The Pontoon.*—The pontoon is made of coppered iron, is in two halves, weighs 34 cwt. and has a buoyancy of $12 \cdot 7$ tons.

The motor pontoon weighs $8 \cdot 2$ tons, has a buoyancy of 8 $11 \cdot 5$ tons, and is propelled by a 35 h.p. petrol engine, type "Ikegai," which is situated in the rear half of the pontoon. A speed of 10 kms. per hour may be attained in calm water.

CHAPTER X

CHEMICAL WARFARE

1. General policy

The U.S.S.R. is a signatory of the Geneva Protocol of 1925 forbidding the use of poison gas, and bacteriological methods in War.

Russian chemical warfare achievements during the war 1914-18 were not spectacular, but since then, of all countries, Soviet Russia appeared to devote the greatest effort to developing the chemical arm, but the practical success attained is problematical. It has been said that they are the most " gas minded " of all nations, and there is much evidence to support this statement. The nation as a whole is constantly being reminded that chemical methods will be decisive in the next war; this conviction is exemplified by the prominence given to the subject in newspapers and periodicals, by the frequency of practice " gas alarms " and the thoroughness with which they are carried out in frontier districts and in industrial centres.

2. Organization, administration and strength

In the U.S.S.R. the controlling body is the Military Chemical Administration of the R.K.K.A., while the Central Institute of Gas Defence, in Moscow, aided by Scientific and technical societies, acts as the Scientific Advisory Committee. The Department is under the jurisdiction of the Deputy Commissar for Defence.

3. Defence

(a) *Organization, administration and strength.*—(i) *Army.*—There is a Chief of the Chemical Services on the Staff of all formations, and a Chemical Instructor on the Headquarters of all regiments and equivalent units, who is responsible for advising on chemical warfare matters and for supervising chemical warfare training. In addition to these she is stated to possess trained anti-gas instructors in every unit.

Chemical platoons, troops, and detachments are attached to each infantry, cavalry and field artillery regiment respectively, and a section to each engineer battalion. They are intended essentially for defensive work and equipped with complete protective clothing, decontamination apparatus, gas alarms, detectors, and warning signs; they are also equipped so as to be employed in offensive operations to a limited extent.

The schemes of training laid down in the Russian handbooks are extraordinarily thorough and the standard of proficiency expected exceedingly high, too high indeed to be attained by the general body of troops.

The centre of training for the higher posts is the Central Gas Training School, Moscow, instruction is also provided in the Chemical Departments of the Military Technical Academy, the Aviation School, the Veterinary College, and Naval Academy. Certain chemical battalions also act as training schools. A school at Nicolsh provides instruction for army personnel and lectures for civilians.

(ii) *Civilian population.*—The official Air Defence League (the Osoaviokhim) has been responsible for propaganda and instruction in civil defence for many years. It has a very large membership throughout the country, has undoubtedly done much good work and organized in most large towns a reasonable A.R.P. service, but it is questionable if the average Soviet citizen has derived much benefit from such instruction. Many millions of reasonably efficient civilian masks (Model G.T.3) have been issued, also special childrens' masks, but issue must be far from complete, while the number of efficient shelters is practically negligible except in the largest factories.

The organization of chemical platoons and troops is believed to be:

Infantry regiment, chemical platoon

(a) *Organization*
Headquarters.
Three Chemical Warfare Sections.
One Transport Section.
Strength about 45 men.

(b) *Equipment.*
Ten per cent. reserve respirators for the regiment.
Four decontamination sprayer outfits.
Fifteen sirens for gas alarms.
Chloride of lime.
Toxic smoke candles.
Smoke producing apparatus.
Forty anti-gas suits (War Establishment).
Sixteen horses.
Eight vehicles.

Cavalry Regiment. Chemical troop.
  Peace Establishment—
      Officer Commanding.
      One Chemical Warfare Instructor.
      Five other ranks.
  War Establishment (reported)—
      Seventeen other ranks.
      Nineteen horses.
      Two carts.
Artillery chemical department.
  No details available.
Engineer chemical section.
  No details available.

(b) *Equipment.*—(i) *Respirators.*—The Russian service respirator is known as the 1935 B.N. mask, with which it is understood that most units are equipped, some still have the older B.N. and possibly the T.T.S.

1935 *B.N.*—The facepiece consists of a light grey press-moulded rubber mask with five-point harness, plain glass eyepieces set in annular grooves, and disc inlet and top hat outlet valves housed in one moulding. The container is made of ribbed tin and is similar in shape to the British Type A. The top half contains a cotton-wool particulate filter and the lower half is filled with wood charcoal of low activity. The respirator has a special pencil with which the eyepieces are rubbed from inside to prevent dimming. It is kept in a canvas bag consisting of two compartments, one for the facepiece and tube, and a larger one for the container. The bag is carried on a strap with buckle on the left side. Usually the connecting tube is about 40-cm. long, allowing the wearing of the respirator with the bag carried at the side. Some have connecting tubes only 24-cm. long for use with bag carried on the chest.

B.N.—This respirator is arranged in the same way as the 1935 B.N., but has a red rubber hood or helmet covering the greater part of the head. For wiping the eyepieces there is a " shoot " in the form of a finger.

T.T.S.—Has the same facepiece as the B.N. but a differently constructed container. The chemical absorbent consists of muslin soaked in chemical and the particulate filter is made of felt. After eight hours in a medium concentration the filter begins to fail.

B.S.4.—Very similar to the B.N. Type. Used for experimental purposes in chemical warfare units and finally to replace the B.N. for all troops.

Civilian respirators.—Obsolete military types were originally used but a special civilian type, the G.T.3 has been evolved, which gives approximately one-third the protection afforded by the B.N. A similar but lighter respirator for children exists and anti-gas devices for small children have been developed.

Insulated respirators.—These exist for special service by doctors, engineer and artillery observers, decontamination, etc. Various types with arrangements for an oxygen reserve are usual, weight between 8 and 12 kgs. Reference has been made in literature to a new T.C. respirator.

Horse respirators.—Issue for horses is now reported to be general. The respirator is of the nose-bag type with canvas " biting pad," and is of a coarse apparently unimpregnated textile material of greyish colour. It is made up of six layers of fabric, and fitted with four wooden stiffeners. Impregnation of the fabric is reported to take place on mobilization. In order to preserve the impregnant, the respirator is kept in a bag treated with rubber. Respirators for messenger dogs are also in use. (Note for Types of Respirator, *see* Appendix B.)

(ii) *Protective clothing.*—Full protective clothing is issued only to chemical troops.

It consists of a combination overall, made from rough linen treated with boiled oil, rubber boots and gloves. The fabric resists penetration by mustard gas for about three hours, but decontamination is difficult. The adverse physical effects when wearing this clothing is appreciated and frequent exercises in full anti-gas clothing are carried out in order to accustom personnel to its use.

It is proposed to issue all ranks of the Red Army with light oilskin cloaks for protection against aerial spray, and overboots to traverse contaminated areas. It is believed, however, that no general issue has yet been made, but training exercises in the use of the cloak are frequent. Cavalry, will, it is understood, have protective cloaks for their horses and protective covering for troops have been reported.

As far as is known experiments have been unsuccessful and no pervious protective clothing is available in the U.S.S.R. Special underclothing affording protection against vesicants, and air ventilated anti-gas suits in which the air is passed through filters, have however, been reported. Reports have also made reference to protective cloaks made of paper.

(iii) *Decontamination.*—The subject of decontamination has received marked attention. An exhaustive manual on the subject, has been issued giving on the whole very sound and practical instruction.

Weathering, treatment in running water and steam treatment are recommended for decontamination of clothing and equipment, boiling is regarded as a possible treatment for woollens.

Bleaching powder is the usual substance for ordinary decontamination work.

They apparently envisage large scale decontamination of ground with bleach distributed by hand or mechanical means. Three types of decontamination apparatus have been described :—

R.P.D.I.	Hand atomiser—the container is carried on the back. Weight 14 lbs. empty—36 lbs. full.
V.P.D.1.	A transportable drum on wheels capable of decontaminating with bleach a strip 1 metre by 140 metres.
A.D.T.I.	A tractor trailer for spreading large quantities of bleaching powder.

In addition, a " sieve " decontaminator for small areas and a " hand scoop " for awkward positions, are mentioned, also the possible adaption of agricultural machinery.

Some reference has been made to dispersal of gas in trenches by the use of special " burning packets."

(iv) *Personal decontamination.*—Individual anti-gas outfits for the personal decontamination are issued to all personnel. The outfit consists of a small tin box containing about 20 tampons of gauze and cotton-wool impregnated with paraffin. A mirror is fitted in the lid of the box for use when decontaminating the face.

Protective ointments have also been prepared.

(v) *Gas detectors.*—No definite information available, but specially treated paper slips, which change colour in the presence of gas, have been reported.

(vi) *Collective protection.*—Gas-proof shelters have been reported, some are fitted with air filters and others are sealed with material soaked in a special mixture. Battalion, Regimental Headquarters of higher formations and medical units are mentioned as having tent shelters with positive **air** pressure inside.

4. Offensive

(*a*) *Organization, administration and strength.* — The Russians are convinced of the utility of specialized troops for conducting large scale gas operations and have been very ambitious.

Commencing with a chemical regiment of two battalions for offensive gas warfare, and one for training, they have subsequently developed independent chemical battalions, organized as corps troops, one battalion to be attached to every Army Corps. In peace, battalions are responsible for the training of all Regimental Chemical Instructors in the corps area, as well as carrying out their normal training, and such experimental work as is required by the Military Chemical Department.

(i) *Special gas units.*—Adequate confirmation of the reported organization of a C.W. battalion is at present lacking.

The following establishment may still be largely experimental.

The Battalion consists of :—

Headquarters.

Reconnaissance platoon.

Strength 20 all ranks includes a meteorological station in a 30-cwt. lorry.

Signal platoon.

Includes cable, visual, wireless and D.R. section.

Anti-aircraft platoon.

Four pairs of anti-aircraft machine-guns, each pair mounted on a lorry.

Two trench mortar companies, each of :—

Headquarters with reconnaissance and signal sections.

Three mortar platoons of six mortars each. Ammunition supply section of six lorries.

Two chemical companies, each of :—

Headquarters with reconnaissance and signal sections.

Four platoons each of four chemical lorries, and 20 portable gas cylinders. Reports refer to the inclusion of six-wheeled lorries with flame throwers in the equipment.

Ammunition and chemical supply company, includes :—
One repair section.
11 five-ton chemical lorries.
26 lorries for—135 chemical mines.
6,000 toxic smoke candles.
6,000 non-toxic smoke candles.
Two mobile disinfecting chambers.
Two motor ambulances.
Four mobile shower baths.

It appears that in peace, some battalions have only one of each of the two types of company.

The mechanization of all chemical warfare battalions, if not yet complete is being carried out. It is reported that the ammunition and supply companies are in all cases completely mechanized.

(ii) *Gas in other arms.—Tank units.*—Certain tanks apparently are fitted with ejectors for gas or smoke.

(b) *Gases for offensive use.*—(i) *General.*—All types— blister, choking, tear and nose gases are likely to be used.

In the following tables the main gases likely to be met are given. Experimental work on a wide variety of other gases has been reported from time to time, and although it is not thought that any important new war gas has been discovered, indications of possible new developments are included in the tables—

Table I

(ii)	Blister gases	Common (and chemical) names
	1. Mustard gas, H.S.	Dichlorodiethylsulphide.
	2. Lewisite, I. ..	Chlorovinyl dichloroarsine.
	3. Dick	Ethyldichloroarsine.
	4. Vesicant toxic smoke.	—

Note.—1. The Russians are very interested in Lewisite.

2. Mixtures of mustard gas with Lewisite may be used in cold weather.

Table II

(iii)	Choking gases	Common (and chemical) names
	1. Phosgene, C.G. ..	Carbonyl chloride.
	2. Diphosgene ..	Trichloromethyl chloroformate.
	3. Chloropicrin, P.S.	Trichloro-nitro-methane.
	4. Dick	Ethyldichloroarsine.
	5. Chlorine	—

Note.—There have been frequent references to mixtures of choking gases, such as phosgene, diphosgene, and chloropicrin, which are stated to be more effective than the individual gases.

Table III

(iv) Nose gases (toxic smokes)	Common (and chemical) names
1. D.A.	Diphenyl chloroarsine.
2. D.C.	Diphenyl cyano-arsine.
3. D.M.	Diphenylamine-chloroarsine (and other names).
4. Vesicant toxic smoke.	—

Table IV

(v) Tear gases	Common (and chemical) names
1. C.A.P.	Chloroacetophenone.
2. B.B.C.	Bromobenzyl cyanide.
3.	Bromoacetone.
4.	Benzyl bromide.
5.	Xylyl bromide.

Table V

(vi) Miscellaneous	Common (and chemical) names
1. H.C.N.	Hydrogen cyanide.
2. Camouflage or fake gases.	—

Note.—The Russians are said to favour the use of camouflage or fake gases for tactical purposes and to economize in the more deadly gases.

(c) *Offensive weapons and equipment.*—(i) *General.*—Since the war 1914–18, the Russians have studied the influence of meteorological factors and topography on the tactical use of gas and smoke. It may be anticipated, therefore, that conditions from the offensive and defensive aspects suitable and unsuitable for the use of gas have been approximately but clearly defined, and an accurate estimate made of the value of different types of weapons. The Red Army General Staff looks on aerial methods of chemical attack as the most effective. The possible development of some ingenious new gas weapon cannot be ignored, but as far as our information goes the following types may be used:—

(ii) *Aerial spray.*—The importance attached to this weapon may be gauged by the fact that an issue of anti-spray cloaks to all ranks is envisaged.

Considerable work has been carried out on aerial spray. They regard low altitude spray (25–75 metres) as an effective weapon both against personnel and for ground contamination. Some work has apparently been done on high spraying. Information as to designs of spray apparatus is meagre and of little value since many factors have a material influence on results. Containers of 300 to 500 litres capacity have been mentioned, both pressure and gravity types. Mustard gas or lewisite may be used and mixtures of these two gases have also been mentioned. Practices include attacks on troops and ships with a harmless mixture.

There is evidence of close collaboration between the civil organization for combating agricultural pests and chemical warfare units ; experience in the handling of toxic compounds and spraying them from the air is thus obtained by military personnel and opportunities for experimental work are also provided by this means. The possibility of spraying phosgene in winter has been put forward.

(iii) *Chemical aircraft bombs.*—Marked attention has been paid to aircraft gas bombs. The following types have been mentioned :—

> Large bombs up to 250 or 300 kg. with non-persistent chargings (phosgene or diphosgene).
>
> Bombs from 15 to 250 kg. capacity with persistent chargings ; fitted with small or large bursters to give heavy or scattered contamination : large types may have time fuses for air burst spray effect.
>
> Slow burning toxic smoke bombs and H.E./Toxic smoke bombs with varying ratios of H.E. to gas, including 1,000 kilo design with H.E. for predominating effect.
>
> Glass capsules filled with a vesicant.

(iv) *Projectors.*—No reference has been made to any efforts to increase the range or improve the mobility of this weapon. Phosgene, mustard gas and apparently toxic smokes are considered suitable chargings.

(v) *Artillery shell.*—The use of gas shell on a considerable scale by the artillery is envisaged. Nevertheless, they realize the limitations of artillery shell as a gas weapon. All field medium and heavy artillery batteries carry a proportion of gas shell of both persistent and non-persistent types, which form about 20 per cent. of the total number of rounds carried. Choking gas chargings are favoured for the larger shell, and blister gases for all calibres. They may also use shell not only with toxic smokes but also with C.A.P. or B.B.C. chargings.

(vi) *Mortars.*—The Russians claim to have trench mortars in 3- and 4-in. calibres with stream-lined bombs having a range of 2,000 metres, or with rifled mortars, 3,000 metres.

Reports all mention mortars of 107, 152 and 240 mm.

(vii) *Gas grenades.*—No information available.

(viii) *Gas cylinders.*—Portable gas cylinders are included in the equipment of Chemical battalions, concentrated point sources may be used in the form of " beam " attack.

(ix) *Gas mines.*—No information available.
Large mortar and projector bombs could be used for this purpose.

(x) *Bulk contamination.* — Chemical lorries — mobile cisterns, mounted on 5-ton lorries fitted with pressure spray apparatus—each cistern is said to be adequate to contaminate about 6 acres. They form part of the equipment of all chemical battalions.

Tanks and armoured cars are also stated to be equipped with apparatus for spraying gas and smoke.

Hand sprayers, used for heat contamination, capacity 32 kg. of mustard gas.

(xi) *Toxic generators.*—The Russians are reputed to possess generators of the intimate mixture type, chargings D.A. or D.C. These are issued to chemical warfare platoons.

5. Research, and research establishments

Since the establishment of the U.S.S.R. much research has been carried out on C.W. methods, a close liaison on C.W. was maintained with pre-Nazi Germany, and every effort was made to develop a chemical industry capable of turning over to war production of chemicals, if necessary.

Research work in connection with chemical warfare is a particularly closely guarded secret. The wide dispersion of research establishments, some of which are situated in inaccessible areas, adds to the difficulty of penetrating the screen of secrecy.

Experimental work and field trials were formerly carried out at the Central Chemical Range, Moscow, but latterly most of this work was transferred to a larger station near Volsk, known as Scientific Research Chemical Range (presumably the same as or part of, the Central Military Chemical Polygon on the R. Volga, 18 miles from Volsk). Research is also carried out by :—

> The Central Institute of Gas Defence, Moscow. (Acts as an Advisory Committee to Military Chemical Departments.)
>
> The Chemical departments of—Military Training Academy Aviation School, Veterinary College, Naval Academy.
>
> Independent Chemical Warfare Battalions—in special areas (*e.g.* in the Far East and Central Asia).

Mention has also been made of a chemical range at Vladivostok and an experimental laboratory under the War Department at the Akhtaba Chemical Works.

6. Manufacturing establishments and depôts

The Russian chemical industry has made great advances during the past ten years and has unquestionably been planned to meet war needs. The War Chemical Trust (Vokhim Trust) is responsible for all factories connected with the manufacture of toxic gases and chemical equipment and also for the maintenance of adequate reserve plant to provide increased supplies in emergency.

(i) *Gas.*—Reliance will be placed on industrial plant for the production of the majority of gases. On the whole, it is probable that output would be equal to Russian requirements, but it is unlikely that any surplus would be available. It should be noted that factories are not confined to Europe and some production is possible in the Far East; some three factories have been mentioned and a storage depot near Lake Baikal.

For the production of mustard gas, however, it is understood that the Berzol Works (also known as State Factory No. 15) was expressly constructed some time ago at Chapaevsk near Samara and capable of producing 200 tons per month. The Russian mustard gas is stated to be inferior in persistency to the German product.

(ii) *Respirators.*—Some five or six factories have been reported as engaged in the production of respirators, and a factory in Leningrad produces activated charcoal.

The Kharkov factory is stated to have an output of 500,000 respirators per annum.

As the entire Russian Army was re-equipped with B.N. respirators in the course of about three years, while large amounts of civilian respirators were also made, it is clear that this industry in the U.S.S.R. must be gigantic.

7. Smoke

(a) *Smoke units.*—No information available.

(b) *Equipment.*—Iron containers holding 100, 200 and 300 litres of smoke producing liquid, are fitted to aeroplanes and armoured fighting vehicles. The liquid, reported as " Chlorossulfron," is led under slight pressure into the main exhaust of the engine.

White phosphorous shell in all calibres is, however, available for the artillery, and smoke bombs for mortars.

A pack smoke-producing apparatus carried by one man is reported. It weighs about 60 lb. and discharges smoke for about 10 minutes, and said to be capable of producing an effective screen of about 300 metres long. This forms part of the equipment of infantry chemical platoons. Recently, references have been made to the use of coloured smokes—green, black, and yellow—for concealing aerodromes, these being regarded as preferable to white smoke for this purpose.

8. Incendiary

(*a*) *Bombs.*—The Russians have a very high opinion of the offensive value of incendiary bombs, particularly as a means of attack on rear area and civilian centres. The bombs principally considered are of the " electron " type, containing a thermite charging in a casing of metallic magnesium, of small size (2, 5 and 10 kilos.), and are released from aircraft in large numbers against suitable targets.

The device consists of a container, about 7 ft. high, for a large number of small bombs : it holds 125 of the 2 kg. type or a smaller number of the larger incendiary bombs. In falling, vanes in the tail cause the container to spin, the sides then open and its contents scattered.

In addition bombs of 50 kg. were used in Finland, containing an explosive charge and filled naphtha or having the front section filled thermite and the rear portion naphtha.

N.B.—There is a tendency in foreign practice to insert a small explosive charge in the larger types of incendiary bombs to prevent interference with them during the burning period.

(*b*) *Shell.*—Approximately, 5 per cent. of shell carried by divisional and corps artillery are incendiary ; in anti-aircraft artillery, the proportion is not known. No details of the construction or performance of incendiary shell are available.

(*c*) *Flame-throwers.*—The Russians do not appear to have the same enthusiasm as Germany and Italy.

They appear to have developed three types :—

The pack type.—A steel reservoir with flexible hose and jet, filled with liquid fuel and compressed air.

Total weight charged is 50-lb. A continuous or intermittent jet of flame, range from 15 to 30 yards; duration of continuous flame about 50 seconds.

The heavy or trench type.—Similar to the pack type but larger, weight charged 400 lb. Range from 35 to 55 yards, duration of continuous flame about one minute.

The fougasse type.—A long cylinder with a piston at the bottom. Beneath the piston a space for a powder cartridge. It is filled with liquid fuel. The powder charge drives the piston forward, forcing out the liquid fuel which is ignited as it passes a jet at the top of the cylinder. Weight charged 65 lb., range 50 yards, produces an instantaneous jet for one or two seconds.

Reference has also been made to the inclusion of six-wheeled vehicles with heavy flame-throwers, forming part of the equipment of Chemical Battalions.

Experiments on the use of flame-throwers as an anti-tank weapon have been recorded, the range of such a weapon is stated to be 300 feet.

9. Bacteria

It is of interest to note that Germany claims to have positive proof that the Russians have been studying bacteriological warfare. It will be recalled that at one time a liaison* on chemical warfare matters existed between Russia and Germany.

It has been reported that certain Russian laboratories have studied the rapid cultivation of typhoid colonies. Spraying of virus of " foot and mouth " disease, dispersed by anthrax spore, and pollution of water supplies by enemy agents, are specially mentioned.

CHAPTER XI

UNITS EQUIPPED WITH ARMOURED FIGHTING VEHICLES

1. General organization, administration and strength

Units of the Red Army equipped with armoured fighting vehicles are organised in :—

Mechanized Corps.
Mechanized Brigades.
Tank Brigades.
Independent Tank Battalions.
Armoured Trains.

They are administered by the Department of Mechanization and Armoured Forces of the Commissariat for Defence. The Chief of the department is directly responsible to the Deputy Commissar for Defence who is in charge of supply of ordnance material of all kinds.

The Red Army authorities are particularly secretive regarding the number, and developments in the organization, of units equipped with armoured fighting vehicles ; and any reliable figure for strengths is consequently impossible to obtain, particularly as many of the organizations are still experimental. It is estimated, however, that at the present time the Red Army has in service a minimum of 10,000 tanks of all types. It is probable that the armament of each type of formation is not always identical. (For details *see* Appendix ' F.')

2. Organization of independent formations and units.

(*a*) *The mechanized corps.*—A mechanized corps comprises :—

Headquarters, containing a reconnaissance battalion.
Two Mechanized Brigades, each of three battalions of light medium tanks.
One Motorized Brigade of three infantry and machine gun battalions.
Mechanized engineer, signal and administrative units.
Corps flight of aircraft.

The formation thus approximates to a division rather than to a corps.

Mechanised brigades of mechanised corps.—These brigades, formerly equipped with T.26 tanks, are now being armed with B.T. tanks, and their probable organization is :—

Three tank battalions each of :—

Battalion Headquarters—two tanks.

Three companies of three platoons of three tanks, plus one company headquarters tank—total per company, ten tanks.

One Reconnaissance Platoon of five to seven amphibian tanks.

One Training Battalion.

One Reconnaissance Company of 16 amphibian tanks (one headquarters tank and three platoons of five), and possibly some armoured cars.

One " B.O." Battalion containing units of ancillary arms and services as described in para. 2 (*c*).

Motorised brigades of mechanised corps.—These brigades contain the holding units and are believed to be organized as follows :—

Three motorised "infantry and machine gun" Battalions.

One training motorised "infantry and machine gun" Battalion.

One " B.O." Battalion of ancillary troops (*see* para. 2 (*c*)).

One Reconnaissance Company of 16 amphibian tanks.

Possibly one artillery group (two batteries of 76-mm. guns "portee."

The " infantry and machine gun " battalions each contain three companies each of twelve machine-guns and one rifle company. Motorised brigades also probably have a " regimental artillery " group.

(*b*) *Other brigade formations.*—(i) *Independent mechanised brigades.*—These brigades, formerly containing T.26 tanks, are now equipped with B.T. tanks. They are " T.R.G.K." troops, *i.e.*, tanks at the disposal of the higher command.

They are organized as follows :—

Three Tank Battalions (organized as in paragraph 2).

One Training Battalion.

One " B.O." Battalion of ancillary troops (*see* paragraph 2 (*c*)).

One Reconnaissance Company.

Brigade Park (with workshop and base).

They also contain a motorised battalion similar in composition to those in motorised brigades.

(ii) *Mechanised brigades of cavalry corps.*—There are certain other mechanised brigades, organized and equipped similarly to the independent mechanised brigades described above, but which, instead of being T.R.G.K. troops, are either allotted or earmarked for employment with certain definite cavalry corps.

(iii) *Tank brigades.*—The heavier natures of tank are organized in tank brigades which are at the disposal of the higher command and can be allotted to formations to supply extra hitting power as required.

They are organized as follows :—

> Three Tank Battalions (organized as in para. 2).
> One Training Battalion.
> One " B.O." battalion of ancillary troops (*see* paragraph 2 (*c*)).
> One Brigade Park.

While the majority of tank brigades are equipped with T.28 type medium tanks, it has been reported that light tank brigades equipped with T.26 light tanks also continue to exist, and recently the new T.35 heavy tank has been issued to these formations.

(*c*) *The " B.O." battalion.*—The " B.O." battalion (Battalion Boegovo Obespecheniya) which forms a part of all mechanised and motorised brigades appears to consist of units of the ancillary arms and services grouped together under one commander presumably for purposes mainly of administration.

It contains the following, but may have certain additional sub-units :—

> One Motorised Signal Company (equipped with four " 6—PK " and one " 5—AK " wireless transmitting sets).
> One Motorised Sapper Company.
> One Motorised anti-aircraft Defence (" P.V.O.") Company or Platoon (equipped with anti-aircraft machine guns).
> One Traffic Control Company.
> One Park Company.

(*d*) *The independent tank battalion.*—Independent tank battalions have from time to time been identified and would appear to comprise :—

> (i) Independent units in districts in Central Russia where there are no large concentrations of troops.

(ii) Battalions originally formed independently, but later incorporated in divisions as divisional tank battalions (*see* paragraph 3 (*b*)).

(iii) Battalions containing special natures of tanks, such as the T.35.

These battalions generaly consist of a headquarters and three tank companies.

The headquarter staff of the battalion is organized in two sections :—

    Operations Section.
    Administration and Personnel Section.

The Commanding Officer is assisted by an Adjutant, Technical Assistant and Political Assistant. The following sub-units are directly under battalion headquarters :—

    Reconnaissance Platoon.
    A.A. Platoon.
    Signal Platoon.
    Sapper Platoon.
    Chemical Platoon.
    Traffic Control Platoon.
    Medical Detachment.
    Supply Detachment.
    Maintenance Detachment.
    Political Personnel and Club.

The reconnaissance platoon usually consists of from five to seven light tanks and possibly two armoured cars.

The anti-aircraft platoon is armed with four pairs of coupled machine guns or four 20-mm. anti-aircraft guns, mounted on lorries.

No details regarding the organization or equipment of the other sub-units are available.

Companies are usually homogeneous and consist of headquarters and three platoons. Each platoon has three tanks. Company headquarters has one tank and three motor-cycles. Units with the heavier natures of tanks may contain a smaller number of tanks in the battalion.

3. Organization of divisional units

(*a*) *General.*—The role of units equipped with armoured fighting vehicles which form part of infantry and cavalry divisions appears to have evolved from one of pure reconnaissance, where any appreciable striking power was supplied by an attached tank unit, to one in which power both to reconnoitre and to strike with some effect is provided.

Earlier organizations were equipped with light tanks, armoured cars, and later, with amphibian tanks. Striking power was added in the form of an attached tank battalion when necessary. The present organization aims at providing a divisional tank battalion and a divisional reconnaissance battalion as part of each infantry division.

A mechanized cavalry regiment now forms part of each cavalry division.

(b) *The divisional tank battalion.*—One tank battalion is allotted to each infantry division in addition to the divisional reconnaissance battalion. It is not yet established, however, that such tank battalions exist on the establishment of every infantry division throughout the Red Army.

Infantry divisional tank battalions are organized as follows :—

> Battalion Headquarters (two T-26 light tanks).
> One Reconnaissance Platoon (three to seven Amphibian tanks).
> One Signal Platoon.
> One Anti-aircraft Machine Gun Platoon (" PVO ").
> One Sapper Platoon.
> One Chemical Platoon.
> One Traffic Control Platoon.
> Three Tank Companies (each of three platoons, each of three T-26 tanks. Total, with Company Commander's tank, ten T-26 tanks per company).
> Motorized Park.

The total number of tanks per battalion thus appears to be :—

> Five to seven Amphibian Tanks.
> Thirty-two T-26 Tanks.

In war there may also be a reserve company of ten T-26 light medium tanks on the establishment of the battalion.

(c) *The divisional reconnaissance battalion.*—This is believed to be organized as follows :—

> Headquarters with Signal Sapper, and chemical platoons.
> One Squadron of cavalry.
> One Company of sixteen T-37 tanks, and generally also some armoured cars.
> One Company of motorized infantry.
> One Battery of four anti-tank guns.

(*d*) *The mechanized cavalry regiment.*—Each cavalry division has, in addition to its four horsed cavalry regiments, a mechanized cavalry regiment, consisting of :—

    One Squadron Armoured Cars.
    One Squadron of T-37 Tanks (amphibian).
    Two Squadrons of B.T. Tanks.
    One (" B.O.") Squadron.

and possibly the following :—

    One Training Squadron.
    One Motorized Infantry Company.
    One Battery of four close-support tanks with 76 mm. guns.
    One Anti-tank Platoon.
    One Anti-aircraft machine gun Platoon.

4. Armoured car units

The only armoured car units known to exist in the Red Army are those included in mechanized cavalry regiments, though there are probably a few armoured cars in the reconnaissance detachments of all mechanized units.

5. Regimental specialists

It is believed that, while recruits for units equipped with armoured fighting vehicles are most carefully selected, they join for the normal period of service, i.e. two years. There is, however, a very high proportion of re-enlisted men in these units.

Commanders of individual tanks, and in most cases tank drivers, are junior N.C.Os. : and in tank units the school for junior N.C.Os. has a much greater strength than is the case with other arms.

6. Regimental transport.

7. Maintenance in the field

As all mechanized fighting units of the Red Army are under the same department, a single organization controls the repairs of all types of vehicles. Engineers and technical personnel repairing vehicles belong to the same corps as the users. The system appears to work smoothly and efficiently.

Each formation appears to be accompanied by a number of 30 cwt. four-wheeled tank lorries carrying 350–400 gallons of petrol.

8. Details of the various types of tank are given in Appendix " F."

CHAPTER XII

SIGNAL SERVICE

1. Organization, administration and strength

The signal service of the Red Army is organized in :—
  Telegraph and telephone units :—
    Independent signal regiments.
    Independent signal battalions.
  Wireless units :—
    Independent wireless regiments.
    Independent wireless battalions.
  Signal units with formations :—
    Corps signal battalions.
    Cavalry corps signal groups.
    Divisional signal battalions.
    Cavalry divisional signal squadrons.
    Signal units of mechanised formations.
    Fortress signal companies.
  Special signal units :—
    Carrier pigeon units.
    Messenger dog units.

Signal sub-units of infantry, cavalry and artillery regiments are dealt with in Chapters VI, VII and VIII respectively. Personnel of these sub-units do not belong to the signal service.

The signal service is administered by the signals department of the N.K.O. Technical training is periodically tested by the Inspector of Signals, who is a member of the department.

There is a Chief of Signal Services in each military district, and he is responsible for the training and administration of all signal units in the district.

2. Signal units

(a) *The independent signal regiment.*—Independent signal regiments consist of :—
  Headquarters.
  Chemical Detachment.
  Medical Detachment.
  Repair Shops.
  Signal Equipment Store.
  Supply Unit.
  Three or four Battalions.

The organization of the battalions is similar to that of independent signal battalions described in paragraph 2 (b) below.

The peace strength of a signal regiment of four battalions is approximately 1,000, and the war strength approximately 1,700 all ranks. Its role in war is to provide line communication for an Army or Front Headquarters. In peace it acts as a training centre, and provides the necessary communication for the headquarters of the military district.

(b) *The independent signal battalion.*—Independent signal battalions contain three companies, viz. :—

    One Telegraph Line Construction Company.
    One Field Pole and Cable Company.
    One Operating Company.

No details of these units are available.

(c) *The independent wireless regiment.*—Independent wireless regiments consist of :—

    Headquarters.
    Two Wireless Battalions.
    One Wireless Interception Company.
    One Depôt and Workshop.

The organization of the interception company is not known.

The organization of the wireless battalions is as given in paragraph 2 (d) below.

(d) *The independent wireless battalion.*—Independent wireless battalions consist of :—

    Headquarters.
    Three Wireless Companies.
    One Depôt and Workshop.

Each company contains three platoons, each of which has four wireless sets.

(e) *The corps signal battalions.*—Corps signal battalions consist of :—

    Headquarters.
    Headquarter Company.
    Wireless Company.
    Two or three Field Pole and Cable Companies.
    Medical Detachment.
    Supply Detachment.
    Transport.

In peace the battalion has only one field pole and cable company, but has an N.C.O.s' training cadre in addition.

The headquarter company contains personnel for manning the terminals at Corps Headquarters ; for maintaining a D.R. relay service : and for a ground-interception platoon.

The wireless company consists of four platoons, each of two stations, for communication with Army Headquarters, and flank and subordinate formations as required. It also includes one direction finding and interception station.

Field pole and cable companies maintain line communication with subordinate formations.

(f) *The cavalry corps signal group.*—The expansion of cavalry corps signal squadrons into groups is not yet completed in all cavalry corps, and information on the subject is still conflicting. The organization aimed at is reported to be :—

    Group Headquarters.
    Headquarter Squadron.
    Two Telegraph and Telephone Squadrons.
    Wireless Squadron.

No further details are available.

(g) *The divisional signal battalion.*—Divisional signal battalions consist of :—

    Headquarters.
    Headquarter Company.
    Wireless Company.
    Field Telephone Company.
    Carrier Pigeon Platoon.
    Medical Detachment.
    Transport.

The headquarter company contains personnel for manning the terminals at divisional headquarters and for maintaining a D.R. relay service.

The wireless company has fifteen mobile wireless sets, carried in mechanized transport.

The field telephone company has three platoons, and maintains line communication with the units of the division and with the division on the right flank.

(h) *The cavalry divisional signal squadron.*—No details are available regarding the organization of cavalry divisional signal squadrons. They are reported to consist of headquarters and three troops.

(i) *Signal units of mechanized formations.*—Little is known of the organization of signal units forming part of mechanized formations and it is probable that various experimental establishments are still being tested.

One establishment reported as being for a mechanized brigade (*vide* Chapter XI, paragraph 2) contains :—
    Wireless Platoon (for long-range work).
    Wireless Platoon (for short-range work).
    Tankette Platoon (for D.R. work).
    Motorcycle Platoon (for D.R. work).
    Air Signal Section.
    Three Signal Aircraft.

The air signal section is a ground unit, used for operating visual and wireless terminals communicating with aircraft.

(*j*) *The fortress signal company.*—No details of the organization of fortress signal companies are available. They are believed to include wireless, as well as line communication sub-units.

3. Experimental and research establishments

As far as is known, the only establishments where experimental and research work is carried out is the Engineering and Technical Academy of Signals at Moscow, and the Signal School at Leningrad.

4. Signal service in the field

There is a Chief of Signal Communications on the staff of every formation, to whom the commanders of all signal units in the formation are subordinate.

Responsibility for the maintenance of signal communication lies with the higher of the two formations or units concerned. Laterally, formations and units are responsible for maintaining communications with their *left* flank neighbours.

Artillery and cavalry are normally responsible for maintaining communication with the infantry with whom they are co-operating. Soviet manuals specifically lay down that the above general rules do not in any way absolve a commander from taking steps to maintain communication as a particular situation requires.

5. Wireless interception service, and ground listening organization.

No information on this subject is available, but it is to be noted that the Russians have always made most efficient cryptographers, and mention is made in the training manuals to the necessity for interception and listening-in.

6. Cipher personnel

7. Messenger dog units and dogs

Dogs are used for carrying messages in forward areas, and for reeling out short lines of light cable.

Messages are carried in a small pouch attached to the collar. A drum of wire is carried, with the axis vertical, on a small pack saddle. Dogs are trained to work in gas masks. The facepiece of the dog gas mask covers the jaw and extends up to the ears, being kept in place by straps round the neck and across the poll. The container is carried on the back at the side of the pack saddle and is connected to the facepiece by corrugated flexible tubing.

No details are available regarding the organization or number of dog units. There is a Dog Training and Breeding Establishment in Moscow, where dogs are trained not only for signal duties, but also to carry S.A.A. or first-aid panniers, and to assist in guard duties at frontier posts, stores, etc.

8. Carrier pigeon units and pigeons

Carrier pigeon units are of two kinds, stationary and mobile. Stationary units have from one to five sections, each of 200 birds, and their radius of working is up to 100 miles. Mobile units, attached to formations as required, have between 20 and 40 birds, and their radius of working does not normally exceed 20 miles.

The number of units maintained in peace is not known. There is a Central Carrier Pigeon Training and Breeding Establishment in Moscow where the breeding and training of pigeons, and experimental work, is carried out. Specialist officers are also trained there. The training of other ranks is normally carried out in Military Districts. Osoaviakhim (*see* Chapter XIII, paragraph 11) also maintains a number of pigeon stations where pigeon keepers are trained prior to their entry into the Red Army.

All pigeons have an aluminium ring attached to one leg marked with the station or unit number, the pigeon's number, and the year of birth, e.g. N6—172—36, indicating

Unit Number	N6
Pigeon number	172
Year of birth	1936

This ring is left on for life ; but if the pigeon is moved to another station or unit, a new ring is affixed to the other leg, bearing the new station or unit number only.

9. Despatch riders

Motor cycle despatch riders are included in the establishment of Signal units of Divisions and higher formations. In the signal companies or platoons of regiments and smaller units, cyclists and mounted orderlies are used.

10. Telegraph codes

11. Armament of personnel

Signal personnel are normally armed and equipped as Infantry (*see* Chapter VI, paragraph 12), but those employed with Cavalry formations are armed and equipped as Cavalry (*see* Chapter VII, paragraph 15).

12. Equipment

(*a*) *Line telegraph.*—With the exception of the morse instrument, of which there is a separate army pattern, all telegraph instruments in use in the Red Army are identical with the instruments used in civilian telegraphs, thus ensuring an ample reserve in the event of war.

There are several patterns in use, both of foreign and Soviet manufacture, the most important of which are :—

Foreign patterns

(i) *The morse army signals* pattern instrument is used by signals from Divisional to Corps Headquarters.

The range is :—

On permanent cable lines—up to 800 km.
On field copper wire and insulated cable—up to 75 km.

The instrument is set up in 15 minutes.

Working speed is 500 words per hour; in alternating messages—300 words per hour.

Weight is 45 lbs.

(ii) *The Hughes letter-typing instrument* is used by signals from Corps upwards. Its range is up to 600 km., or even further with relay.

The instrument can be set up by well trained personnel in about one hour and dismantled in about half and hour.

Working speed is 1,000 words per hour; in alternating messages—600–700 words per hour.

Weight is 220 lbs.

(iii) *The " Bodo " (Beaudot) letter-typing* instrument is used by signals at Army and Military District Headquarters, and at larger stations on the L. of C.

One to three pairs of instruments can use the same line. Working speed is 2,000 words per hour; in alternating messages up to 1,200 words per hour with one pair of instruments.

(iv) *The Wheatstone morse-typing automatic* instrument.

Range is up to 6,000 km.

Average working speed is 450–900 words per hour, maximum possible is up to 3,000 words per hour.

Soviet pattern

(v) *The Shovin letter-typing " start-stop "* instrument. Up to 4 pairs can use the same line.

Working speed is 240 letters and signs per minute in " long range messages."

The weight is 50 lbs.

It is constructed on the " typewriter transmission " system, with Russian and Latin alphabets. It is claimed that it can work with any type of electrical energy and also with relays.

The minimum current required is 60–70 M.A.

It was designed to replace other instruments (including the " Bodo ") and it appears that the 1930 pattern has been accepted for universal introduction.

(vi) *The Treml* instrument. It appears that this instrument is only in the experimental stage, but when a successful pattern has been evolved it will have two advantages over the " Shovin " :—

    (a) Minimum current required is 30–35 M.A.
    (b) Weight is only 25 lbs.

(b) *Line telephone instruments.*—(i) *Telephones.*—The principal types of telephone instruments in use in the Red Army are :—

    (i) UNA F.28.
    (ii) UNA F.31.
    (iii) UNA I.28.

UNA F.28.—The ranges claimed are :—

With telephone cable, ground line ..	15 kms.
With telegraph cable, ground line ..	30 kms.
With field pole and cable line ..	89 kms.
With telegraph line	90–100 kms.

It is worked by two 1·5 volt dry cells. The total weight of the instrument is approximately 7½ lbs.

UNA F.31.—An improved model of the F.28.

UNA I.28.—A ringing telephone which is in other respects largely similar to the F.28, with the same range of action. It is used chiefly in Infantry units, from Battalion to Regimental Headquarters. The total weight of the instrument is approximately 12 lbs.

Ordonans artillery (buzzer) instrument is used only in Artillery units. It is either used with a switchboard unit of 4 lines or by itself.

(ii) *Switch units.*—The switch units in most general use are :—

The *KOF*.28 (Kommutator oblegchonni-fonicheski 1928) is used in Infantry regiments and battalions, and in Artillery regiments and groups. Works 6 lines. Its approximate dimensions, including container, are 185 × 176 × 90 m/m. (7½ in. × 7 in. × 3¾ in.) and the weight complete is 3¾ lbs.

The *R.E*.12 is used from Regimental Headquarters upwards and works 12 lines. Its dimensions, including containers are 410 × 235 × 160 m/m (16½ in. × 9½ in. × 6½ in.) and weight complete is 15 lbs.

The Soviet pattern " *Erikson* " *type* " ringing switchboard " is also used from Regimental Headquarters upwards and works 12 lines. Its weight complete is approximately 14½ lb. The *R*.20 (ringing) switch unit is used from divisional headquarters upwards and works 20 lines.

The *R*.60 (ringing) switch unit is also used from divisional headquarters upwards, and works 60 lines.

(c) *Intercept sets, W/T direction finders and ground listening sets.*—(i) *Intercept sets.*—It is known that special troops are trained and are issued with special equipment for the service of interception, but there is no reliable data available as to the organization of this service or the type of instruments employed.

(ii) *W/T direction finders.*

(iii) *Ground listening sets.*

(d) *W/T " Jamming " devices.*—No information is available as to the equipment or methods used in " jamming " hostile radio transmissions.

(e) *W/T instruments.*—There are several types of wireless set issued to the Red Army, from small portable battalion sets to the large Corps 1½ kilowatt station.

(i) *The battalion set.*—The usual type for use in the battalion is the 6-Pk. type. It can be carried in pack by 2 men and can be set up in 2-3 minutes. It is worked normally by 3 men, and can maintain transmission for 1½ days without recharging. It works on a wavelength which precludes the reception of its signals by regimental sets. It is a W/T and R/T set, and the range is 10-15 kms. for morse. Three sets are carried in one 2-wheeled cart.

Other small sets in use (*e.g.*, between O.P. and battery or group) are :—
    1 K.P.
    No. 2.T.
    No. 2.G.
but no details of their construction and performance are available.

(ii) *The regimental set* is much more powerful, having a range up to 50 km. It is mounted and carried either in a small car, 1½-ton lorry or two-wheeled cart, and can operate either on the move or stationary, in the vehicle or on the ground. It is a W/T and R/T set ; no details of performance are known.

The Siemens-Halske, 1915, 1923 and 1924 patterns are frequently used for working from regimental to divisional headquarters.

(iii) *The divisional and corps set* is the 1½ kilowatt Telefunken mobile set, with a range of 200–250 km., and is transported by motor or horsed transport. It is worked by 12 men and can be set up in 15 minutes.

(*f*) *R/T instruments.*—The majority of W/T instruments at present in use in the Red Army can be used for R/T with a considerable reduction in range. No details other than those given in sub-paragraph (*e*) above are available.

(*g*) *Visual signalling.*—(i) *Lamps.*—The following types of signalling lamps are found in the Red Army :—

Lucas Lamp   Similar to the British pattern.

S.P. 95 ..   A Soviet design of electric lamp for use in infantry units. It has a range of 2,000 yards by day and 7,000 yards by night.

Zeuss lamp   (Large and small).—The diameter of the mirror of the larger lamp is 25 cm., and its range with an oxy-acetylene flame is 12 miles by day and 36 miles by night. With acetylene only, these ranges are greatly reduced. The weight of the complete apparatus is 130 lb.

(ii) *Heliographs.*—There are three sizes of heliograph in use, all of normal pattern, viz :—

The 76-mm. cavalry type. Range up to 7 miles.
The 140-mm. standard type. Range up to 17 miles.
The 250-mm. long-range type. Range up to 60 miles.

(iii) *Flags.*—Flags are not larger than 20 in. square, and are of single colour—red, orange or yellow according to light conditions. Regulations lay down 600 yards as the maximum range for the use of flags.

(*h*) *Visual equipment for air co-operation.*—No details are known.

(*i*) *Light signals.*—The light signal pistol in the Red Army is of 26-mm. bore. No details of the range of colours of the cartridges, or of any code, are available.

(*j*) *Message throwers and projectiles.*—A wooden message carrier, shaped like a grenade, can be fired from a rifle fitted with the Diakonov grenade cup.

Two types of grenade are in use, one with a wooden and one with a metal base. The grenade is solid with the exception of a slot in the forward end into which an empty cartridge case containing a message can be inserted. Ranges are said to be :—

      With wooden base .. Up to 150 yards.
      With metal base .. Up to 250 yards.

(*k*) *Line construction.*—

(*l*) *Vehicles.*—The only special signal vehicle about which information is available is the A.T.K.V. - 1 (Avtomashina Telegraphno-Kabelnovo Vzvoda) cable layer.

The apparatus can be mounted in any light lorry : when cable is being laid, the cable drum runs freely : and in reeling up, the drum is driven off the rear wheels.

It is claimed that cable can be laid at the rate of 12 miles per hour. The equipment carried includes 12 miles of cable, 2 telephones and lineman's maintenance and repair material. The crew consists of a commander, driver, and six signallers.

13. Regimental transport

No details are known.

CHAPTER XIII

POLICE, INTERNAL SECURITY TROOPS AND SEMI-MILITARY ORGANIZATIONS

A. Police and internal security troops

1. Introduction

The responsibility for internal security in U.S.S.R. was in the hands of the O.G.P.U. (Unified State Political Department) from 1922 until July, 1934, when a decree was published abolishing the O.G.P.U. and transferring responsibility to the N.K.V.D. (People's Commissariat for Internal Affairs). It is probable that the abolition of the notorious O.G.P.U. was primarily a sop to public opinion both at home and abroad for it appears that the change was really only one of nomenclature and that the former methods and organization of the O.G.P.U. continue. In the following paragraphs, therefore, a brief sketch of the history and organization of the O.G.P.U. is given.

The O.G.P.U.—or G.P.U. as it was originally called—was founded in November, 1922, when, after the framing of the constitution of the U.S.S.R., it was decided to revise the functions of the Cheka.

The functions of the O.G.P.U. was laid down as follows :—

(i) Suppression of anti-Soviet risings.

(ii) Suppression of brigandage.

(iii) Counter espionage.

(iv) Protection of roads, railways, waterways and industrial undertakings.

(v) Political defence of the frontier.

(vi) Prevention of illegal frontier traffic.

(vii) Performance of any special tasks allotted by the Soviet Government.

The role of the O.G.P.U. may, in fact, be said to have been the preservation of the Communist regime in the U.S.S.R.

The directing organ of the O.G.P.U. was the Collegium, the President of which was responsible through the State Prosecutor ot the U.S.S.R. to the Sovnarkom or Cabinet.

For purposes of control, the U.S.S.R. was divided into thirteen Regions, each of which had its own Regional G.P.U. with similar functions to those of the O.G.P.U. at Moscow. The Regional G.P.U.s were directly subordinate to the O.G.P.U. at Moscow, except in those Regions forming a part of a National Republic where they were subordinate to the Sovnarkom of their respective Republics. At the head of each Regional G.P.U. was a representative plenipotentiary who was appointed by the Collegium of the O.G.P.U. and commanded all the internal security troops in the region. Each region was further subdivided into provincial and district organizations.

For the performance of its duties the O.G.P.U. possessed, in addition to secret police, its own troops. These were organized into units and included internal security troops, frontier guards, and at one time units of special designation (Ch.O.N.).

At the same time there existed the Militia, corresponding roughly to police in this country, and escort troops, both of which, though nominally under the direct control of the Commissar for Internal Affairs, were in fact subordinate to the O.G.P.U. and were controlled through the O.G.P.U. organization.

2. Functions and organization of the N.K.V.D.

The Decree of July, 1934, authorized the formation of a new "All Union Commissariat for Internal Affairs" (N.K.V.D.) which was to supersede the O.G.P.U. and to which the former O.G.P.U. troops were subordinated. Although the old Collegium of the O.G.P.U. was officially disbanded, former heads of the O.G.P.U. became chiefs of the various directorates of the new Commissariat.

Under the Decree, the Commissariat is charged with :—
  (i) The security of the revolutionary regime and safety of the State.
  (ii) The guarding of socialist property generally.
  (iii) Compilation and maintenance of civil records.
  (iv) Frontier defence.

The branches of the Commissariat which carry out these functions are as follows :—
  (i) Central Directorate of State Security.
  (ii) Central Directorate of Frontier Guards.
  (iii) Central Directorate of Military Guards of Ways and Communications.
  (iv) Central Directorate of Penal Labour Camps and Settlements.
  (v) Central Directorate of Workers and Peasants Militia.
  (vi) Department of Civil Records (equivalent to Somerset House).
  (vii) Administrative and Economic Directorate.

The system of control throughout the country is closely analagous to the former O.G.P.U. system, and it is probable that the O.G.P.U. provincial etc. organizations are continuing to function as before, but under a new name. The regional representative plenipotentiary has disappeared and his functions are now performed by a Republican N.K.V.D. in the seven Union Republics and by Directorates of the N.K.V.D. in the Autonomous Republics.

The judicial powers of the various N.K.V.D. institutions are somewhat more limited than were those of the corresponding O.G.P.U. institutions. All cases tried by them must be sent forward to the judicial organs after the conclusion of the enquiry. There is, however, in the All-Union Commissariat a special council having the power to put into effect, on its own authority, sentences of exile, banishment, confinement in penal labour camps up to five years, and deportation.

The troops and other personnel, through whose agency internal security is maintained, remain as before, namely :—

Secret Agents—*see* paragraph 3.
Internal Security Troops—*see* paragraph 4.
Frontier Guards—*see* paragraph 5.
Escort Troops—*see* paragraph 6.
Militia and Militarised Guards—*see* paragraph 6.

3. Central directorate of State security (G.U.G.B.)

The Directorate is divided into the following departments :

(i) Operations Department—which is, in fact, the executive and carries out searches and arrests.

(ii) Foreign Department—which is in charge of all N.K.V.D. agents abroad.

(iii) Internal Department—which is in charge of N.K.V.D. agents in the U.S.S.R.

(iv) Intelligence Department.

(v) Counter-Espionage Department.

(vi) Ciphers Department.

(vii) Economic Department.

(viii) A Special Department responsible for the political control of the Red Army.

(ix) Transport Department which is in charge of security work on all transport in the U.S.S.R.

(x) Messengers Corps which is responsible for the carriage of N.K.V.D. secret mails.

It will be apparent that this organization carries on the work of the former O.G.P.U. secret service. It works through its secret police but also has the power to invoke the aid of the other security troops, when necessary.

4. Internal security troops

(i) *General.*—The internal security troops are under the control of the Central Directorate of State Security. These troops which, with the frontier guards, constitute a military force of considerable size, are not a charge on the military budget of the U.S.S.R., but have a budget of their own which is shown in the general budget of the N.K.V.D. As a military asset—except in so far as they protect the frontier areas, cover mobilization and relieve the active army of internal security duties—their value is limited, as their duties necessitate wide dispersion. They are, however, of vital importance for the maintenance of the Soviet régime.

(ii) *Organization and strength.*—The internal security troops are organized in :—

Divisions.
Regiments (of which four are cavalry).
Groups.

In addition to the above, there are in the C.A.M.D. three or four " Grazhdanski " cavalry divisions, specially formed to deal with Basmachi bands.

The division and regiments are organized, armed and equipped on similar lines to corresponding units of the Red Army.

The division in Moscow comprises :—

Two Infantry Regiments.
One Technical Regiment, including a Mechanized Detachment equipped with tanks and tankettes.
Divisional Artillery Regiment.
Divisional Cyclist Group.
Divisional Sapper Company.
Divisional Armoured Car Group.
Divisional Cavalry Regiment.

Groups are of varying strength but normally consist of :—

Two Infantry Platoons.
One Machine Gun Platoon.
One Cavalry Troop.

There exists also an Air Arm containing at least 32 machines.

(iii) *Recruiting and terms of service.*—Recruits are obtained from volunteers or men of the annual contingents, specially selected for their political reliability, and include as many members as possible of the Communist Party or the Komsomol (Communist League of Youth).

The terms of service are a training period of three to six months, followed by two years in a unit.

In October, 1935, a system of ranks, similar to that in the Red Army, was introduced for commanding personnel of internal security troops.

(iv) *Accommodation and welfare.*—Units are quartered in barracks similar to the Red Army, but receive special consideration in questions of pay, rations, accommodation, etc.—their requirements being given priority over those of the Army.

5. Frontier guards

(i) *Functions.*—The Frontier Guards (which include the Customs Guard, 1,800) are under the control of the Directorate of Frontier Guards. They are responsible for the collection of customs duties and the protection of the sea and land frontiers of the U.S.S.R.

The jurisdiction of frontier guard troops extends to a distance of 30 kilometres within the frontier and this area is divided into :—

(*a*) The 40-metre patrol zone, which is cleared of all obstacles to movement, and into which entry is forbidden, except at certain control points established by the frontier guards.

(*b*) The 500 metre zone, where residence and cultivation of crops are not permitted.

(*c*) The $7\frac{1}{2}$ kilometre zone, to enter which a special pass is required.

(*d*) The 22 kilometre zone, which usually marks the limit of frontier guard control.

(ii) *Strength and organization.*—The total strength of the force is about 65,000 men organized in units whose strength varies from 500 to 2,000 men, according to the importance of the frontier sector for which they are responsible. For example, units on the western frontier of the U.S.S.R. are responsible for a sector averaging about 60 miles in length.

Units normally consist of :—
  Headquarters
  Three to four detachment (Komandatura).

Headquarters comprise sections dealing with operations and intelligence, political work and administration, and also include signals personnel, supply and transport, and a mobile reserve of one cavalry troop and three rifle platoons.

Each detachment, which is equivalent, on an average, to about a company of infantry, consists of a headquarters, organized on the same lines as the detachment headquarters, and five to fifteen piquets. A piquet, containing twenty to forty men and one to two machine guns, is responsible for organizing the requisite number of posts and patrols to cover its sector, which is usually about two miles of frontier.

Units employed on the protection of coastal areas, etc., have a special organization and equipment including motor boats and glisseurs.

(iii) *Recruiting, etc.*—The personnel is recruited and administered similarly to the men of internal security troops.

There exist five training regiments and some ten training battalions for the training of recruits.

(iv) *Arms and equipment.*—Arms and equipment of the frontier guards include :—

> Rifles.
> Heavy and light M.Gs.
> Artillery.
> Motor boats with light guns and M.Gs.
> Glisseurs.

6. Escort troops

(i) *Functions.*—Under the control of the Central Directorate of Penal Labour Camps and Labour Settlements are the escort troops who are utilized for guard duties at prisons and camps and for the escort of persons under arrest. These troops are quite independent of the internal security units at the disposal of other Directorates but may in emergency be called upon to assist them.

(ii) *Organization and strength.*—Their total strength is estimated at about 30,000 men ; they are quartered in barracks like military units and are organized in formations and units as follows :—

> 6 divisions.
> 7 independent brigades.
> 13 regiments.
> 35 battalions.
> 91 companies or detachments.

Exact information on the above is hard to obtain and it is possible that the larger formations may include some of the smaller units.

(iii) *Conditions of service.*—Conditions of service in the escort troops are similar to those in the Red Army and recruits are drawn from annual contingents.

(iv) *Commanding personnel.*—Officers are obtained by transfer from the Red Army or by promotion of N.C.Os.

(v) *Arms and equipment.*—Escort troops are armed with rifles and carbines.

7. The militia, or workers' and peasants' police forces

(i) *Functions and organization.*—The militia is under the control of the Central Directorate of Workmen's and Peasants' Militia and carries out the functions of civil police in a normal country.

The militia is divided into—

(a) *The general police* or police proper, who in addition to carrying out normal police duties, have the following special functions :—

Carrying into execution sentences of the courts in cases of exile and banishment and of keeping a record of such persons :

Taking measures to prevent the evasion of obligatory military service :

Maintaining records of horses, carts, mechanical transport and other items required by the army on mobilization.

(b) *Militarized guards* (Vokhr) who are organized for the special protection of particular enterprises, buildings, property, etc., by arrangement between main (or local) militia directorates within the framework of the All Union Commissariat of Internal Affairs.

The Vokhr may also be called on to perform normal police duties as well as the special roles outlined above.

The militia is not organized in formed bodies or quartered in barracks.

All personnel are dismounted, except small bodies in some of the larger towns and districts.

(ii) *Strength.*—The strength of the workers' and peasants' militia is as follows :—

General police :—

Higher personnel ..	19,000
Subordinate personnel	90,000

Militarized guards :—

(a) River and forest guards ..	12,500
(b) Railway guards	14,000

(In addition there are a further 1,500 railway guards at the disposal of the Central Directorate of State Security, Transport Department.)

(c) Factory guards, at least 8,000.

(d) Other groups, such as agricultural police, of which the strengths are not known.

(iii) *Terms of service and method of recruiting.*—Recruiting for the militia is carried out locally and is entirely voluntary : both men and women are eligible.

Terms of service for subordinate personnel are for not less than two years, with further re-engagement periods of not less than two years, and a liability to be called up in case of emergency up to the age of 40.

No details are available in the case of higher personnel.

(iv) *Training.* — Subordinate personnel first under two-months' course with the local militia, comprising :—

(a) The study of service regulations.

(b) The study of the Constitution and policy of the Soviet Union.

(c) Revolver shooting and physical training.

Men selected to become high personnel attend a course of from 5½ to 12 months at one of the 12 militia schools in the U.S.S.R., at which the syllabus is similar to that for subordinate personnel, but more advanced.

(v) *Arms, equipment and clothing.*—All the militia wear the same uniform and identical badges of rank.

Arms consist of the revolver only, except that militarized guards have 10 per cent. rifles.

Equipment and clothing are issued free from a central source under the same procedure as issues to the Army.

(vi) *Pay.*—The pay of the militia corresponds to that of a " worker of average skill ".

(vii) *Discipline.*—Members of the militia are subject to military discipline and can be tried by courts-martial for desertion and military offences and by the civil courts for other offences.

(viii) *Cost of upkeep.*—The cost of upkeep of the militia is borne by the National republic, Autonomous republic, district, town, etc., concerned, except in the case of militarised guards, when it is borne by the special enterprise for which they are employed.

B. Semi-military Organizations

9. Military settlers

Ex-soldier farmers are being settled in all the frontier regions of the U.S.S.R.

In the Far East, these military settlers are believed (1935) to number some 50,000 and to be organized somewhat loosely in three " Divisions " in the areas Ulan-ude (ex-Verkhneudinsk), Poyarkovo and Iman. Each military farming unit forms a unit or sub-unit.

10. Red guard and partisan units

The personnel of these units consist of men who participated in the Revolutionary and Polish wars and are faithful adherents of the Soviet régime.

The units have occasional training rallies in peace and would probably be employed in war for internal security purposes in their home districts.

The numbers of such units existing is not known.

Numerous organizations for promoting " defence-mindedness " exist in the U.S.S.R., all of which enjoy the direct support and encouragement of the Soviet authorities. Any organization which did not tend to the definite support of the Government would be immediately suppressed.

11. Osoaviakhim

The most important of these semi-military organizations is the Osoaviakhim. (The Union of Societies of the Friends of the Defence and of Air and Chemical Construction of the U.S.S.R.), the object of which is to assist in training the man power of the nation and in preparing the population generally in defence, especially against air and gas attacks.

Although financed largely by public subscription it receives Government support in the way of funds, equipment and instructors.

It was founded in 1927 when the Aviakhim Society (the air and chemical defence society) was merged with the OSO Society (the defence of the U.S.S.R. Society) and the new body the Osoaviakhim came into existence with some 2,000,000 members.

Since then its membership and its " OSO " (Military) activities have been markedly increased and its strength was reported in 1935 to be 20 million members of both sexes. Of the 20 million members of the " OSO " 215,000 are " Voroshilovskie Strelki," *i.e.*, 1st and 2nd Class riflemen.

The Society is the chief instrument of the Soviet authorities for the propogation among the masses of " warmindedness," or as it is euphemistically described, " preparedness for defence." In March, 1934, a Plenary Session of the Central Council decided to reorganize the Osoaviakhim. The reason for this was that it had been found that collective responsibility for the activities of the various branches was not giving good results. Responsibility is now vested in the hands of one individual.

(i) *Activities of Osoaviakhim.*—The activities of the Osoaviakhim are even more comprehensive than its title would suggest, for it plays a part not only in the strengthening of the defensive capacity of the Soviet Union and the development of its air and chemical power, but also in the industrialization of the country and the socialization of agriculture. It also promotes the technical development of civil aviation and of the military, naval and air forces, and educates the masses on the subject of national defence, by means of "military circles," of which some 60,000 are said to exist.

It organizes naval, military, aeronautical and chemical instruction among the workers, promotes the practice of rifle shooting, and does military, political and general educational work among the officers and other ranks of the armed forces. In the sphere of aviation, it conducts experiment and research, maintains flying schools and clubs and promotes the establishment of aerodromes and the organization of airlines. In the field of chemistry, it educates the masses in the principles and practice of aero-chemical defence, surveys the chemical resources of the country and promotes the "chemicalization" of the national economy. It collaborates in the militarization of sport and of all forms of physical culture. It organizes aerial observation posts, riding schools, rifle ranges, naval stations, camps, laboratories, research institutions and many other such concerns.

(ii) *Military training.*—The purely military side of the Osoaviakhim's activities takes three main forms :—

(*a*) Pre-military training.

(*b*) Training during the period of normal army service.

(*c*) Refresher training for reserve N.C.Os. and officers.

(*a*) *Pre-military training.*—All fit men during each of their 19th and 20th years are liable to do one month's pre-military training. This training is now largely carried out by the Osoaviakhim which has organized 3,000 fixed centres for this purpose, and hundreds of training centres for officers and N.C.Os.

In general, the Osoaviakhim training takes the form of courses in the winter, 120 hours being quoted as a normal programme, while in summer, camps are held at which personnel are, as far as possible, grouped for tactical and administrative purposes into platoons and companies, etc.

Courses are classified as Grades one, two and three, in order of difficulty, and men who pass grades one and two are exempted from carrying out pre-military training : a slight reduction in "training outside the army" (paragraph (*b*) below) is also granted to those who pass any of the above three grades. Since the beginning of 1934, a number of naval clubs and training centres have been founded for pre-conscript naval training.

(b) *Training during the period of normal army service (22nd to 27th years).*—In each annual contingent there is a category of about 100,000, which the regular and territorial armies cannot absorb for training. These men, therefore, receive in lieu what is termed *training outside the army*, totalling in theory six months spread over five years, the carrying out of which is now entrusted to the Osoaviakhim. Till recently, however, probably only quarter to half of this category could be given this "outside training." With the development of the Osoaviakhim great progress has been made and since 1931 it is believed the large majority of men who are not taken for either the regular or territorial forces receive training in this form.

The basic unit of organization and training is the detachment, often only 20 to 30 strong, in schools, villages, farms, factories, etc., all over the U.S.S.R.

Till recently these detachments were formed into units, such as companies and battalions, only for special exercises: now, however, complete Osoaviakhim battalions regularly take part in training, manœuvres and 1st May celebration parades, alongside army formations. One complete Osoaviakhim division is also believed to exist, whose personnel do not live in barracks but are periodically called up from their homes for training and 1st May parades. The efficiency of some OSO units in all forms of training is of a very high standard.

The foregoing shows that the military training activities of the Osoaviakhim have greatly developed in scope and quantity in recent years. A feature of the activities of the Osoaviakhim which merits special mention, is its relation to railway transport services—existing railway personnel are given training in railway military duties, while civilians are given training in railway transport duties in order to fit them to take over these duties in an emergency.

(c) *Reserve training and refresher courses.*—It is not certain whether the Osoaviakhim conducts post-military courses for rank and file reservists but it is highly probable that the latter take part in lectures, rifle shooting and other activities organized by the Osoaviakhim.

Special refresher courses are, however, carried out by the Osoaviakhim for N.C.Os. and officers on the reserve, viz :—

(a) Courses for reserve N.C.Os. totalling 220 hours' instruction.

(b) Courses for reserve officers, both junior and senior, totalling 150 hours' instruction.

(iii) *Financial activities.*—Although partly assisted by Government funds, this society, through the subscriptions of members and by the sale of lottery tickets raises considerable funds which are expended on the purchase of war material, such as aeroplanes and tanks, or in making donations to Army funds.

(iv) *General.*—Women are also accepted into the Osoaviakhim and are trained mostly as hospital nurses affiliated to the " Red Crescent."

All members wear a badge on the breast which depicts a gasmask on a horizontal propellor, superimposed on a hammer and sickle in a diamond shaped frame. The Osoaviakhim has a *uniform which corresponds in cut and colour to that of the Red Army* and which may be worn by those who are able to provide it.

(v) *Mechanical transport section (formerly Avtodor).*— Avtodor or the Society of friends of motor transport was organized in 1927 to encourage the study of motor transport in all its aspects, including design, driving construction, etc., and to assist in providing mechanical vehicles of all sorts for the use of the Red Army.

Its activities were subsequently extended on the same lines as those of the Osoaviakhim to include the pre-military train:ng of men selected from M.T. units, and the building up of a general reserve of drivers, mechanics, etc. It also assists in road development.

It has a membership of about 2,000,000 (1930) organized in about 20,000 units.

In 1936, Avtodor was abolished in name, its organization being absorbed into Osoaviakhim.

12. Odr—(The society of friends of wireless).

A voluntary society for the encouragement of wireless amateurs.

The society is under the control of the Inspector of Signals of the R.K.A.A. and close co-operation with the army is maintained. During the 1929 manœuvres, for example, 13 short wave stations were organised and manned by amateurs, who were attached to formation headquarters.

13. Women's organizations

No purely women's organizations are known to exist though as in Russia women have equal rights to men they are eligible for membership to all the various societies, etc., referred to in this chapter.

14. Juvenile organizations

There are also a number of important juvenile organizations, which are junior branches of the All-Russian Communist party. These organizations are thus semi-political, aiming at training and instructing selected and politically reliable young people of all ages and both sexes in the tenets of communism, with a view to increasing the reliability of the youth of the country towards the communist régime. These organizations are :—

(a) *The Komsomol* (Communist League of Youth), numbering 3,000,000 members, of both sexes, between the ages of 14 (or 16?) and 23. Members, of whom about 150,000 are serving in the R.K.K.A., are expected to act as active devotees and a mouthpiece of the Communist Party and their activities are mainly directed towards the preparation for war, and towards supporting the policy of the Soviet Government.

Formerly, also, whenever a crisis arose in agriculture or industry, " shock brigades " of Komsomol were formed with the object of restoring the situation by their example and energy, and by detecting and exposing hostile elements—commonly termed " saboteurs," restore the critical situations which have arisen. In 1935, however, Stalin announced that the activities of the Komsomol were to be confined strictly to the education of youth. It appears that the interference, often unauthorised, of headstrong and inexperienced young Komsomols in the direction of industrial undertakings had only led to great confusion.

(b) *The Pioneers*, numbering nearly 4,000,000, are boys and girls from the age of 8–14 when they become candidates for the Komsomol, which directs the Pioneer organization. Although the pioneers were evolved from the former boy scouts, they do not form part of the boy scout movement, which they affect to despise as a bourgeois institution. They wear a simple uniform the distinctive mark of which is a red scarf and are encouraged to take an interest in military training, and the assimilation of the doctrines and policy of communism.

(c) *Little Octobrists.*—A similar organization to the Pioneers caters for those below the age of 8. Though of no military value, the existence of such an organization shows the importance attached by the authorities to the inculcation of communist teaching among even the very young.

CHAPTER XIV

UNIFORM

Note.—Plates illustrating uniform and badges of rank and distinguishing badges are given in the short note on the Red Army, Part II.

1. General notes

Uniform is, with the exception of that for Cossack units, khaki in colour, and severely plain. The aim is the production of a serviceable and comfortable kit, with the minimum of regard for ornamental effect.

A concession to appearances was however made in October, 1935, after the reintroduction of ranks into the Red Army, by the provision of a close fitting jacket and slacks or overalls for use as a walking-out or evening dress. This order of dress is very similar to that of the Turkish Army.

Political officers wear the same uniform as combatant officers.

Cossack units have a special uniform, described in paragraph 2(x).

2. Home service uniform

For illustrations of certain articles of uniform, colours of gorget patches and piping and cap bands for the various arms of the service, *see* short note on the Red Army Part II.

The following articles comprise the home service uniform of the R.K.K.A. :—

(i) *Headdress*.—Peaked cap, or cloth helmet with side flaps, which can be worn up or buttoned under the chin.

(ii) *Greatcoat*.—Dark khaki woollen material. The greatcoat of mounted arms is longer than that of the dismounted arms.

(iii) *Jacket*.—Dark khaki cloth for all arms except Air Force and mechanized units, which are dark blue and steel grey respectively. Jackets are close-fitting, and fasten at the neck. They are *never* worn on parade.

(iv) *Smock*.—Dark khaki, fastening at the neck and with turn-down collar. The smock is worn outside the breeches.

(v) *Breeches*.—Dark blue woollen cloth, except in case of mechanized units, when they are steel grey.

(vi) *Trousers.*—Worn only with the jackets. They are of same material and colour.

(vii) *Footwear.*—Black leather ankle boots and leggings or knee boots. The latter are the normal order for all ranks, both mounted and dismounted.

(viii) *Belt.*—Officers wear a belt of Sam Browne pattern, and other ranks an ordinary leather waist belt.

(ix) *Special uniform.*—Leather jackets and caps are issued to mechanized units. Felt boots are issued to troops in very cold districts. A panama hat is issued to units serving in the C.A.M.D. and T.C.M.D. for wear in summer.

(x) *Cossack uniform.*—*Don Cossacks.*—Tall fur hat of black with red top trimmed with two rows of fine black braid, sewn on to form a cross (in the case of officers with gold braid) ; cap with red cap-band, dark blue top and red piping ; greatcoat ; khaki-coloured tunic shirt ; loose tunic of dark blue piped with red ; grey hood ; dark blue full knee breeches with a broad red stripe down the outer seam ; knee breeches with a broad red stripe down the outer seam ; knee boots ; normal cavalry equipment and sword.

Terek and Kuban Cossacks.—Kubanka (special form of round fur hat), black in colour with light blue top for Terek Cossacks and red top for Kuban Cossacks, and with lace or braiding on top as for Don Cossacks ; cap with blue capband and khaki-coloured top with black piping for Terek Cossacks and red piping for Kuban Cossacks ; coloured hood with long ends ; tunic shirt of light blue with black collar and piping for Terek Cossacks and of red with black piping for Kuban Cossacks (those of officers are edged with gold lace) ; long waisted Cossack tunic coat of grey lined with medium light blue for Terek Cossacks and of dark blue lined with red for Kuban Cossacks ; circular riding cloak of black.

Gorget patches of all cossacks are blue with black pipings, while officers also have gold lace.

3. Field service uniform

Field service uniform consists of a steel helmet of French pattern, smock, breeches and knee boots. Leather equipment is worn, and the greatcoat, when not in use, is rolled and strapped round the pack. The latter is of the

" ruksack" type and is made of stout canvas with leather bindings. Cossack units wear home service uniform and do not wear the steel helmet.

4. Badges of rank

Badges of rank are in red enamel or red cloth and are worn on the gorget patches of tunic and greatcoat and on the sleeve. A complete list of badges of rank of officers is given in the short note on the Red Army.

The gorget patches are coloured according to the arm of the service (for table of colours see short note on the Red Army).

5. Regimental crests and badges, distinguishing marks, etc.

Regimental crests and badges do not exist in the Red Army. Distinguishing badges of specialists must not be mistaken for Regimental badges. Regimental numerals, which were formerly worn on the shoulder, have now ceased to be issued. There is therefore no visual means of identifying the unit to which a Red Army soldier belongs.

Distinguishing marks and flags for formations and divisional, etc., signs are given in the short note on the Red Army under Topographical signs.

6. Staff distinctions

Nil.

7. Uniform worn by semi-military bodies

(a) Troops of the Commissariat of Internal Affairs (N.K.V.D. previously known as the O.G.P.U.), which includes internal security troops, frontier guards and escort troops, wear uniform of standard army pattern. The cap has a blue top and red capband, except in the case of frontier guards who wear a khaki cap with a green hatband.

(b) *Militia.*—Militia also wear standard army uniform, but wear a crest in silver of the sickle and hammer on the headdress, and turquoise gorget patches with red edging with the sickle and hammer crest on the top outer corner.

(c) *Osoaviakhim.*—The uniform can be worn by persons undergoing military training with any organization of the Osoaviakhim, as well as by the permanent staff. It is similar to the uniform of the Red Army except that leggings or stockings are worn by persons undergoing training. Short padded coats may be substituted for greatcoats in the event of shortage of cloth. All personnel wear the

Osoaviakhim badge on the head-dress. Distinguishing marks for the different arms are identical with those of the Red Army, and are worn by officers exclusively.

There are four marks, identically the same in size and shape for all categories. In addition a metal red enamelled star (diameter $0 \cdot 6$ inch) with silver or white metal edges, is worn by officers as follows :—

First category	— junior	— one star.
Second category	— intermediate	— two stars.
Third category	— senior	— three stars.
Fourth category	— highest	— four stars.

Buttons are polished and are similar to those worn in the Red Army. Commanders and staffs (including political) of instructional centres, personnel in schools of anti-aircraft defence and motor schools, and employees of the Central and Local Councils of Osoaviakhim have for daily wear a tunic shirt of Army cut, breeches, and also a double-breasted overcoat of dark grey colour.

Aviation workers wear the same uniform, with, for ceremonial occasions, an open jacket. Their badge represents an aeroplane. A special uniform for pupils in aviation, gliding and parachute work consists of a tunic of dark grey cotton, dark grey breeches, and a dark blue beret.

8. Identity discs

These are *not* issued.

9. Distinguishing marks of specialists by arms

See short note on the Red Army.

10. Personal kit

Officers and other ranks are provided with personal clothing, etc., on the following scale :—

> One serge shirt.
> Three undershirts.
> Five pairs of pants (three thin and two thick).
> Three towels.
> Three handkerchiefs.
> Two pairs of gloves.
> One blanket.
> Three sheets.
> Two pairs of foot bandages (instead of socks).

11. Orders, decorations and medals

Orders and decorations are of two kinds: those for military personnel only, and those obtainable by either military or civilian personnel.

(a) *Military.*—(i) *For valour.*—The medal may be awarded to Service personnel of all ranks for personal bravery during engagements with the enemies of the Soviet Union in war areas, in defending the inviolability of Soviet territory, or in the struggle with diversionists, spies and other enemies of the Soviet Union. Recipients of this medal receive a pension of ten roubles a month, and have the right of free travel on the tramway system of any town in the Soviet Union.

(ii) *Order of the Red Banner.*—Can be awarded to both individuals and units for outstanding merit. It consists of a 5-pointed red star, surrounded by a wreath of laurel in metal, and bearing a red flag, which occupies the greater part of the upper portion of the design. A number superimposed on the decoration indicates the number of times it has been awarded.

(iii) *Honorary Standards.*—Awarded to units for distinguished military action.

(iv) *Honorary Arms.*—Awarded to higher commanders for distinguished military action, and consist of a sword or revolver suitably inscribed, and with the badge of the Order of the Red Banner mounted on the handgrip.

(v) *Order of the Red Star.*—Consists of a red 6-pointed star with the picture of a Red Army soldier carrying his rifle at the port, in the centre above the inscription " U.S.S.R. (C.C.C.P.) ". Round the edge of the medallion is the motto " Proletarians of all countries—unite ! " It is worn on the left breast, and is awarded for special services in the interests of the defence of the U.S.S.R. either in peace or war.

(vi) *Two decorations for tank personnel only.*—" For distinguished driving."

It consists of a diamond-shaped medallion with a tank superimposed on the diamond and a star at the top point of the diamond.

" For distinguished shooting."

It consists of a 5-pointed star, on which is superimposed a circular target with a tank on top.

(b) *Military or civil.*—(i) *For military service.*—The medal may be awarded to military or civilian personnel for distinguished service in a war area or in defending the inviolability of the frontiers or in the struggle with diversionists, spies and other enemies of the Soviet Union. Recipients of this medal receive a pension of five roubles a month, and have the right of free travel on the tramway system of any town in the Soviet Union.

(ii) *The Order of Lenin.*—It consists of Lenin's portrait, surrounded by a wreath, with the badge of the hammer and sickle at the top, and the inscription " U.S.S.R." (C.C.C.P.) at the bottom. It is awarded to individuals, bodies or associations for achievements in various departments of military or economic life.

(iii) *The Order of the Red Standard of Labour.*—Awarded for distinguished service in all branches of labour. It is very similar to the Order of the Red Standard.

(iv) *Hero of the Soviet Union.*—A title awarded to individuals for outstanding feats contributing to the honour and material development of the Soviet Union.

(v) *Order of Merit for Technical Conquest.*—It consists of an embossed picture of Stalin, surrounded by the words " During the reconstruction period technical skill decides everything."

CHAPTER XVI

THE SERVICES

1. General organization

The peace organization of the services in the R.K.K.A. is so designed that it can be used as the basis for expansion in war.

All services are controlled as regards policy, both in peace and war, by the appropriate "Directorate of the Commissariat of Defence (N.K.O.). There is a directorate for each service.

At each military district headquarters there is a principal administrative officer known as the "Assistant for Ordnance and Supplies." This officer controls the various departments for food, artillery, technical supplies, etc. His control, however, is largely of a co-ordinating nature, and the heads of the departments within the district itself are permitted to correspond direct with the Directorate of the N.K.O. on matters affecting their own service.

Mobilization stores in military districts are not as a rule large, and consist chiefly of explosives and ammunition, and articles of personal equipment. Impressment on a large scale will be instituted to make up deficiencies in other stores. A considerably higher scale of mobilization stores is kept by formations in frontier districts than elsewhere.

Representatives of services in the R.K.K.A. are included in the permanent establishments of formations and units. Personnel of services, however, are quite distinct from the combatant personnel of the formation or unit of which they form a part, and are specially recruited.

2. Supply services

(*a*) *General.*—Supplies of all natures in the R.K.K.A. are dealt with by two directorates of the N.K.O. These directorates are :—

(i) Directorate of the Chief of Ordnance, which deals with all artillery and technical supplies.

(ii) Directorate of Supplies, which deals with the supply of rations and forage, clothing and non-technical equipment and *horse* transport.

(*Note.*—M.T. is dealt with by a separate directorate of the N.K.O. known as the Directorate of Mechanization and Motorization.)

The detailed organization of the two above directorates is shown in the accompanying diagrams.

(b) *Supply services in the field.*—(For ordnance supply *see* sub-paragraph (c).)

On mobilization, military districts become Front or Army Zones and the responsibility for maintaining the troops in these zones rests with the Commander and Staff of the Front or Army concerned.

The system by which in peace the district commander has an assistant for ordnance and supply duties (with staff) responsible for the organization and maintenance of depots and stores in the military district is adapted as follows in war :—

(i) Military district depots, etc., become in war the advanced bases of the Front or Army under the Assistant for Ordnance and Supplies.

They are termed " Intermediate Stores " and their replenishment from the " Main Depot " or base is the responsibility of the directorate concerned in the N.K.O.

(ii) Additional subsidiary depots may also be formed by the Assistant for Ordnance and Supplies if required.

(iii) The maximum distance over which division and corps transport columns can normally operate is considered to be $3\frac{1}{2}$–4 unit marches. The Assistant for Ordnance and Supplies is responsible for ensuring that a day's supply of rations and forage is always available within this radius. This is done either by the formation of advanced stores, or by the use of army transport columns or of the rail services.

At the headquarters of the corps and divisions there is also an Assistant for Ordnance and Supply Duties with the necessary staff who is responsible for similar duties in the formation concerned.

The responsibility for bringing supplies to within $3\frac{1}{2}$–4 marches of units is the responsibility of the Army Headquarters concerned. Forward of this point, where there may be located either an advanced stores, a railhead or the delivery point of a transport column, corps headquarters assumes responsibility, supplies being drawn by the corps supply transport.

Corps supply transport moves one day's march in rear of the divisional supply transport, and these two formations are the main supply agencies in the zone of corps responsibility.

Corps and divisional supply transport was previously entirely on a horsed basis, but it is clear that in view of the increased size of corps and divisions, and the extent to which mechanized transport is becoming available, the future organization will be partly on a mechanized basis.

It will always be essential, however, to retain a large proportion of horsed transport, owing to the existence of large tracts of country unsuited to M.T.

(*Note.*—Divisions fighting in Finland 1939–40 appear to have had about 500 cars and lorries, part of which must have been unit transport.)

The organization of corps and divisional supply transport is given in paragraph 3 (*c*) below. In the case of the former, the total weight required to be lifted is approximately 600 tons, and in the case of the latter approximately 200 tons.

Corps supply transport delivers to one of the sections of the divisional supply transport, which marches one day in rear of the division. Divisional supply transport delivers to regimental transport, which marches a half day's march in rear of units.

The total rations which *can* be carried in front of railhead, are :—

On man	One day's reserve.
In travelling kitchens	Current day. (One kitchen per company or equivalent unit.)
In regimental transport ..	Two days.
In divisional transport ..	2 days.
In corps transport	2 days.

(*c*) *Supply of ordnance material and stores.*—Ordnance units as such do not exist in peace, and there are apparently no arrangements for their formation in war.

At the headquarters of military districts, the Assistant for Ordnance and Supply Duties, in his capacity as chief administrative staff officer, exercises a general supervision over ordnance matters, and is responsible that the correct scale of ordnance stores is maintained in the district.

Subject to this general supervision, which is chiefly of a co-ordinating nature, the chiefs of the various arms (*i.e.*, engineer, artillery, signal, chemical, etc.), are responsible for ordnance matters affecting their own arm, and deal *direct* with the appropriate section in the Directorate of the Chief of Ordnance in the N.K.O.

In corps and divisions, representatives of the Chief of Ordnance are similarly the Chiefs of Arms, who are responsible for ordnance matters affecting their own arm, and deal with the corresponding Chief at the headquarters of the district. Chiefs of Arms at headquarters of military districts and corps and divisional headquarters have an "Assistant i/c Ordnance Supplies " on their staffs.

Ordnance stores come under two main headings, viz :—
Artillery stores ; and
Military engineer stores.

Artillery stores.—These are either main artillery stores or *military district* artillery stores which are again subdivided into the following three categories :—
Artillery, armoured fighting vehicles, machine gun, rifle, artillery transport, etc., stores
Ammunition stores.
Chemical warfare stores.

All the above are classed as Grades I or II according to size.

Military engineer stores.—These come under four main headings :—
Main engineer stores.
Military district stores.
Fortress stores.
Signal equipment stores.

They are classified in Grades I, II and III according to their importance.

Workshops form part of the equipment of all artillery engineer stores.

Main artillery stores and main engineer stores which are generally combined, are under the ordnance department of the N.K.O., which is responsible for keeping them replenished.

Military districts stores come under the Chiefs of Artillery and Engineers of that military district, who are responsible to the Assistant for Ordnance and Supplies, that stocks are maintained at the correct scale.

In war, unit requirements are met by corps and divisional artillery parks, who draw on the appropriate store.

(d) *System of supply of petrol, oil and lubricants.*—Stores of the above are held in military engineer stores, and in peace are issued to units by the officer in charge of the store.

Owing to the undeveloped state of M.T. in the R.K.K.A., little is known of the proposed system of supply in war, but so far as mechanised forces are concerned, it is believed that the multiple-delivery tanker lorry is favoured.

(e) *Water supply.*—Specialist officers, who are responsible for the preparation of water supply plans, and for the supervision of their working, are included in the staffs of Army and corps headquarters.

Purification of local drinking water supply is carried out by the medical personnel of lower formations and units.

The main water supply system of the field armies is provided by water companies, of whom six are known to exist, but their work is supplemented by other sapper units as required.

(f) *Field bakeries and butcheries.*—(i) *Bakeries.*—In war, field bakeries on the scale of one per division and one for corps troops, accompany the divisional or corps supply transport. These are of two types :—

    Collapsible, consisting of 18 ovens.
    Non-collapsible, consisting of 16-oven vehicles.

A new type of tractor-drawn trailer-oven which bakes bread while on the move has been experimented with. No details of its construction are available.

(ii) *Butcheries.*—All fresh meat for issue to troops in the field is slaughtered under local arrangements by the regimental or unit supply personnel, etc.

Herds of cattle accompany the division or corps supply transport and used to consist of :—

    Divisional herd 125 .. 150 head of cattle.
    Corps herd .. .. 250–300 head of cattle.

Six sheep or four pigs equal one ox.

When motorised transport has been substituted, it is probable that these herds will be dispensed with and an army slaughter house organized, meat being delivered from the latter to units in specially equipped lorries.

3. Transport and transportation services

(a) *General organization.*—The control and administration of all military transport and transportation agencies in the Red Army is vested in the " Directorate of Military Communications " (UPVOSO), which is the third Directorate in the People's Commissariat of Defence (N.K.O.).

The provision and maintenance of M.T. is dealt with by the directorate of mechanisation and motorisation of the N.K.O., and that of H.T. by the appropriate branch of the directorate of supplies in the N.K.O.

As regards railway transport, " mobilization departments " form a branch of the administration of each railway district. These are responsible for detailed organization ; consequently the directorate of military communications, being free from detailed administrative problems, is able to devote itself to wider questions of policy, organization and technical matters.

At the headquarters of military districts there is a " Chief of Military Communications " (referred to as " Z.O.") who with his staff is directly responsible to the directorate of military communications of the N.K.O. for all technical matters. For command and administration, however, he is subordinate to the commander of the district.

The following transportation units exist in peace, and are described in turn in this paragraph:—

> Cadre M.T. units (for army transport only).
> Cadre H.T. units (except regimental transport, which has a full peace establishment).
> Railway units.
> " Etappe " (L. of C.) units. " Etappe " units (from Russian " Etap " meaning " stage "), are units specifically earmarked for work on the L. of C. and are *not* employed on other tasks.

On the outbreak of war a line will be fixed in rear of which transportation services will remain under the control of the Director of Military Communications, but in front of which they will be controlled by G.H.Q. or armies.

Each army in the field will be allotted its own L. of C. area, which will be immediately under the command of a Chief of Army L. of C. (" Nachvoendor ") assisted by a Corps Transport Committee (*i.e.*, staff), comprising transport representatives from each corps in the army.

The " Nachvoendor's " sphere of control will include the advanced railway sector (*i.e.*, that portion of the railway system in rear of railhead, the operation of which has been taken over by railway troops) and all transport echelons in advance of railhead as far forward as the areas under corps headquarters.

Each army will be allotted one or more L. of C. brigades. These brigades, the exact composition of which will vary according to circumstances, will consist of:—

> Railway regiments.
> Army transport units (mixed M.T. and H.T.).
> Etappe units (classed as army troops).

Forward of railhead, transportation services are carried out by the corps and divisional units as described in paragraph 2.

In circumstances where it is not possible to establish a railhead within reach of corps supply units, army transport units form the link between railhead and corps supply units. Each sector or stage on the L. of C. is controlled by special *etappe units* organized in battalions and companies, who are responsible for the defence and maintenance of their portion of the L. of C., and for feeding, accommodating and looking after all troops and casualties passing through their area. Areas vary in length according to whether they are in front or in rear of railhead. In the latter case, the length is generally that of a day's march of 15 miles.

It is believed that in war the battalion will consist of headquarters and four companies, the normal task of a company being the maintenance of 4,000 men *en route* through their area.

The following diagram shows the organization of the L. of C. :—

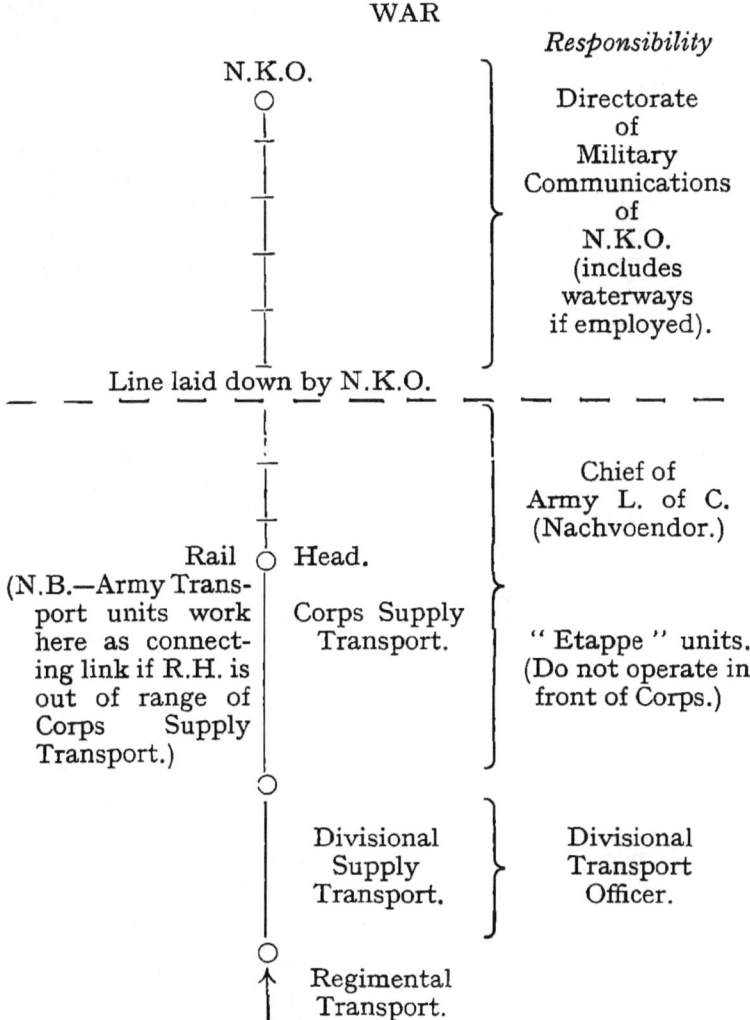

(b) *Mechanical transport.*—The poor and undeveloped state of the existing road systems in most parts of the U.S.S.R. and in the frontier districts of neighbouring countries makes it doubtful whether, even if adequate supplies of M.T. were available, the horse transport at present existing could profitably be replaced on a large scale by mechanical transport vehicles. Furthermore, the provision of the necessary vehicles for an army so large as the Red Army is bound to present some difficulty, but the enormous reduction in recent years in the number of horses available in the Soviet Union must necessitate an increasing effort being made to overcome this difficulty.

It is believed that every infantry division is being provided with a divisional M.T. company of thirty lorries, but this would not appear sufficient without some H.T. for the necessary daily lift. On occasions, however, divisions have been allotted a large number of extra M.T. vehicles for some special operations. In addition, it is believed that M.T. regiments are being formed each of three battalions of four companies, each company containing thirty lorries. These regiments form a part of M.T. "at the disposal of the high command" and are, therefore, in peace, directly under the commanders of military districts. In war they will presumably be available either for supply duties in rear of the corps boundary or for strategical and tactical moves of infantry units. The number of such M.T. regiments allotted to any district in peace, or any army in war, will depend on the local situation and on the amount of M.T. available.

In addition, there are certain motor-car and motor-cycle units, and also army M.T. units which, like railway units, are employed under the Directorate of Military Communications at the N.K.O.

(c) *Horsed transport.*—Although an extended use of mechanized transport is envisaged for the future, under the existing organization all normal transport echelons in front of railhead, *i.e.*, corps, divisional and regimental 1st and 2nd line, are horse-drawn.

The following are the horsed transport formations in the field :—

Regimental :	1st line ..	Light limbers for automatics. S.A.A. reserves.
	2nd line ..	Supply carts, etc.
Divisional transport	..	*Supply section,* divided into two platoons, each capable of carrying one day's rations and forage (less hay) for the division. Platoons probably work on double echelon system.
		Ammunition park, divided into three sections, one each for light artillery, divisional artillery and S.A.A.
		Engineer section.
		Medical section.

Corps transport ..	*Supply section*, divided into two echelons, which work on double echelon system, each echelon being capable of carrying one day's rations and forage for the corps. Included are also a herd of cattle and three field bakeries. *Ammunition park.* *Engineer section.* *Medical store section.*
Army transport ..	A variable pool of mixed horse and mechanized transport for use if required between railhead and corps.

With the exception of regimental transport, all transport mentioned above exists in peace only in cadre form, and has to be formed on mobilization. Regimental transport, however, forms an integral part of peace establishment of all units and is maintained at approximately war scale.

Carts.—Since the greater part of the horsed transport will be requisitioned from civilian sources, the many types of civilian carts found in the U.S.S.R. will form part of the army's transport. Types are on the whole fairly similar, being mostly long, narrow, four-wheeled and highly flexible, and taking loads of 500–1,000 lb. The chief drawback in the multiplicity of types is that each requires a different form of harness. The two types of cart found chiefly in the army at the moment are :—

    Two-horse cart (1884 type) .. .. load 1,000 lb.
    One-horse cart (military) .. .. load   430 lb.

Great efforts, however, are being made to standardize all carts throughout Russia, and in 1925 a type known as the " Tsupvoz " was evolved for universal use in the army and in civilian life. This is a four-wheeled cart adaptable to either pole or shaft draught, with a detachable body and a wheel track of 42 in. Its full load is 1,000 lb., and it is now being turned out in large quantities.

Sleighs.—In winter the local Russian sleigh, normally one horse, will be used instead of the cart. Its carrying capacity is 430 lb.

d) *Railway transport.*—Owing to an inadequate and indifferent road system, the U.S.S.R. will be peculiarly dependent on her railways in the event of war.

Railways in the U.S.S.R. are state-owned, and the " Directorate of Communications " of the N.K.O., which is primarily responsible for all military transportation agencies, has a special branch which deals with railways.

Special railway troops, classed as engineer troops, exist in the Red Army and are organized in :—

Railway regiments.
Independent railway battalions.
Training battalions.

The regiment is organized into two battalions in peace.

Duties in war.—The duties of railway units in war are :—

The construction and repair of lines.
The operating of advanced sections.
The construction and working of light railways.
Changing of foreign railways to Russian gauge.
Destruction of railways on retirement.

It is claimed that a constructional battalion, with the addition of labour and carpenter battalions can lay daily from $2\frac{1}{2}$–4 miles of new broad-gauge track for steam, or 3–6 miles for horse-drawn traffic, or thoroughly repair 12 miles of track.

An operating battalion can completely take over and run 55 miles of broad-gauge line with three stations and traffic to capacity.

The following are certain particulars concerning Russian railways :—

Speed and tonnage.—The efficiency of Russian railways is lower than the standard of Western Europe. Owing to the very great differences in track, which varies from metal ballast on certain main lines to sand in Central Asia, it is difficult to lay down a general average speed for the whole of the U.S.S.R. but it may be assumed that such an average will be considerably below that of Western European systems.

The average lift of trains may be taken as 350 tons military stores.

Maximum number of trains daily in each direction.—In theory it should be possible to allow 24 trains in each direction on double and 12 on single lines daily. In practice, however, it has been found that it is more accurate to reckon on 18 and 10 respectively.

Capacity of trucks.—The standard truck will accommodate 32–36 men (50 for very short distances), or eight light draught or six heavy horses. For carriage of personnel, trucks are equipped with special timber berths or seats, Trucks so equipped exist in peace, but material for converting additional trucks is held in mobilization stores.

Composition of trains and numbers required.—The standard train consists of 40–50 trucks.

The number of trains required to move certain formations is given below, but must be regarded as approximate only :—

    Infantry division .. 43 trains (with regimental artillery, but NOT including corps troops).
    Cavalry division .. 56 trains.
    Cavalry brigade .. 26 trains.

Loading Times.

	High platform whole length. minutes.	Low platform or ground. minutes.
Infantry and cavalry	30	45
Field artillery ..	45	60
Special units (*i.e.*, medium artillery, pontoons, etc.)	60	90

4. Medical service

The Medical Directorate of the Red Army is directly subordinate to the Commissariat for Defence (N.K.O.), but receives instructions regarding its general policy and the co-ordination of its activities, with those of the civilian medical organizations, from the Peoples' Commissar for Health of the R.S.F.S.R., who acts in consultation with the Commissars for Health of the Union Republics.

There are nine main medical supply depots distributed among the main military districts, the central medical store being situated in the Moscow District.

All requirements of medical stores, etc., are obtained by the Medical Directorate of the N.K.O. and stored at the central medical store, whence they are issued to the depots in military districts, and to medical and other units as required.

The regulations for the medical service of the R.K.K.A. lay great stress on the importance of correct classification of wounded and sick from the earliest stages of evacuation.

Wounded are given a ticket at the regimental aid posts on which particulars of wounds and treatment received are recorded. These particulars are amplified at each stage of evacuation, and the ticket therefore becomes a temporary medical history sheet.

The stages of evacuation are as follows :—

Auxiliary aid post to regimental aid post by stretcher or stretcher cart.

Regimental aid post to main field dressing station by vehicle of divisional ambulance convoy and thence to divisional hospital by a special pool of 50 vehicles under divisional medical officer.

Divisional hospital to corps hospital and thence to ambulance train by ambulance convoy under corps.

No details of the composition of this convoy are available.

It is laid down that supply routes will be used for evacuation of wounded, and that as far as possible vehicles of the supply columns returning empty will be used for the transport of casualties.

Each regiment has a medical detachment, the establishment of which is as follows :—

One military doctor, 1st or 2nd rank.
One military doctor, 2nd or 3rd rank.
One assistant surgeon.
Three medical orderlies.

The above establishment may be increased according to circumstances. During operations the medical detachment opens a regimental aid post, normally about $1\frac{1}{2}$ miles in rear of the front line, and auxiliary aid posts in battalion areas. Here casualties receive preliminary treatment and are then evacuated to the regimental aid post.

At the regimental aid post casualties receive first-aid only, and after classification and registration are evacuated to the main field dressing station.

A divisional ambulance convoy consists of 25 2-horse and 35 1-horse 2-wheeled ambulance carts. There is also the pool of 50 vehicles in the hands of the divisional medical officer.

The one or two-horsed ambulance cart is sprung, and its capacity is two lying cases or four sitting. There is no seat for the driver, who leads the horse.

Evacuations between division and corps are effected by motor and horse convoys, but their establishments are not known.

It is believed that the Soviet General Staff are contemplating the complete mechanization of their ambulance services, but no details are yet available.

Corps field hospitals, the number of which depends on the situation, are usually situated one day's march behind divisional hospitals, and if possible in close proximity to railhead.

They normally constitute the final stage of evacuation by road, and therefore correspond to the British C.C.S. In cases, however, where it is impossible to site the corps hospital in close proximity to railhead and still keep it one stage from division, a *railhead clearing station* is organized. The latter then becomes responsible for collecting wounded from the corps hospital.

Corps hospitals contain approximately 200 beds.

5. Other services

(a) *Veterinary service.*—The veterinary service of the Red Army is subordinate to the Veterinary Directorate of the R.K.K.A., which is a department of the Commissariat of Defence (N.K.O.).

In each corps or division and in each regiment or equivalent unit there is a veterinary detachment consisting of one or more veterinary surgeons and a number of regimental personnel trained in veterinary and farrier duties.

Detachments normally contain a farriers training shop and a veterinary hospital.

As in other services, the peace veterinary organization is used as the basis for expansion in war.

Regimental veterinary detachments are capable of opening a regimental hospital, which is normally located with the unit transport. Here only slightly wounded cases and minor ailments are treated, the remainder being evacuated to divisional hospitals.

The latter, which have sections for infectious and non-infectious cases, are situated from ten to fifteen miles in rear, depending on the tactical situation. They appear to have accommodation for only 150 cases, and their first duty is the classification of casualties into cases which can be treated on the spot, and cases for further evacuation to the rear.

From divisional hospitals, casualties may be evacuated either to corps veterinary hospitals, or to base veterinary hospitals. Little is known of the corps hospitals or their functions, but it is thought that they may be only " staging camps " for re-adjusting dressings, etc., of cases passing through.

Garrison veterinary hospitals which exist in peace become base hospitals in war and open convalescent depots.

From base hospitals, recovered animals are passed to convalescent depots and then to base remount depots.

(b) *Labour service.*—Labour is provided by the following:—

(i) Military construction corps, which are organized in military construction battalions, and are employed on the construction and maintenance of military works.

(ii) Independent brigades of rear militia, which are composed of men deprived of the right of service in the Red Army, and are available for military construction work.

(iii) Enforced labour, which is raised as required for a definite purpose, generally of a non-military character, and which is composed largely of political and other prisoners.

Organization of Ordnance and Supply Directorates—Peace

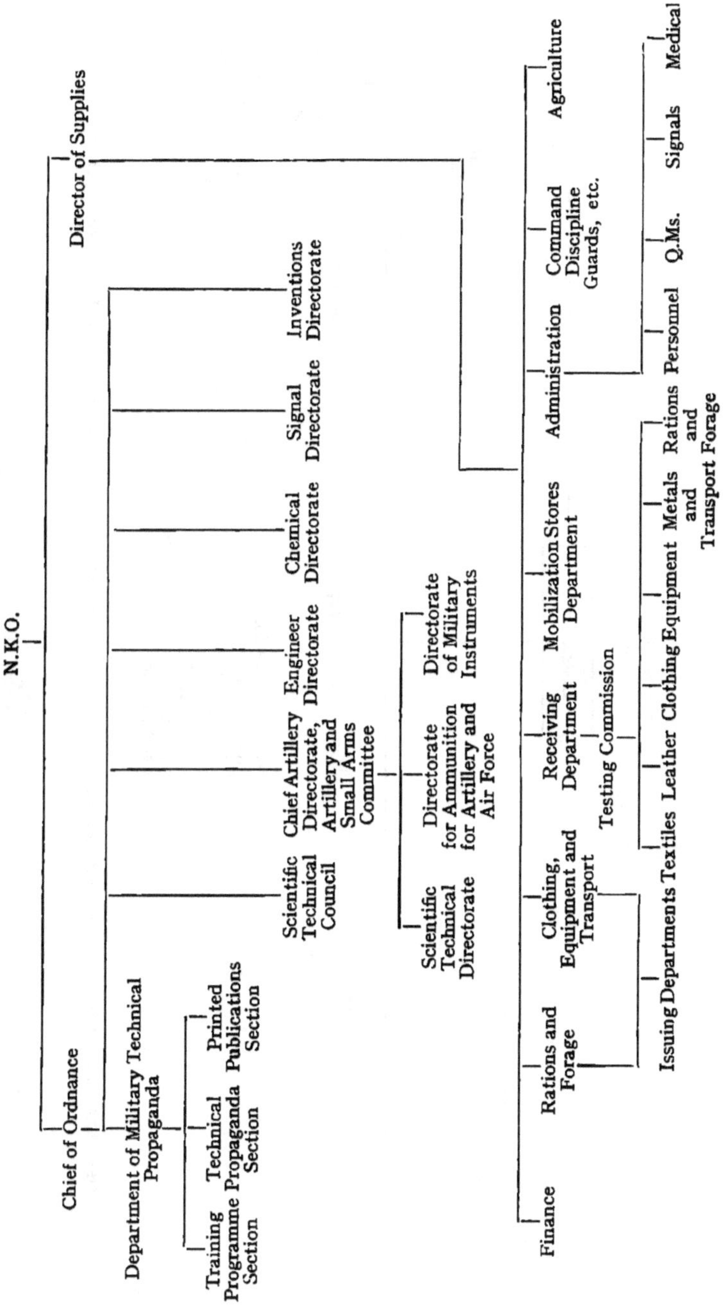

N.K.O.
- Chief of Ordnance
  - Department of Military Technical Propaganda
    - Training Programme Section
    - Technical Propaganda Section
    - Printed Publications Section
  - Scientific Technical Council
    - Chief Artillery Directorate, Artillery and Small Arms Committee
    - Engineer Directorate
    - Chemical Directorate
    - Signal Directorate
    - Inventions Directorate
  - Scientific Technical Directorate
    - Directorate for Ammunition for Artillery and Air Force
    - Directorate of Military Instruments
- Director of Supplies
  - Clothing, Equipment and Transport
    - Receiving Department
      - Testing Commission
    - Mobilization Stores Department
    - Issuing Departments: Textiles, Leather, Clothing, Equipment, Metals and Transport
  - Rations and Forage
    - Rations and Forage
  - Administration
    - Command Discipline Guards, etc.
    - Personnel
    - Q.Ms.
    - Signals
    - Medical
    - Agriculture
- Finance

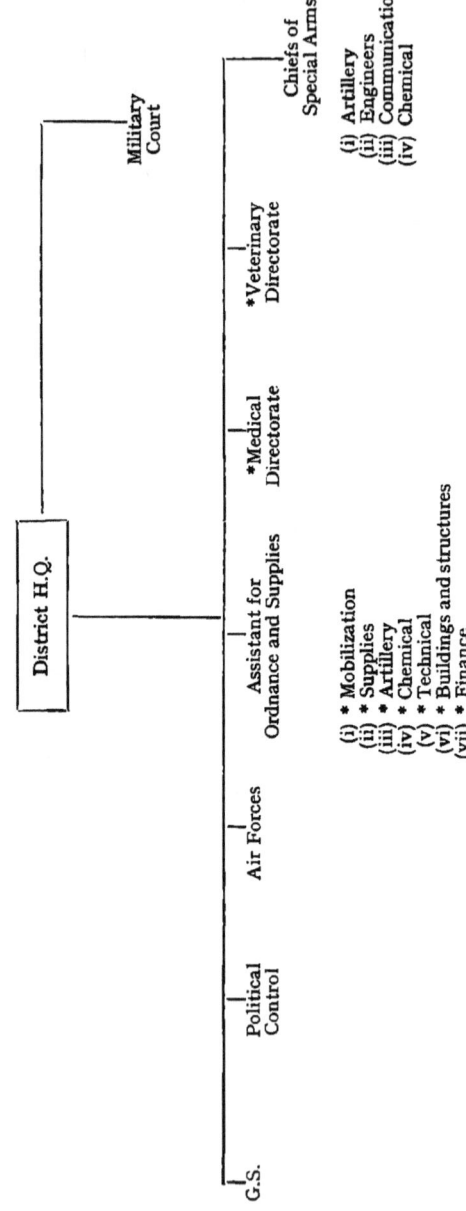

Note.—Departments marked * are entitled to deal direct with the appropriate branch of the N.K.O. on matters affecting their own service.)

CHAPTER XVII
TACTICS AND TRAINING

1. General principles

The principles laid down in the Soviet Field Service Regulations are in general very similar to the accepted military teaching in other countries. They, however, give the impression of being designed to combat some of the inherent weaknesses of the Russian character, while incorporating also some of the German tactical doctrine acquired by the higher Soviet leaders in the pre-Hitler period when military relations between the two countries were close.

Great emphasis is laid on the initiative, due very possibly to the realization that the natural tendency of the Slav, when faced with a complex situation, is to do nothing. Nevertheless, during the Finnish campaign and also in such training activities as have been witnessed, lack of initiative has been very marked and commanders in all grades have generally displayed serious inability to deal with unexpected situations, and a tendency to adhere rigidly to the teaching laid down in the manuals, irrespective of the particular circumstances obtaining at the moment.

The manuals, though giving the impression of a lack of clarity, have at least one great virtue in that they deal throughout with operations by all arms, including aircraft. The necessity for co-ordination and co-operation is thus kept constantly to the fore. Great stress is laid on this in the attack which is designed, whether by penetration or by envelopment, to crush all defensive systems throughout the whole depth of the position. Considerable emphasis is laid on the need for the co-operation of the air arm by bombing or by low flying attacks, and on the use of mechanized forces in almost every situation, with the result that in the defence the first consideration, whether in the siting of the position or in the use of the artillery, is one of anti-tank defence.

2. Battle

(a) *Forward movement.*—The regulations lay down the forward movement should take place on as broad a front as possible.

The general rules laid down for marches do not differ materially from our own. Mechanical vehicles are moved on separate roads from infantry and horsed transport, but this must often be difficult to arrange because of the shortage of roads, and because of the fact that the Red Army division now normally contains a tank battalion and a reconnaissance battalion which is also largely mechanized. Individual columns are generally given two objectives, one which they must secure and a second to which they may advance if they find it possible. A column appears to be at liberty to advance to its second objective quite irrespective of the movements of the columns on its flanks. There is also a tendency to give objectives too far ahead ; cases occurred during the Finnish war when objectives were laid down two or three days ahead.

(b) *First contact with the enemy.*—Divisional commanders are instructed to act energetically and to attack the enemy where met, without waiting for information regarding the general situation, and irrespective of the action of formations on either flank. The aim appears to be the early separation of the enemy columns from each other, in order that subsequent deployment may achieve their defeat in detail.

(c) *Deployment.*—For deployment, a formation is divided into two groups, a striking group and a holding group.

The striking group contains the bulk of the artillery and tanks, and delivers the main attack. It is divided into two echelons, the second of which exploits the success of the first. Units of the first echelon are allotted boundaries ; units of the second echelon are given a general direction only. The holding group is comparatively weak, and has the task of drawing off the enemy's attention from the main attack and of pinning him to his ground.

In defence, the relative strength of the two groups changes, the holding group occupying the defensive position, and the striking group forming the reserve for counterattack.

It appears to be considered that the division is the largest formation which can be deployed off one road when first contact is gained, but this rule is not in practice universally applicable owing to the shortage of roads in most of the theatres in which the Red Army is likely to operate. During the Finnish campaign two and sometimes three divisions operated along a single road.

3. Information

(a) *General system of reconnaissance.*—It is laid down that the collection of information about the enemy and the ground in the theatre of operations is the duty of all units, formations and staffs.

The sources of information considered are :—
    (i) Fighting and ground reconnaissance by land forces, which produce the most reliable information.

(ii) Air reconnaissance, the basic means of strategical and one of the chief means of tactical reconnaissance.

(iii) Observation, by units of all arms in the course of their normal activities, and by special observation posts and patrols sent out by staffs of formations.

(iv) Telephonic and telegraphic interception by troops in close contact with the enemy or by detachments tapping his rearward system of communication.

(v) Wireless interception.

(vi) Documents obtained through agents, by the capture of prisoners, from dead and wounded, and particularly by raids on the L. of C.

(vii) The interrogation of local inhabitants, whose information may often be valuable, but must always be verified by other means.

(b) *Air reconnaissance.*—Distant reconnaissance is carried out by aircraft of the corps reconnaissance flight (which contains six to nine aircraft), often reinforced by one or more flights from army air uuits.

Close reconnaissance is carried out by aircraft of the divisional reconnaissance " Zveno " (two or three aircraft).

A single aircraft is considered to be capable of covering the following areas :—

Close reconnaissance .. Six by eight miles.
Distant reconnaissance .. Three to six miles of front.
Sixty miles in depth.

The minimum heights permissible are 3,000 ft. for close, and 4,500 for distant reconnaissance.

It is remarkable that no mention is made, under air reconnaissance, of air photography, although some slight attention is drawn to it elsewhere.

It would appear to be a frequent practice for staff officers to carry out air reconnaissance for particular purposes such as to observe the progress of their mechanized forces in the attack. The general standard of army co-operation is low.

(c) *Ground reconnaissance.*—Reconnaissance before battle is carried out by the divisional reconnaissance group up to 15 or 30 miles ahead of the main body. For this purpose the group may be divided into parties consisting of two or three armoured fighting vehicles, supported by an infantry detachment carried in lorries.

Moving behind this party may be one or more mobile observation posts, each consisting of an officer and a few other ranks, on horses or in M.T. vehicles (the resources of the divisional reconnaissance group provide for both means of transport).

In mechanized formations, distant reconnaissance is carried out by tanks (one or two platoons), which may be accompanied by infantry, motorized artillery or tanks mounting a 76 mm. gun. The depth of reconnaissance may be up to 15 or 20 miles from the main body. The rate of movement expected is from 6 to 10 miles per hour.

(*d*) *Reconnaissance during battle.*—In addition to the normal reconnaissance carried out by units in contact with the enemy, the divisional reconnaissance group may be detailed to carry out a special reconnaissance of the enemy's dispositions or to locate his flanks. In this case, as information can probably be obtained only by fighting, the group is supported by artillery, and possibly by additional infantry. In the event of such a reconnaissance, the regulations lay down that there will be a demonstration (usually in the form of artillery preparation) on another portion of the divisional front.

Particular emphasis is laid on the necessity for the careful organization of reconnaissance work by the divisional staff, for the establishment of divisional observation posts with their own means of communication, and for the observation from aircraft of the course of the battle by staff officers. The results obtained are, however, generally inadequate.

4. Protection

(*a*) *General principles.*—The principles of protection, and the guiding rules for its attainment laid down in the Soviet regulations, do not differ materially from our own.

(*b*) *Advanced guards.*—The strength of the advanced guard may be up to one-third of the infantry of the column, and one-half of the artillery. Heavy howitzers and long range guns are included in the advanced guard artillery if available.

Another guide for the strength of the artillery is given : a scale of two groups (18 pieces) per infantry battalion is recommended.

(*c*) *Flank guards.*—Flank guards are considered almost entirely from the point of view of anti-tank defence. Small bodies of infantry, with battalion anti-tank weapons, form picquets covering approaches to the column. The normal distance of flank guards from the column is given as between 2 and 3 kilometres. The regulations give no details of the method of employment of these anti-tank flank guards, but it is implied that owing to the scarity of roads in Russia, they normally work as standing picquets, rejoining the rear of the column. They are not provided with M.T., so that their rate of movement would not be sufficient to enable them to occupy successive tactical features on the flanks of the line of march.

(*d*) *Rear guards.*—The Red Army regulations regard night withdrawals as normal but little attention appears to be paid to the administrative difficulties involved, nor to the careful staff work required to overcome them. The withdrawal of the rear guard by bounds is envisaged, but no guidance as regards timing, or order of withdrawal of units is given. Particular emphasis is laid on the necessity for counter attack by A.F.V.s, in co-operation with aircraft, against the flanks of the advancing enemy. It is foreseen that the enemy will probably make energetic use of his own aircraft, and, in addition, to a well planned anti-aircraft defence lay-out, the avoidance of crowding in areas devoid of cover from air observation is enjoined. The importance of a demolition belt, combined with the use of gas, is not overlooked, but it is remarkable that no mention is made here of anti-tank defence, despite the fact that the Soviet teaching for the pursuit involves the use of A.F.V.s in large numbers.

(*e*) *Protection at rest.*—The dispositions for outposts are on the same lines as those given for defence on an extended front. The frontage for a battalion may be up to three miles; and the outpost line is normally three miles in advance of the main body.

It is laid down as an invariable rule that outpost troops shall not be detailed as protective troops for the subsequent move. In the case of an advance a fresh advanced guard is always detailed, and after passing through the outpost troops, the latter close and join the main body. In the case of a withdrawal, a rear guard takes up a position in rear of the outpost line, after which the outpost troops withdraw through it to join the main body.

Protection of formations and units in billets and bivouacs behind the lines is treated separately in the manuals. Instructions cover anti-tank, anti-aircraft and anti-gas defence, and it is laid down that alarm posts for each of these means of defence will invariably be organized for any body of troops, whether in the battle zone or on the L. of C.

(*f*) *Tactical camouflage.*—In theory camouflage in all its forms receives great attention in the Red Army, but the practical results are not always satisfactory. Apart from any special camouflage equipment issued, men are trained to cover their weapons, vehicles, etc., and themselves with branches, brushwood, hay or any material available, whenever overhead cover is lacking. There is ground for supposing that this is sometimes overdone, and that objects are made more conspicuous, particularly in movement, than they would be if no attempt at camouflage had been made. It is notable that, at the beginning of the campaign in Finland, only a very small proportion of the Soviet troops had been provided with the white smocks necessary to camouflage them against the snow, and that during the February offensive on the Carelian isthmus a large number of batteries and some very large dumps of munitions were entirely without camouflage. It is unlikely that this was wholly due to the knowledge that the enemy was poorly equipped with air forces and long range artillery.

5. Attack

(a) *General.*—It is laid down that a successful attack requires the concentration of superior force, and the maintenance of its strength and momentum in the direction laid down for the main blow.

By the co-operation of all arms, the attack should seek to crush simultaneously all defensive systems throughout the whole depth of the position.

This, Soviet doctrine lays down, is achieved by :—

(i) Air action against reserves and rear organization.

(ii) Destruction by artillery of the tactical layout throughout the whole depth of the position.

(iii) Penetration by long range tank units into the furthest limits of the defensive position.

(iv) Infantry attack closely supported by tanks.

(v) Attack by cavalry and mechanised units on the enemy's rear.

(vi) By the lavish use of smoke to hide the movement of attacking troops and to deceive the enemy.

Where there is an open flank, the main attack should be directed round the flank of the enemy and towards his rear. Open flanks, and points of junction between neighbouring formations and units, are the defenders' most vulnerable points. By outflanking a hostile position, it is possible to launch a direct attack on his artillery, headquarters, signal communications and transport.

The plan of attack, whether it be against the flank of the enemy or whether it involves penetration of his front, should aim not at driving him back, but at surrounding him and capturing his material.

The most important element is surprise, and it is therefore essential to preserve the greatest secrecy during the period of preparation.

An outflanking movement requires speed and boldness in execution, combined with adequate measures for self protection especially on the pivotal flank. Tanks and aircraft facilitate outflanking movements, and it is when employed in this manner that they give the most decisive results. Long-range fast tanks should be directed across the enemy's line of retreat to attack him from the rear. Mechanised brigades and cavalry divisions should be used for the outflanking movement, while infantry formations make a frontal attack.

If the enemy has no exposed flank, orders should be issued for a break-through. A concerted attack by infantry, long-range tanks, and aircraft, with artillery support, should bring about, even in the absence of an open flank, the destruction of the enemy and the capture of his material.

The attack is thus envisaged almost exclusively as a crushing blow. There is hardly a hint of guidance in the possible event of only partial success; nor is mention made of attack when aircraft are not available, when tanks cannot operate, or when circumstances make any but a very limited offensive impossible. This is perhaps due to a realization of the limitations of the average commander, whose powers of initiative and individual thought are possibly below the average, and whom it therefore pays to imbue thoroughly with one main idea rather than with several alternatives.

(b) *Gaining of contact.*—No clear picture is given in the manuals of what happens between the time when the advanced guard is first held up and the main attack launched.

They state :—

" The forward movement of main bodies is covered by advanced guards and other protective detachments. When the advanced guards become committed in an engagement with hostile protective detachments, main bodies should be concentrated in concealed positions within their respective divisional boundaries, some three to four kilometres from the nearest enemy detachments. During this period all units should organize their own local protection, particularly against air, gas and tank attack.

" In addition, divisional artillery commanders should carry out a reconnaissance over ground likely to be used in the attack, and under cover of the infantry, arrange for such deployment of the artillery as the plan of the command requires. 'Reconnaissance by all available means should take place on a wide front. If a further advance or an attack is to take place at dawn on the following day, night reconnaissance must be carried out in order to discover, as far as possible, hostile dispositions. Aircraft dropping flares will often reveal hostile movement.

" Care must be taken that reconnaissance measures do not reveal to the enemy the proposed main line of advance.

" As a result of information gained by all means available and verified by staff officers carrying out a special reconnaissance in aircraft, the corps commander should make his plan of attack and issue his orders. Orders should lay down divisional boundaries for the attack, the allotment of corps troops, and zero hour."

There is no mention either of the reinforcement of the advanced guard, or alternatively of the assembly of units to take part in the main attack. The emphasis laid on the necessity for reconnaissance during this period, and the employment of staff officers in aircraft for this purpose is noteworthy.

In practice on making first contact with the enemy Soviet troops generally consolidate their position and dig in before making any further move. Efforts to obtain further information are generally very restricted and the main body is often committed without adequate information about the enemy's strength and position. In this connection the manuals imply that, if the advance guard is definitely held up, an attack by the whole formation should be launched, and it appears that Red Army commanders tend to follow this guidance too literally.

(c) *General conduct of the attack*.—This is treated largely from the point of view of a corps, and attention is in the main confined to methods for control of direction and for ensuring mutual support and co-operation.

" When contact with the forward elements of the defensive position has been gained, the commander makes his final plan and issues his orders for the attack.

" In the case of a corps seeking to outflank the enemy's defensive position, boundaries for attacking divisions should be defined only up to the enemy's flank. Further movement is controlled by defining a general direction of advance, which is adjusted in accordance with the situation.

" If there is only one group of long-range tanks, corps artillery should generally be responsible for their fire support. If the number of such tanks available is sufficient to allow of their organization in two groups, their fire support should normally be arranged by divisions. The corps commander should attach a liaison officer with wireless to each group of tanks, and a staff officer should watch their progress from the air."

(*d*) *Infantry in the attack.*—The regulations are definite on the subject of frontages. They give the following as named frontages for the attack :—

Infantry company	250 to 300 metres.
Infantry battalion	500 to 600 metres
Infantry regiment	1,200 to 2,000 metres
Rifle division	2,500 to 4,500 metres

Between the limits given, frontages are to be varied according to the strength of the defensive position.

The scale of support laid down for an attack on a well-organized position is 75 to 200 tanks per division according to the strength of the position attacked, and two batteries for every kilometre of front. On the assumption that the supporting arms enumerated are in addition to those included in the composition of an infantry division (53 tanks and 54 to 78 guns and howitzers), from 17 to 40 guns and howitzers per kilometre of front and from 128 to 253 tanks per division are normally to be employed.

Only very general instructions are given for the conduct of the attack. The following extract is an example :—

" The commander of an infantry regiment normally arranges attacking battalions in two echelons, accompanying the second echelon himself, since it is upon the timely intervention of this latter that the success of the infantry attack depends. Close support is provided by the regimental artillery groups which frequently use direct fire methods. Additional artillery, and infantry support tanks, are provided from the division.

" After deployment, infantry units will take every opportunity of advancing, by bounds at the double, or by crawling, with the object of getting nearer to the enemy and so reducing the distance to be covered when the signal for the assault is given."

The instructions that infantry should attack in echelons are apparently interpreted to mean attacking in line. The practice of advancing in line at the double has, no doubt, grown up side by side with the idea that infantry will always be supported by tanks. The difficulty of timing the two elements of such differing economical speeds to reach the objective simultaneously, has led to the abandonment of attempts to stage separate and converging attacks, so the infantry now accompany the tanks and have to run in order to keep up with them.

The fire plan and control of battalion weapons (37-mm. guns, M.Gs., and light automatics), is frequently found to be sketchy.

During the Finnish war, Soviet attacks conformed on the whole to these instructions, but the co-ordination of the various arms was bad and the troops were inclined to lose direction. The speed with which the infantry dug themselves in as soon as they were checked was remarkable, and it was evident that Soviet commanders would never abandon any ground they had won even if it entailed holding a most unsuitable defensive position.

(e) *Artillery in the attack.*—Artillery is charged with the following tasks :—

During artillery preparation—destruction of hostile artillery, tank obstacles and defensive works.

During attack by long-range tanks—support of the attack by fire against hostile anti-tank and artillery weapons.

During attack by infantry and supporting tanks—protection of the forward movement of the tanks by fire against hostile anti-tank and small arms weapons and the support of the infantry by fire (and by movement where necessary) during the whole course of the attack.

Further instructions given are :—

" The minimum period for artillery preparation, in cases where the allotment of field artillery is from 30 to 35 pieces per kilometre of front, and that of tanks is two battalions per infantry division, is $1\frac{1}{2}$ hours. With fewer tanks this period may be as long as three hours, and in cases where the enemy is occupying a carefully prepared position, it may be considerably longer. In certain circumstances, however (where it may facilitate surprise, where the enemy is in a hastily occupied position, etc.), preliminary bombardment may be limited to 10 or 15 minutes and subsequent support afforded by a creeping barrage.

" The most successful means of artillery support for long-range tanks is by a moving barrage, lifts being arranged in accordance with the probable speed of the tanks in the prevailing circumstances. An artillery group (9–12 pieces) can cover from 300 to 400 metres, either along the front, or in depth. Where the lay-out of the hostile anti-tank defences can be discovered, support may take the form of concentrations on successive areas, but a considerable time is required for reconnaissance if this method is to be used successfully. In any case tanks, whether carrying out reconnaissance or the main attack, must not be sent into action without artillery support."

During the Finnish campaign the handling of the artillery did not altogether correspond with these instructions. In the battles of the Karelian Isthmus, artillery preparation was generally long, up to eight hours, but it was not sufficiently concentrated except during the final battles of the war, when the number of guns available was so great that the production of concentrated fire presented no difficulties. Special attention was paid to the destruction of Finnish strong points and M.G. positions, and on occasions, unsupported infantry attacks were made in the sector where a major attack was being prepared, with the object of forcing the Finns to open fire and reveal the position of their strong points and machine guns which were then systematically pounded by the Soviet artillery. Artillery support during the attacks was generally comparatively ineffective, as the Soviet artillery did not appear to be capable of firing a barrage or a co-ordinate fire plan.

(*f*) *Armoured fighting vehicles in the attack.*—The Red Army Command has a child-like faith in tanks, which are used in very large numbers in support of every major attack quite irrespective of whether the terrain is not suitable for the action of such weapons.

In Red Army manuals, tanks are classified according to their tactical role as long-range tanks, infantry support tanks, or cavalry support tanks.

> " The role of long-range tanks is to penetrate to the furthest limits of the whole defensive system, destroy the hostile reserves and headquarters, and cut off the enemy's retreat. Their action should be planned so that the infantry and their supporting tanks, taking advantage of the disorganization effected by the long-range tanks, may move forward and prevent any reorganization of the defence."

The action of these tanks is likely to have considerable effect, as the Red Army has made a special study of the type, and the B.T. tank is an excellent weapon. It seems, however, possible that the scale of anti-tank weapons envisaged by the Soviet regulations is lower than that of most first-class powers, and that the very difficult problem of artillery support for these tanks has not received enough attention. The speed of the tanks is such that support by low-flying aircraft is often employed in lieu of artillery support, but the difficulties of co-ordinating the action of two such different arms are such as to prevent satisfactory results being achieved by an army whose standard of staff work is so unsatisfactory. According to the Soviet regulations, artillery support must be pre-arranged, and whether by barrage or concentrations, or by a combination of both, will be liable either to outstrip or to impede the tanks, even if it neutralises the hostile field and anti-tank guns. This is realised to some extent, for the manual refers to the possibility of control of lifts from the air, and to the necessity for attacking in waves at short intervals, so that anti-tank defences, once neutralised, will never have time to recover. Where it has been possible to observe the work of long range tanks during training, their action has been in accordance with the teaching of the manuals; but there has always been an air of artificiality about such exercises which aroused a suspicion that adequate artillery support could not have been arranged in the time available.

The following extracts from the regulations deal with infantry support tanks :—

> "The attack by infantry and their supporting tanks should take place simultaneously along the whole front. Where the ground occupied by the forward defences of the enemy is unfavourable for tank action, it may be necessary for the infantry and their supporting tanks to precede the long range tanks. In this case the task of the latter will be to exploit the success of the infantry attack.
> "Infantry supporting tanks should always have artillery support. This is normally provided by the battery or group allotted to an attacking infantry battalion, and fire is directed against the hostile anti-tank lay-out. The task of the tanks is then to destroy the hostile machine guns."

The present type of infantry support tank is very unsuitable for its role, as it is lightly armoured, comparatively fast and unsteady.

The terrain over which the battles of the Finnish campaign were fought is very unfavourable for the employment of tanks, but it appears that, on the whole, the Soviet commanders endeavoured to put into practice the theories laid down in their regulations. A proportion of the tank forces employed in the big attacks generally attempted to break through and attack the rear of the Finnish positions, while the remainder co-operated with the infantry. Soviet tanks fired both halted and on the move but their fire on the move was most inaccurate. The best results were achieved when tanks could halt just behind a crest near the Finnish position so that only their turrets showed over the crest.

(g) *Cavalry in the attack.*—Field Service Regulations for the Red Army make little mention of cavalry in the attack. The only examples of its use to be given are :—

" In outflanking movements, they co-operate with mechanised brigades.

" When the infantry have succeeded in making a gap in the hostile defences, they are enjoined to keep it open and fully to protect the cavalry and mechanised units which are to be passed through in pursuit."

(h) *Engineers in the attack.*—The duties of engineers in the attack are laid down as :—

(i) Continuous engineer reconnaissance of the locality and of the enemy's defences.

(ii) Preparation of routes and avenues of advance.

(iii) Camouflage of assembly areas.

(iv) Water supply.

(v) Preparations for assisting the advance across obstacles (ladders, steps, bridges, etc.).

(vi) Construction of defences in captured areas, and provision of obstacles.

(vii) Construction of roads and bridges in back areas. Emphasis is laid on the necessity of a reserve of engineer personnel and material in all formations.

During the Finnish war engineers were also responsible for clearing mines and booby traps left behind by the retreating Finns.

(i) *Aircraft in the attack.*—Aircraft with the field army, apart from reconnaissance machines, are classified as :—

Storm aircraft—used primarily for low-flying attack.

Light bombers—for bombing troops and light construction work.

Fighters (lit. " destroyers ")—for protection of light bombers and storm aircraft, and of formations, against attack by hostile aircraft.

Bombers—for bombing heavier construction work, brigades, railways, depots, etc.

The roles of aircraft in attack are given as :—

To attack the hostile rear organization with storm and light bomber units immediately prior to, and during, the main attack.

To concentrate their attack during the later stages on such enemy units as have avoided the outflanking movement, and turn withdrawal into a rout.

The general tendency appears to be to carry out light bombing or gas spray attacks from a very low height of 100 metres or less.

The regulations mention parachute units, whose descent is to cause complete disorganization of rear headquarters and services, but no details are given of the way in which they are to be employed. Since aerial descents have been a feature of most Red Army manœuvres since 1934, however, some details of their execution can be given.

The following appears to be the normal procedure :—

Preliminary operation

Reconnaissance machines are sent out to report on conditions in the area selected for the landing. On receipt of a favourable report, the heavy bombers carrying personnel take off, preceded by storm aircraft which machine-gun the selected area. Simultaneously a heavy bombing attack is carried out on some important target in another sector, with a view to distracting the attention of enemy aircraft from the landing.

1st Phase

The 1st (light) group, consisting of from 1,000 to 2,000 lightly-equipped infantry, armed with rifles, revolvers, and light automatics, carries out a parachute descent from a height of about 4,000 ft. Some heavy machine-guns, packed in straw and sacking, are also dropped by parachute.

Undue dispersion is avoided partly by dropping off in quick succession, and partly by the use of a second smaller parachute which each man carries, and which appears to enable the direction of descent to be controlled. Immediately after landing, battle units are formed and positions covering the approaches to the captured areas are occupied, so as to provide a protected landing ground for the remainder of the force.

2nd Phase

The remainder of the air landing force is carried in heavy bombing machines which actually land on the captured ground. The 2nd (heavy) group consists of about 1,500 infantry with heavy machine guns and cycles. The 3rd (heavy) group includes some light artillery, amphibian tanks, light armoured cars, signal vehicles and light lorries, the guns and vehicles being carried below the fuselages of the machines between the landing wheels. The guns are drawn up into the lorries and carried as artillery portee.

For this type of operation, open country, such as predominates in Eastern Europe, would be essential. Even then it may be doubted whether storm aircraft could ensure that the landing would not be opposed. It appears probable that such tactics could only be used in the pursuit of a demoralised and badly equipped enemy ; in co-operation with a mechanised corps, to seize an unoccupied position and hold it for a very limited time ; or in desperate situations, in order to create diversion. This would most likely entail the virtual annihilation of the landing party, but the morale of the carefully picked and trained troops appears to be such that they would act with resolution in such circumstances.

During the Finnish campaign aircraft were largely used to give fire support during the attack as well as for attacks on headquarters and lines of communication ; parachute troops were not used on any large scale, though groups of up to 20 men were dropped. The results of the air bombardments were insignificant owing to the very wooded nature of the country, and the parachutists dropped at random in the forests generally lost their way, either perished or emerged completely exhausted.

(j) *Special methods of attack.*—(i) *Chemical.*—A note at the beginning of Field Service Regulations for the Red Army (1937 edition) states :—

" Chemical means of attack, to which these regulations refer, will only be resorted to by the Red Army in cases where the enemy employs them first."

As the equipment of chemical warfare battalions includes apparatus for the offensive use of gas and as a percentage of gas shell is invariably included in all echelons of artillery ammunition supply, it can hardly be doubted that the above note is for foreign consumption only, and that the Red Army will employ gas offensively from the very beginning of a war of the first magnitude. In view, however, of the note, and of the desirability of retaining the element of surprise in the use of gas, the regulations do not give details of its employment.

In the attack the use of persistent and non-persistent gases, choking gases and poison smokes is recommended. With favourable winds, and particularly at night, poison and smoke is preferred.

Chemical warfare units are employed in the attack primarily to cover the advance by smoke, and for decontamination duties.

(ii) *Propaganda.*—The Soviet authorities regard propaganda as an important weapon, to be employed within and in rear of the hostile armed forces by every possible means. The means employed will naturally vary with the nationality and circumstances of the enemy, and the execution of plans is the duty of the political sections of formations and units.

There can be little doubt, however, that great attention will be given to this form of attack by all available means, which even include the use of special artillery shells which, on bursting, produce a flood of literature.

(k) *The attack in trench warfare.*—Beyond remarking that for the attack in trench warfare more detailed reconnaissance, a greater mass of artillery of all natures and particularly of the heavier calibres, more tanks, aircraft and engineer units are required, the Red Army manuals merely state that " attack will be carried out in accordance with the general instructions already laid down."

6. Defence

(a) *General principles.*—The Red Army authorities envisage a hostile attack being made largely in accordance with their own doctrine, that is by all arms, including low flying and bombing aircraft, with large numbers of tanks, and simultaneous assaults in front, in flank, and against rear services. The regulations consequently lay down :—

" Defence should be planned to meet superior enemy forces attacking simultaneously throughout the whole depth of the position and should aim at :—

Destroying the hostile infantry in front of the foremost defended localities.

Preventing enemy tanks from breaking through beyond the main position.

In the event of a break through by tanks breaking down their attack by anti-tank weapons, and at the same time separating them from the accompanying hostile infantry by pinning the latter with small arms fire.

Destroying any enemy who have succeeded in penetrating into the main position by counter attacks carried out by tanks and other arms.

Modern defence is primarily anti-tank defence, composed of the fire of anti-tank and field artillery in conjunction with a system of natural and artificial obstacles, anti-tank mines and chemical defence measures. The use of ground in conjunction with interlocking belts of fire and the sighting of some machine-guns in the anti-tank defence zone, should produce favourable conditions for paralysing the attack of the hostile infantry and separating the latter from the accompanying tanks."

The normal defensive layout appears to be as follows :—

(i) A belt of obstacles is prepared mainly by engineer and chemical warfare units some 12-km. from the main position. The use of demolitions contaminated with persistent gases is implied. The belt is defended by "small units of infantry with some artillery," but the regulations give no real indication of the organization, degree of resistance expected, or action on withdrawal of these units. If time permits of the construction of such a belt, it would seem uneconomical to hold it only lightly, and to allow the enemy some 6 or 8 km. in which to reorganize before he reaches even the protective belt.

(ii) A protective belt is constructed from 1 to 3 km. in front of the main position, and is held by strong protective detachments. The organization of this belt is not described, nor is it clear whether the troops holding it are found from the main position or from a reserve.

(iii) Behind this lies the main defensive position. Favourable ground for anti-tank defence is the primary consideration to be borne in mind in the selection of this main defensive position. The bulk of the anti-tank weapons are sighted within the position, but in front of the field artillery battery positions and main observation posts, so that a tank attack may not reduce the amount of observed artillery fire which can be brought to bear on the hostile infantry.

Protective detachments are put out in front of the main position. Their duty is laid down as being to prevent reconnaissance of the main dispositions and to give warning of attack while, at the same time, avoiding being drawn into any serious engagement.

(iv) A rear defensive position may be organized at a distance of 12 to 15 Km. from the main position, but its organization does not appear to be considered as always essential. The regulations leave it to the discretion of the higher commander, and state that the corps or general reserve will be located in its vicinity. The considerations governing its location are laid down as facilities for anti-tank defence, the range of the hostile artillery, and the necessity or otherwise for retaining at all costs a particular area of ground.

Observers at Red Army exercises have frequently reported on the absence of any arrangement for defence in depth, emphasising the impression that the whole conception of defence in the Red Army appears to be linear. It seems certain that the regulations are responsible for this conception. There is depth in so far as there is one position behind another : there is depth in the main position, in that it appears to be divided roughly into an infantry zone, anti-tank zone and an artillery zone : but there is no hint that defended localities should be mutually supporting from front to rear as well as across the front.

(b) *Counter-attacks.*—Counter-attacks are considered as the tasks of divisional and regimental reserves only. Battalions and smaller units are taught not to stage local counter-attacks, but to organize themselves for all round defence if overrun, relying on the regimental reserves to restore the situation.

The direction and strength of the counter-attack, the allotment and tasks of artillery (and in the case of the divisional reserve, of tanks) for its support, are laid down by divisional and regimental commanders in the orders for the conduct of the defence.

If hostile tanks break through, the mobile reserve of anti-tank guns are brought into action, and a tank counter-attack launched at once. In the confusion resulting from this counter-attack, and from those started locally by regiments in the line, the divisional commander launches his reserve in a counter-attack with artillery support. Counter-attacks by a corps reserve are supported by storm and light bombing aircraft.

Counter-attacks against parachute descents are organized by army or corps commanders.

(c) *Infantry in defence.*—It is laid down that the main position will be organized on an infantry corps or divisional basis, and the protective belt on an infantry regiment or battalion basis.

The following are laid down as suitable frontages and depths:—

	Frontage.	Depth.
Infantry division ..	8–12 Km.	4–6 Km.
Infantry regiment ..	3–5 Km.	2½–3 Km.
Infantry battalion	1½–2 Km.	1½–2 Km.

In organizing their sectors, commanders of all units are responsible for covering by fire all ground within 400 metres of their front and flanks. Emphasis is laid on the necessity for withholding fire and maintaining concealment until the enemy is sufficiently close for fire to reach its greatest effect.

Some heavy machine guns are always to be sited in the anti-tank gun area, in concealed positions from which they can enfilade the hostile infantry following behind the tanks.

(d) *Anti-tank defence.*—The Red Army regulations pay more attention to anti-tank measures than to any other form of defence. In the selection of a defensive position, the siting of the anti-tank gun area is first considered, and the disposition of other weapons decided in conformity with the anti-tank defence plan.

The anti-tank gun area is divided into sectors, each sector having all round defence, and its fire zones interlocking with those of neighbouring sectors. Emphasis is laid on the importance of concealment, and of siting some anti-tank weapons on reverse slopes. Ditches, mine fields, and other obstacles are to be covered by anti-tank guns. Anti-tank gun areas are laid down by divisional commanders. Infantry regimental commanders are then responsible for organizing and manning sectors within their regimental boundaries. The regulations do not indicate what happens to the anti-tank weapons of units in reserve, but they are presumably used as a mobile reserve or given a special task by the divisional commander. Divisional and regimental commanders are enjoined to have available a reserve of mobile anti-tank weapons : but definite guidance is limited to the organization of the anti-tank gun area, and the possibility of any large number of tanks getting through this area does not seen to be regarded seriously.

The anti-tank aspect of artillery defence is discussed in the paragraph that follows.

(e) *Artillery in defence.*—The idea of anti-tank work is predominant in the instructions for artillery in defence. It is laid down that every battery position must either afford facilities for direct-laying up to a range of 800 metres, or alternative gun positions which allow of this, and to which guns can move rapidly in the event of a tank attack, must be selected. Natural and artificial obstacles must be utilised to the full as protection against tanks. When the division is on a wide front, or in very close country, a group from the divisional artillery regiment is normally placed under the command of each infantry regimental commander.

When hostile tanks approach the forward edge of the main position, all batteries which can bring effective fire to bear on them are ordered to do so. As soon as the tanks pass through the defensive fire zone, and come under fire of shorter-range weapons, the bulk of the artillery fire is transferred to the hostile infantry following the tanks, which remains the principal target unless tanks approach so close to the battery position that they can be fired at by means of direct-laying. The separation of the infantry from the tanks immediately preceding them appears in fact to be the primary consideration in any fire plan. The artillery reverts to counter-preparation when it becomes clear that the forward elements of the attack have been held up.

(f) *A.F.V.s in the defence.*—A.F.V.s are used in the defence for counter attack ; and, in the case of a hastily organized defensive position, to form strong points in the defensive system. When used for the latter purpose they are generally covered with sods of earth, and the crews dig themselves dugouts just behind their tanks.

7. Night operations

Soviet regulations lay down that night operations must be regarded as normal in modern warfare, and that troops must be accustomed to march and manoeuvre at night from the very beginning of their training. Great emphasis is laid on the necessity for a simple plan.

The regulations lay down that on a moonlit night the rate of movement should be the same as by day, but on a dark night, and over indifferent roads, the pace may fall as low as 1 Km. per hour. In night marches normal distances are reduced, and, when possible, units are allotted to different roads according to their rate of movement.

Night attacks are usually carried out by battalions, and only rarely is a whole infantry regiment employed. A night attack by a division is considered most exceptional.

The regulations state that night attacks should have only very limited objectives and must be so timed that any exploitation of success can be carried out in daylight. Emphasis is laid on the need both for careful reconnaissance in daylight, and also for the instruction of guides who will lead units to the starting line, beyond which all movement will be straight to the front.

No firing of any kind is permitted until the enemy opens fire when artillery and machine-gun fire is opened on targets which have been previously registered by fire or by survey methods.

8. Warfare under special conditions

(a) *General principles.*—The Soviet manuals do not attempt to lay down general principles which can be applied to warfare under all the widely differing conditions in which their troops may have to fight.

(b) *Bush fighting.*—Bush, of the type found in the tropics, does not exist within the borders of the Soviet Union. The extent of wooded country is, however, so great as to call for special instructions for operations in it, and, although the woods and undergrowths are less dense than in most bush country, and the visibility less restricted, conditions are somewhat similar to those found in bush warfare.

Marches through woods are protected by strong reconnaissance bodies and where the depth of the woods permits, the forward edge and exits are seized before the main body enters. Where the depth of the wood is too great for this, the main body is split into columns, each with its own artillery and engineer troops, according to the number of tracks available. Protective detachments are sent forward along each track bounding from one lateral path or clearing to the next, and making contact with neighbouring protective detachments on each bound.

The attack in wooded country is treated in two phases; the assault on the forward edge, and the subsequent fighting within the wood. In the first phase control is centralized and artillery preparation is considered of first importance. It is considered that circumstances may arise in which the use of tanks may be possible. In the second phase, the Regulations state that the attack must become a dog fight, carried on by battalions with small artillery, engineer and possibly chemical units under their command.

The regulations mention the possibility of burning the wood but no guidance is given regarding the method to be employed. It is thought possible that incendiary bombs dropped from aircraft might be used.

It is noteworthy that no reference is made to the use of gas. As the Red Army makes a speciality of chemical warfare a possible explanation of the omission lies in an appreciation of the fact that the advance of an attacker may be prejudiced later if gas has been used.

In dealing with the defence of woods the regulations recommend that the forward edge should not be held. The defence is organized on a system of defended localities within the wood, having all round defence and covering natural and artificial clearings.

During the Finnish war the Red Army did not distinguish itself at forest fighting. Its failures were largely due to lack of individual initiative and leadership and to a strong inclination to cling to the roads and a consequent failure to patrol to sufficient depth into the woods. In addition the Russians have an instinctive fear of the dark.

(c) *Desert fighting.*—The Red Army manuals have little to say on the subject of desert fighting, and nothing which differs to any extent from the normal teaching. Mechanized units and aircraft may be expected to form the bulk of any Red Army formation taking part in desert operations.

(d) *Mountain warfare.*—Included in the Red Army are a number of mountain cavalry and infantry divisions which are stationed in mountainous districts and are recruited largely from local tribes.

Mountain warfare is regarded largely as the work of these special formations. If other formations are to be employed it is laid down that a certain proportion of mountain units, and of officers having experience in mountain warfare, should be attached to each column.

Emphasis is laid on the effectiveness of the mortar as a close support weapon. The regulations urge, however, that the artillery of mountain divisions should be brought up whenever roads are sufficiently good.

Considerable use is made of aircraft for reconnaissance, photographic survey, bombing transport and intercommunication. Owing to the special conditions affecting flight in mountainous regions, some special preliminary training is considered necessary for flying personnel before participating in mountain warfare.

It is laid down that marches shall not be of longer duration than ten hours. Long halts are given after six or seven hours marching. A ten-minute halt is given every hour and when ascents are steep additional halts of two or three minutes every fifteen or twenty minutes are allowed. The system of flank protection by pickets appears to be similar to our own.

(e) *Other special conditions.*—(i) *Built-up areas.*—The Soviet regulations place considerable value on built-up areas on account of the cover from view and from small arms fire which they afford, and also because of the ease with which they can be strengthened for defence, particularly against tanks. The system adopted in the attack of built-up areas is for heavy artillery and bombing aircraft to destroy the more heavily constructed buildings and then for infantry attacks to be launched usually round a flank so as to cut off the enemy still holding out in the centre.

(ii) *Winter warfare.*—Winter in Russia is characterized by intense cold, deep snow and usually short hours of daylight. The snow adds greatly to the difficulty of movement off roads, except for personnel on skis. On the other hand, the passage of rivers, lakes and marshes, which are numerous in western frontier regions, is greatly facilitated by winter frost. The short day, coupled with the fact that most movement can take place only on roads, frequently necessitates night marching.

The duration of a march is generally limited to six or seven hours. The size of columns is governed not only by the tactical situation, but by the amount of shelter which can be found at the end of the march. Marches must terminate in a village, wood, or other locality, where shelter from the wind is afforded, and where supplies of fuel can be obtained. Protection is afforded by infantry on skis, with battalion and regimental artillery weapons mounted on sleighs and drawn by gun crews when off the roads. The length of columns is reduced by marching the personnel on skis along the sides of, or across country in proximity to, the road. The general direction of an attack must usually be along a road, but every effort is made to bring about a surprise attack against one or other of the enemy's flanks. For this purpose a special group is organized with its mounted personnel on skis and guns mounted on sleighs hauled by their own crews, or in some cases being drawn by tracked or half-tracked vehicles. Tanks are also employed in the attack where possible. The movement to the starting line as a rule takes place at night, but the use of smoke to cover this movement, as well as of the frontal attack, is considered essential if the advance is by day.

The pursuit is carried out by infantry on skis, drawn by horses or tanks. A light tank normally draws a section of infantry. The general rule for the operation of tanks across country is that the depth of snow shall not be more than one foot.

Defensive positions, owing to the need for protection against cold, are usually so located that towns, villages or woods can be included in them. The line of forward defended localities must afford adequate protection of these sheltered areas.

It is often impossible to dig down, and in default of time and material, breastworks must be packed snow from six to twelve feet thick. Camouflage is regarded as of particular importance in winter and issues of white cloaks and hoods are made.

In practice Soviet commanders appear to have disregarded the importance of providing adequate shelter and food for their troops when operating under arctic conditions, and in Finland many cases occurred where men slept in the open and had to exist for two or three days without food merely because the advance was ordered without reference to administrative possibilities. The Soviet ski units which fought in Finland were inadequately trained and of little value.

Soviet troops appeared to be remarkably proficient at digging in, in spite of the frozen condition of the ground; dug-outs two or three stories deep were found in some of their positions.

9. Combined operations

(a) *General.*—It is probable that for any combined operations a commander for the whole operation would be appointed.

Two main types of combined operation are envisaged, namely landings, and the protection of the seaward flank of land forces.

(b) *Landings.*—Landings are envisaged normally as small operations in co-operation with land formations already engaged in the vicinity, and in which the landing party does not exceed an infantry regiment with its own artillery and possibly a company of tanks. The task of the landing party would be to attack against the flank or rear of the enemy.

No details are given regarding the method of execution or the special material available for employment in combined operations. It is, however, known that an exercise has been carried out in which amphibian tanks were launched from warships, and landed under their own power, but this was achieved only in a flat calm.

(c) *Protection of the seaward flank.*—It is laid down that protection of the seaward flank of land forces is achieved by :—

(i) A co-ordinated artillery fire plan, ships' guns engaging targets which cannot be reached by land armaments.

(ii) The installation, on temporary or permanent mountings, of coast defence guns.

(iii) The manœuvres of the fleet in being, or of such units of it as are in the neighbourhood of the land operations.

10. Conventional signs used in map reading

The conventional signs used, and methods of indicating units and formations on maps and sketches are given in Appendix " H."

CHAPTER XVIII

MILITARY AIR FORCES

1. General organization, distribution and strength

(a) *Organization*.—The air forces of the U.S.S.R. do not constitute a separate service but are part of the Red Army. They are divided into—

Air forces of the naval commands.
Air forces of the military districts.

They are all commanded by the Chief of the Air Forces under the supreme command of the N.K.O. and are administered by the Department of Military Air Forces, which is one of the Departments of the General Staff of the Red Army.

The air forces are subordinated for operations to their respective naval and military district commanders. They are, further, commanded by the local senior air force officer, who also acts as adviser to his naval or military commander.

The air forces of the naval commands are organized into air brigades, which consist of from three to six squadrons. The U.S.S.R. possess no aircraft carriers, though there are approximately 40 vessels in the Soviet navy which can carry aircraft.

The air forces of the military districts are organized similarly to those of the naval commands. There are also numerous independent flights or squadrons for co-operational duties with the army, and these move with the formations to which they are attached.

The air forces of the military districts comprise in the main fighter squadrons and the army co-operation units, consisting of bomber reconnaissance and "storm" (low-flying attack) aircraft. The army co-operation units and a majority of the fighter squadrons are located to correspond with the geographical organization of the army. Other fighter squadrons are distributed in accordance with the need for defending vital centres and points of strategic importance. It is believed to be the intention to allot permanently one reconnaissance squadron to each infantry corps, and possibly also to each mechanized corps.

There are indications, however, that the air forces of the military districts will be organized into air divisions. The air brigade consists of some three to six squadrons, and a quadron has three flights of two or three Zvenos (Links). A Zveno may consist of two or three aircraft, depending on the type of unit. It is the smallest tactical unit in the Russian air force.

The Red Air Force contains a number of independent flights. These units are self-contained and usually consist of nine army co-operation aircraft. This type of unit was evolved to meet the demand of the army for co-operation in outlying districts.

Each air brigade has an air park, the functions of which are to relieve the units in the brigade of the various ancillary ground services. Thus the air park, in addition to providing supply and minor repair services for units in the brigade, holds units' reserve aircraft, is in charge of guards and aerodrome labour and also contains the signals, photographic, meteorological, chemical and transport sections. Thus the units in the air brigade are purely flying units : they are not mobile on their own transport as they are moved by the air parks.

2. Distribution

The following table shows the general distribution of the Red Air Force in 1939 :—

Area.		Fighters.	Bombers.	Bomber Transport.	Storm and Army co-operation.	Naval.	Total.
	Military District.						
North-west	Leningrad M.D. Kalinin M.D. White Russia M.D. Moscow M.D. Baltic Sea (N).	648	676	72	580	72	2,048
South-west	Kiev M.D. Kharkov M.D. Orel M.D. Black Sea (N).	399	300	36	310	92	1,137
South-central	N. Caucasus M.D. Trans Caucasus M.D. Central Asia M.D. Pri Volga M.D. Ural M.D.	224	36	12	200	—	472
Far East	Siberian M.D. Trans Baikal M.D. Far East M.D. Pacific (N).	368	120	108	490	96	1,182
	Total	1,639	1,132	228	1,580	260	4,839

Over 80 per cent. of the Red Air Force is equipped with obsolete or obsolescent types.

(N) = Aircraft under Naval Command.

The U.S.S.R. claims to have 100,000 reserve pilots, but this figure is undoubtedly a gross exaggeration and includes glider pilots and members of model aeroplane clubs.

3. Air material

(a) Types and performance.—

Fighters

Type.	Description.	Maximum Speed.		Cruising Speed.		Service Ceiling.	Armament.	Bomb Load.
		Speed.	Endurance.	Speed.	Endurance.			
D.16	Two-seater single-engined biplane.	223 m.p.h.	—	—	—	32,000 ft.	—	110 lb.
I.15	Single-seater single-engined biplane.	220 m.p.h.	—	—	—	—	4 M.G.s	110 lb.
I.16	Single-seater single-engined biplane.	248 m.p.h.	1 hr.	190 m.p.h.	2¼ hrs.	—	2 or 4 M.G.s	—
I.16	Single-seater low-winged single-engined monoplane.	260 m.p.h.	0·85 hr.	200 m.p.h.	2 hrs.	31,500 ft.	2 or 4 M.G.s	—
I.17	Single-seater low-winged monoplane, single-engined.	—	—	—	—	—	—	—
Seversky	Two-seater low-winged, single-engined amphibian monoplane.	—	—	—	—	—	—	—

Military Aircraft

Type.	Purpose.	Description.	Maximum Speed.	Bomb Load.	Armament.	Endurance Range.
R.5	Army co-operation	Single-engined two-seater biplane.	143 m.p.h.	660 lb.	2 M.G.s	510 miles at 115 m.p.h.
S.S.S.	Ground attack ..	Single-engined two-seater biplane.	165 m.p.h.	660 lb.	5 M.G.s	—

Bombers

Type.	Description.	Maximum Speed.	Armament.	Bomb Load and Range at Cruising Speed.		
				Cruising Speed.	Bomb Load.	Range.
T.B.3	Four-engined high wing monoplane.	130 m.p.h. to 160 m.p.h.	6 M.G.s	125 m.p.h.	4,400 lb.	1,850 miles
T.B.6	Four-engined high wing monoplane. (Very few of this type in existence.)	280 m.p.h.	4 M.G.s 1 cannon	244 m.p.h.	5,500 lb.	950 miles
S.B.	Two-engined mid wing monoplane.	240 m.p.h. to 250 m.p.h.	4 M.G.s	220 m.p.h.	1,100 lb.	848 miles
	Ditto, later type ..	260 m.p.h.	4 M.G.s	228 m.p.h.	1,100 lb.	784 miles
Ts.K.B.	Two-engined low wing monoplane.	250 m.p.h. to 275 m.p.h.	3 M.G.s	200 m.p.h.	3,300 lb.	1,600 miles

(b) *Distinguishing marks and silhouettes.*—The distinguishing mark is a red five-pointed star which is shown on the outside of the main wing and on the fuselage.

4. Tactics and training

(a) *General principles.*—The primary role of the air forces now seems to be to afford direct assistance to the ground forces, its status being comparable to that of the tanks and artillery. In the event of the U.S.S.R. being engaged in a major war in the near future, medium and heavy bombers are likely to be employed at the outset in gaining ascendancy, and this will be achieved by the bombing of enemy aerodromes and air bases. What the objectives will be if and when air ascendancy has been obtained is not definitely known, but present policy points to the selection of objectives, the destruction of which will most directly assist the land forces, possibly lines of communication, rear services, etc.

The general efficiency of service training is low when compared with the standards of other major European powers. A point of interest however with regard to service training in the U.S.S.R. is the ease with which arrangements can be made for air firing and bombing practice. There is always a bog, moor or piece of waste land within reach of any service aerodrome, which can be utilised as a range.

Great importance is attached to the low-flying attack, and there is ample evidence that " storm " squadrons are specially trained in these duties. These squadrons in fact are becoming more numerous every year, and are given a very intensive training. They are frequently called upon to assist the infantry (whether held up or not) in taking objectives. In addition to these " storm " aircraft other air units including fighters and bombers are sometimes employed in low flying attacks. These attacks are usually executed by formations of any number of aircraft flying in flights of three in " flight line astern," the flights being Vee formation.

Machine-gun fire is the usual method of low flying attack, full advantage being taken of contours, woods, etc. While bombing is used on occasion in low flying attack this is frequently impossible owing to the very low heights at which these attacks are delivered. Smoke bombs are sometimes used and it it has been found that smoke screens of satisfactory density can be created.

Great importance is attached to the use of gas from the air. On every service aerodrome there is an air park which, apart from its other functions, contains a chemical company responsible for loading aircraft with toxic substances. Aircraft are fitted with spraying apparatus and during training troops are sprayed with liquids representing gas. Percussion gas bombs are also to be used mainly for the contamination of localities such as bridges and railway junctions. In addition to the ordinary gas bombing it is proposed to fill bombs with a non-persistent toxic substance weighing up to 700 lb. for use against enemy concentrations.

During recent years much interest has been shown by the Soviet General Staff in the landing of an armed force from the air behind the enemy lines. It is believed that such landings might be put to the following purposes :—

> The creation of a diversion against an enemy in position, by landing forces behind, and attacking the position from the rear.
>
> The creation of a diversion by landing a force well behind the enemy's main troops, and attacking the rear establishments.
>
> The landing of a force on an enemy key position, immediately after it had been over-run by tanks, for the purpose of dealing with enemy troops still resisting, and of holding the position until the arrival of organized bodies of infantry and artillery.
>
> The landing of a force to seize a bridge-head, aerodrome, etc.
>
> The landing of a force during an approach march in order to anticipate the enemy in an important position.
>
> The landing of trained agitators.

As regards the employment of aircraft for the transport of troops in friendly territory, the Soviet Union has had much experience in this work and no difficulty should be presented provided strategic and tactical conditions are favourable.

(b) *Army Co-operation.*—(i) *Reconnaissance.*—Generally speaking the methods employed by the Soviet Air Force are copied from foreign countries, and notably from France. Army co-operation as we know it has so far been only sketchily developed. There is a marked tendency to divert aircraft from reconnaissance tasks during their execution, in order to employ them for such operations as low flying attacks.

(ii) *Artillery reconnaissance.*—For artillery reconnaissance, artillery officers, usually allotted from the battery firing, are responsible both for making observations and for the defence of the aircraft. All young officers are trained in these duties. The normal method of conducting the shoot is for the observer to take command from the air and issue fire orders. A system somewhat similar to the British method of reporting the fall of the shot in relation to the target and having the necessary corrections applied to the guns, is also used but not generally favoured.

(iii) *Photography.*—Very little is known of the methods of photographic training employed in army co-operation units, and the information available is insufficient to estimate the degree of efficiency attained. It is to be noted, however, that photographic reconnaissance appears to have played a very small part in the collection of information during manœuvres. Experiments have undoubtedly been carried out in infra-red work.

(iv) *Intercommunication.*—Intercommunication between air and ground and vice versa is believed to be poor, judging by reports on manœuvres. W/T and R/T aircraft sets of Russian construction are used. R/T is used regularly during service training. Ground strips are also employed, as well as visual signalling both from air to ground and from ground to air. In artillery reconnaissance, communication is by two-way W/T manned by artillery personnel, but R/T can be used.

CHAPTER XIX

NAVAL

1. Policy

Up to 1935 comparatively little naval construction was carried out, as the requirements of the army and air force were given priority over those of the fleet. Since 1935, however, new construction has steadily increased, and it is the avowed policy of the Soviet Authorities to build a fleet of the first class. Up to the present considerable numbers of submarines and light torpedo craft have been constructed and a few cruisers of modern design have lately been completed. The new dreadnoughts which are under construction will probably not be completed until 1943 ; the existing dreadnoughts are 12-in. gun ships completed in 1911–13.

2. Strength and distribution

The Soviet fleet may be called upon to operate in five widely separated areas :—

        The White Sea.
        The Baltic.
        The Black Sea.
        The Caspian.
        The Far East.

The Soviet Navy may be said to be divided into five commands dealing with each of these theatres. So far as is known, the present distribution is :—

    (a) The Northern Fleet, based on Murmansk.
        4 large destroyers.
        15 small destroyers.
        26 submarines.
        Various auxiliaries.

    (b) The Baltic Fleet, based on Kronstadt.
        2 dreadnoughts.
        2 cruisers.
        3 light cruisers.
        14 large destroyers.
        13 small destroyers.
        57 submarines.
        60 M.T.Bs.
        Various auxiliaries.

(c) Black Sea Active Fleet, based on Sebastopol.
    1 battleship.
    3 or 4 modernised cruisers.
    3 light cruisers.
    22 destroyers.
    48 submarines.
    40 M.T.Bs.
    Various auxiliaries.

(d) Caspian Flotilla.
    2 gunboats.
    4 M.T.Bs.
    A number of armed launches, minesweepers, etc.

(e) Pacific Fleet, based on Vladivostok.
    2 light cruisers.
    12 destroyers.
    92 submarines.
    100 M.T.Bs.
    Various auxiliaries.

And, in addition, the Amur River Flotilla, based on Khabarovsk, consisting of about 20 gunboats and 40 armed launches and a few auxiliaries.

3. Marines

Marines do not exist in the Soviet Navy

APPENDIX "A"

TABLE OF RANKS OF OFFICERS AND N.C.O.s IN THE RED ARMY

Combatant appointment.		Engineer appointment.		Administrative appointment.	Army Medical appointment.	Army Veterinary appointment.	Military Judicial appointment.	Military Political appointment.
Land and Air Forces.	Naval Forces.	Land and Air Forces.	Naval Forces.					
Section Commander.	Section Commander.	—	—	—	—	—	—	—
Junior Platoon Commander.	Petty Officer.	—	—	—	—	—	—	—
Serjeant Major.	—	—	—	—	—	—	—	—
Mladshi Leitenant (Junior Lieutenant) (equivalent of an "aspirant" in the French Army).	—	—	—	—	—	—	—	—
Leitenant (Lieutenant).	Lieutenant.	Military Technician, 2nd Rank.	Military Technician, 2nd Rank.	Technician Commissary, 2nd Rank.	Military Assistant-Surgeon.	Military Veterinary Assistant-Surgeon.	Junior Military Lawyer.	Junior Political Leader.

For equivalent ranks in the British Army *see* Introductory Remarks to the Order of Battle.

Appendix "A"—continued
Table of Ranks of Officers and N.C.O.s in the Red Army—continued

Combatant appointment.		Engineer appointment.		Administrative appointment.	Army Medical appointment.	Army Veterinary appointment.	Military Judicial appointment.	Military Political appointment.
Land and Air Forces.	Naval Forces.	Land and Air Forces.	Naval Forces.					
Starshi Leitenant (Senior Lieutenant).	Senior Lieutenant.	Military Technician, 1st Rank.	Military Technician, 1st Rank.	Technician Commissary, 2nd Rank.	Senior Military Assistant-Surgeon.	Senior Veterinary Assistant-Surgeon.	Military Lawyer.	Political Leader.
Kapitan (Captain).	Captain Lieutenant.	Military Engineer, 3rd Rank.	Military Engineer, 3rd Rank.	Commissary, 3rd Rank.	Military Doctor, 3rd Rank.	Military Veterinary Doctor, 3rd Rank.	Military Lawyer, 3rd Rank.	Senior Political Leader.
Maior (Bn. Commander).	Captain, 3rd Rank.	Military Engineer, 2nd Rank.	Military Engineer, 2nd Rank.	Commissary, 2nd Rank.	Military Doctor, 2nd Rank.	Military Veterinary Doctor, 2nd Rank.	Military Lawyer, 2nd Rank.	Battalion Commissar.
Podpolkovaik (Lieutenant-Colonel).	—	—	—	—	—	—	—	—
Polkovnik (Colonel).	Captain, 2nd Rank.	Military Engineer, 1st Rank.	Military Engineer, 1st Rank.	Commissary, 1st Rank.	Military Doctor, 1st Rank.	Military Veterinary Doctor, 1st Rank.	Military, Lawyer, 1st Rank.	Regimental Commissar.
Kombrig (Brigade Commander).	Captain, 1st Rank.	Brigade Engineer.	Engineer Flag Officer, 3rd Rank.	Brigade Commissary.	Brigade Doctor.	Brigade Veterinary Doctor.	Brigade Lawyer.	Brigade Commissar.

For equivalent ranks in the British Army see Introductory Remarks to the Order of Battle.

Appendix "A"—*continued*

Table of Ranks of Officers and N.C.O.s in the Red Army—*continued*

Combatant appointment.			Engineer appointment.		Administrative appointment.	Army Medical appointment.	Army Veterinary appointment.	Military Judicial appointment.	Military Political appointment.
Land and Air Forces.	Naval Forces.		Land and Air Forces.	Naval Forces.					
Komdiv (Divisional Commander).	Flag Officer, 2nd Rank.		Divisional Engineer.	Engineer Flag Officer, 2nd Rank.	Divisional Commissary.	Divisional Doctor.	Divisional Veterinary Doctor.	Divisional Lawyer.	Divisional Commissar.
Komkor (Corps Commander).	Flag Officer, 1st Rank.		Corps Engineer.	Engineer Flag Officer, 1st Rank.	Corps Commissary.	Corps Doctor.	Corps Veterinary Doctor.	Corps Lawyer.	Corps Commissar.
Komandarm II (Army Commander, 2nd Rank).	Flag Officer of the Fleet, 2nd Rank.		Army Engineer.	Engineer Flag Officer of the Fleet.	Army Commissary.	Army Doctor.	Army Veterinary Doctor.	Army Lawyer.	Army Commissar, 2nd Rank.
Komandarm I (Army Commander, 1st Rank).	Flag Officer of the Fleet, 1st Rank.		—	—	—	—	—	—	Army Commissar, 1st Rank.
Marshal of the Soviet Union.									

For equivalent ranks in the British Army *see* Introductory Remarks to the Order of Battle.

APPENDIX "B"

MINIMUM PERIODS TO BE SERVED IN EACH RANK IN THE RED ARMY IN ORDER TO QUALIFY FOR PROMOTION

Commanders Land and Air Forces.	Commanders, Naval Forces.	Military Political Staff, Land, Air and Naval Forces.	Military Technical Staff, Land, and Air Forces.	Military Economic and Administrative Staff, Land, Air and Naval Forces.	Military Medical Staff, Land, Air and Naval Forces.	Military Veterinary Staff, Land, Air and Naval Forces.	Military Legal Staff, Land, Air and Naval Forces.	Qualifying periods.
Lieutenant	Lieutenant	Political Leader.	Military Technician, 2nd Rank.	Technician Quartermaster, 2nd Rank.	Military Medical Assistant.	Military Veterinary Assistant.	Junior Military Lawyer.	3 years.
Senior Lieutenant.	Senior Lieutenant.	Senior Political Leader.	Military Technician, 1st Rank.	Technician Quartermaster, 1st Rank.	Senior Military Medical Assistant.	Senior Military Veterinary Assistant.	Military Lawyer.	3 years.
Captain	Lieutenant-Captain.	Battalion Commissar.	Military Engineer, 3rd Rank.	Quartermaster, 3rd Rank.	Military Physician, 3rd Rank.	Military Veterinary Surgeon, 3rd Rank.	Military Lawyer, 3rd Rank.	4 years.
Major	Captain of 3rd Rank.	Regimental Commissar.	Military Engineer, 2nd Rank.	Quartermaster, 2nd Rank.	Military Physician 2nd Rank.	Military Veterinary Surgeon, 2nd Rank.	Military Lawyer, 2nd Rank.	4 years.
Colonel	Captain of 2nd Rank.	Brigade Commissar.	Military Engineer, 1st Rank.	Quartermaster, 1st Rank.	Military Physician 1st Rank.	Military Veterinary Surgeon, 1st Rank.	Military Lawyer, 1st Rank.	8 years.

APPENDIX "C"

U.S.S.R. Characteristics of Artillery Weapons
COAST DEFENCE.

Type of gun.	Calibre in inches.	Length of piece in calibres.	Weight of shell (lbs.).	Muzzle velocity, f.s.	Approx. max. range, yards.	Max. rate of fire.	Remarks.
14-in. coast defence	14	—	No details known.			—	There are believed to be some such guns among the coast defence armaments of the 11 defended ports of the U.S.S.R.
12-in. coast defence	12	52	900–1,037	2,500	35,000	?	Thought to be of modern design.
12-in. coast defence	12	40	?	2,900	31,500	?	Thought to be of modern design.
11-in. coast defence (1887)	11	35	760	2,635	13,800	?	
11-in. mortar (1887)	11	11·6	655	2,080	9,400	?	Nil.
10-in. coast defence (1900)	10	45	497	1,015	22,700	1 round every 2 minutes.	
9·5-in. coast defence	9·5	27	No details known.	2,580	—	1	Built at the Bolshevik Works, Leningrad, and was tried out in 1928. Results of trials unknown. Said to have a very long range. The Length of the piece is short compared with the British 9·2-in. gun which has a length of 46¾ calibres. (Shot travel 39 cals.).
9·2-in. coast defence	9·2	—	No details known.		—	—	There are believed to be 20 such guns among the coast defence armaments of the U.S.S.R.
9-in. mortar (1877)	9	11·7	300	1,070	8,500	?	Nil.
8-in. coast defence	8	—	No details known.			?	
6-in. Canet gun	6	45	91	2,635	14,700	?	
6-in. coast defence (1877)	6	22	90	1,535	9,700	?	
130-mm. naval gun	5·1	55	No details known.			?	Nil.
120-mm. Vickers pattern	4·7	50	52	3,100	15,400	?	A modern type of weapon.

Appendix "C"—continued

U.S.S.R. Characteristics of Artillery Weapons

HEAVY AND MEDIUM ARTILLERY

Type.	Calibre in inches.	Length of piece in calibres.	Weight of shell in lbs.	Muzzle velocity, f.s.	Approx. max. range, yards.	Weight in draught.	Weight in action.	Method of transport.	Max. rate of fire.	Time into action.	Remarks.
305-mm. howitzer, 1915.	12	20	850	1,460	15,000	Total 63.	Weight, tons.	Rail	1 rd. every 3 mins.	1¾ days	Nil.
305-mm. howitzer (Vickers).	12	15	740	1,200	11,500	?	?	Tractor	1 rd. every 3 mins.	?	Nil.
280-mm. howitzer (Schneider).	11	11·5	442 (605)	1,380	12,200	15 tons	?	Tractor	1 rd. per min.	1 hour	
250-mm. gun ..	10	45	490	2,575	22,600	Total 45.	Weight, tons.	Rail	1 rd. every 2 mins.	7 days	This is the same as the 10-in. (1900) coast defence weapon.
240-mm. mortar (French).	9·5	—	202	—	1,500	—	—	—	—	—	Possibly obsolete.
235-mm. mortar (British).	9·3	—	253	—	1,200	22 cwt.	22 cwt.	—	—	—	
210-mm. howitzer	8·3	—	—	No details known.		—	—	Kommunar caterpillar tractor.	—	—	A report stated that an increased number of these were on the 1st May, 1933 parade. Possibly confused with the 203-mm. howitzer.
203 mm. howitzer (Vickers).	8	15·9	196	1,320	10,000	170 cwt.	—	Tractor	2 rds. per min.	10 mins.	—

228

Appendix "C"—continued

U.S.S.R. Characteristics of Artillery Weapons. Heavy and Medium Artillery—continued

Type.	Calibre in inches.	Length of piece in calibres.	Weight of shell in lbs.	Muzzle velocity, f.s.	Approx. max. range, yards.	Weight in draught.	Weight in action.	Method of transport.	Max. rate of fire.	Time into action.	Remarks.
203-mm. howitzer	8	—	—	No details known.			—	Kommunar caterpillar tractor.	—	—	Reported to be a new type. "Had three buffer springs, one over the barrel." Vickers knew of no howitzer answering to this description.
152-mm. gun (gun-how.?)	6	30	90	1,980	Greater than 13,000	5¾ tons	5 tons	Kommunar caterpillar tractor.	1 rd. per min.	—	The piece is the same as the old 1904 type, but has been fitted with a "Recoil Check and Silencer." Gun carriage is new. Range is stated to be much greater than the old pattern. A model probably 1933, fitted with split trail maximum elevation about 40° vertical buffers, or recuperators.
152-mm. gun, 1904	6	30	90	1,980	13,000	5¾ tons	5 tons	12 horses or tractor.	1 rd per min.	3 hours	These are being converted by the addition of a "Recoil Check and Silencer" and a new type of carriage.
152-mm. Canet gun.	6	45	90	2,635	14,700	Total 19½.	Weight, tons.	Rail	5 rds. per min.	2 days	The piece is the same as the coast defence 6-in. Canet gun. Manufacture transferred to Perm. Works.

Appendix "C"—*continued*

U.S.S.R. Characteristics of Artillery Weapons. Heavy and Medium Artillery—*continued*

Type.	Calibre in inches.	Length of piece in calibres.	Weight of shell in lbs.	Muzzle velocity, f.s.	Approx. max. range, yards.	Weight in draught.	Weight in action.	Method of transport.	Max. rate of fire.	Time into action.	Remarks.
152-mm. (Schneider ?) gun.	6	45/50	90	2,100	13,500	—	5½ tons	Kommunar tractor.	2 rds. per min.	10 mins.	It is not certain whether this gun is Schneider.
152-mm. howitzer, 1910.	6	13·5	90	1,120	8,600–11,000	3 tons	2½ tons	8 horses or tractor.	2 rds. per min.	10 mins.	With streamline shell range is said to be 11,100 yards.
122-mm. Obukhov. gun.	4·8	50	45	3,100	16,000	11 tons	?	24 horses or 2 tractors.	2 rds. per min.	3 hours	Probably obsolescent. The muzzle velocity stated is very high. A second report has given it as 1,700 f.s. and a maximum range of 14,000 yards.
107-mm. gun, 1910	4·25	28	36½	1,930	13,000	2 tons	2 tons	Kommunar caterpillar tractor or horse-drawn.	4 rds. per min.	10 mins.	—
107-mm. gun, 1910/1930.	4·25	40	36½	1,930	13,000–18,000	2¼ tons.	2 tons	Tractor or horse-drawn.	4 rds. per min. 6–7 ?	10 mins.	This is the same as the 1910 type but has been fitted with a "Recoil Check and Silencer."
122-mm. gun	—	40	—	—	—	—	—	—	—	—	M.A. was not certain whether 40 calibres, 122-mm. guns were on parade 7th Nov., 37, may have been 107-mm. guns (*vide* M.A. 295 d. 9th Nov., 37).

Appendix "C"—continued

U.S.S.R. Characteristics of Artillery Weapons
FIELD, HORSE, MOUNTAIN AND ANTI-TANK

Type.	Calibre in inches.	Length of piece in calibre.	Weight of shell, lbs.	Muzzle velocity, f.s.	Approx. maximum range, yards.	Weight in draught.	Weight in action.	Method of transport.	Maximum rate of fire.	Remarks.
122-mm. howitzer, 1909/1910.	4·8	14	51	1,100	8,400	2 tons	—	—	—	Range with streamline shell said to be 10,500 yards.
122-mm. howitzer, 1910/1930.	4·8	12·8	51	760	8,400	2 tons 6 cwt.	1 ton 9 cwt.	Towed by Citroen-Kegresse car.	4–5 rounds per min.	Fitted with a muzzle brake (one type seen without). Carriage has pneumatic tyred wheels. Same ballistics as 1909 pattern. Said to be an excellent weapon. Barrels of light construction and the pieces sometimes burst at the muzzle end. Box trail. Fires shrapnel streamline shell. No pneumatic tyres on one type.
113-mm. howitzer (British type).	4·5	15·5	34¾	1,000	6,800	2 tons 2 cwt.	1 ton 7 cwt.	6 horses	2 rounds per min.	
90-mm. howitzer	3·56	—	No details known.		—	—	—	4 horses		Said to look like a pack-draught weapon. This is probably the 45-mm. howitzer.
76-mm. gun, 1902	3	30	14	193°	9,300	2 tons	20 cwt.	6 horses	10 rounds per min.	Obsolete.
76-mm. gun, 1913	3	16·5	14·1	900	2,600	11 cwt.	11 cwt.	6 horses	15 (?) rds. per min.	Believed obsolete.
76-mm. gun, 1927	3	16·5	14	1,270	6,900	29 cwt.	15 cwt.	4 horses or carried-on lorries (portee).	6 to 12 rounds per min.	A light and easily transportable gun. No novel features. Falls between three stools: close support, anti-tank and divisional artillery. Box trail. One model fitted with split trail.

Appendix "C"—*continued*

U.S.S.R. Characteristics of Artillery Weapons. Field, Horse, Mountain and Anti-Tank—*continued*

Type.	Calibre in inches.	Length of piece in calibres.	Weight of shell, lbs.	Muzzle velocity, f.s.	Approx. maximum range, yards.	Weight in draught.	Weight in action.	Method of transport.	Maximum rate of fire.	Remarks.
76-mm. gun, 1902/1930.	3	40	14	1,930	11,000	2 tons	1 ton	Tractors or 6-horse team. (Also carried on lorries (portee). Horse-drawn.	6 rounds per min. (maximum 15 r.p.m.).	Fitted with a muzzle brake. Carriage has rubber-tyred wheels and permits of a greater maximum elevation, probably of a box trail type. Improved design of shell. Buffer and recuperator mounted above barrel.
76-mm. Q.F. gun, 1933.	3	55–60 calibres.	15¼	—	12,500 or more, possibly 14,000.	—	24 cwt.	—	—	Carriage manufactured 1934. Maximum traverse 20°. Maximum elevation 45°. Said to be made at Taritsin works. None issued to formations. Split trail. No muzzle brake. Telescopic dial sight. Streamline shell. No pneumatic tyres.
76-mm. mountain gun, 1909.	3	16·5	14 ?	1,270	7,200	1 ton 4 cwt.	12 cwt.	Mule draught or pack	10 rounds per min.	Charge weight 1·76 lbs. Box trail. For pack transport gun and limber divided into eight pack loads.
57-mm. Nordenfeldt.	2·25	—	—	—	6,500	—	—	Limber drawn by 2 horses.	22 rounds per min.	Obsolescent or obsolete.
Close support 45-mm. howitzer (1929).	1·78	26	Complete round 9 (shell 4¾)	1,280	3,400	472 lbs.	—	—	—	Can be transported in sections. Probably only experimental.
40-mm. Vickers	1·59	40	2⅖	2,000	6,000	—	—	Tractor	200 rounds per min.	

233

Appendix "C"—*continued*

U.S.S.R. Characteristics of Artillery Weapons. Field, Horse, Mountain and Anti-Tank—*continued*

Type.	Calibre in inches.	Length of piece in calibres.	Weight of shell, lbs.	Muzzle velocity, f.s.	Approx. maximum range, yards.	Weight in draught.	Weight in action.	Method of transport.	Maximum rate of fire.	Remarks.
37-mm. Rosenberg (1927).	1·46	19–23	1 lb. 5 oz.	1,450	3,500	400 lbs.	400 lbs.	Light 1-horse limber or in an ordinary 1-horse vehicle.	8 rounds per min.	Effective range 1,500 yards.
37-mm. (Obukhov)	1·46	22·5	—	1,500	2,850	400 lbs.	—	—	20 rounds per min.	Obsolete types. Small M.V. short barrels.
37-mm. (Krupp)	1·46	23·5	1 lb. 2 oz.	1,475	2,650	—	400 lbs.	—	—	
37-mm. Hotchkiss	1·46	21·5	—	1,800	4,700	Including mounting, 660 lbs.	—	—	—	
37-mm. Maklen (MacLean?).	1·46	50	1 lb. 1 oz.	2,150	4,000	Including mounting, 670 lbs.	—	Light 2-horse limber or light caterpillar tractor.	20 rounds per min. (30?)	Effective range 1,500 yards.
37-mm. anti-tank gun.	1·46	45	1 lb. 7 oz.	2,650	7,600	Complete, 682 lbs.		Transported in a vehicle or drawn by means of a limber.	20 rounds per min.	Said to be an accurate and powerful anti-tank weapon. Will penetrate armour:— *Range. Thickness.* 50 metres :: 80 mm. 300 ,, :: 45 ,, 500 ,, :: 38 ,, 1,000 ,, :: 20–30 mm.

Appendix "C"—*continued*

U.S.S.R. Characteristics of Artillery Weapons. Field, Horse, Mountain and Anti-Tank—*continued*

Type.	Calibres. in inches.	Length of piece in calibres.	Weight of shell, lbs.	Muzzle velocity, f.s.	Approx. maximum range, yards.	Weight in draught.	Weight in action.	Method of transport.	Maximum rate of fire.	Remarks.
37 mm. (Bofors)	1·46	—	—	No details known			—	—	—	Experimental as infantry close support weapon.
25 mm. gun ..	1	—	Complete round, 1·43 lbs.	—	5,500	Total weight, 400 lbs.		—	100 rounds per min.	15 shells in a belt. Belts are changed automatically. Said to be manufactured at the Tsaritsin works. Not yet been supplied to any formations.
20-mm. automatic anti-aircraft and anti-tank gun.	0·8	65	¼ lb.	2,750	6,200	1,300 lbs. ?		1 or 2 horses (limber with 600 rounds).	200 ? rounds per min.	This gun is considered to be the same or very similar to the Solothurn S.S-100. It has the following armour piercing performance:— 100 metres .. .. 35 mm. 300 ,, ... 24 ,, 500 ,, ... 19 ,, 1,000 ,, ... 12 ,,
20-mm. anti-tank gun (German design), 1926.	0·8	—	—	2,500	1,350	—	220 lbs.	Mounted on motor cycles.	300 rounds per min.	Reports state that three were imported during the summer of 1926, and that probably 250 more will be ordered. Can penetrate 20 mm. of armour up to a range of 550 yards. It is possible that this gun is the same as the one above, *i.e.*, the S.S-100.

Appendix "C"—continued

U.S.S.R. Characteristics of Artillery Weapons

ANTI-AIRCRAFT

(i) Mobile Guns.

Type.	Calibre in inches.	Length of piece in calibres.	Weight of shell, lbs.	Muzzle velocity, f.s.	Approximate maximum vertical range in yards.	Weight.	Method of Transport.	Maximum rate of fire.	Remarks.
4·7 anti-aircraft gun.	4·7	—	—	—	14,000	—	—	—	Maximum elevation, 80°. A report states that 60 of these guns were ordered in 1924, to be made at the State Artillery factory, "Bolshevik."
85-mm. anti-aircraft gun.	3·35				No details known.				A report stated that an order for 15 was to have been completed by 1st January, 1927, and that a further 85 were to be ordered. These guns are of modern design, probably German.
8-cm. Bofors anti-aircraft gun.	3·15	50	17·6	2,500	Vertical, 10,800; horizontal, 18,000.	Draught, 4 tons; in action, 3 tons.	Tractor	—	A report stated that "two or three" were delivered to the U.S.S.R. in 1933, and that the right to manufacture has been purchased from Bofors.
Anti-aircraft	3				No details known.				No details are known. Said to be a new type. Was seen on 1st May, 1932, parade (one battery).
76·2-mm. anti-aircraft gun, 1914.	3	25·3	14⅜	1,935	6,000	Draught, 10 tons, including lorry.	Mounted on lorry.	10 rounds per min.	Of little value against modern aircraft. Central pivot mounting bolted into floor of lorry.

Appendix "C"—*continued*

U.S.S.R. Characteristics of Artillery Weapons. Anti-Aircraft—*continued*

(i) Mobile Guns—*continued*.

Type.	Calibre in inches.	Length of piece in calibres.	Weight of shell, lbs.	Muzzle velocity, f.s.	Approximate maximum vertical range in yards.	Weight.	Method of Transport.	Maximum rate of fire.	Remarks.
76·2-mm. field gun on improvised wooden anti-aircraft mounting "Ivanov."	3	30	14¾	1,960	Vertical, horizontal, 9,400.	On normal fd. carriage, 22 cwt.	Horse-drawn. The special anti-aircraft mounting is drawn separately by a team of four horses.	10 rounds per min.	Is in nature of improvisation. Doubtful if of much value against modern aircraft.
76·2-mm. anti-aircraft gun, 1931.	3	50	14¾	3,000	Vertical, 10,500; horizontal, 15,500.	3¾ tons. In action, 2⅞ tons.	Tractor drawn.	20–25 rds. per min.	Single axle travelling carriage, cross type mounting. Very much like the Bofors 76·2-mm. gun and is probably the standard Russian anti-aircraft equipment. The M.V. given is probably too high; 2,500 f.s. is perhaps nearer.
76-mm. gun, 1915/1928.	3	40	—	2,130	8,400	3 tons 4 cwt.	—	12–15 rds. per min.	This has not the performance of a modern weapon and is probably obsolete.

Appendix "C"—*continued*

U.S.S.R. Characteristics of Artillery Weapons. Anti-Aircraft—*continued*

(i) Mobile Guns—*continued*.

Type.	Calibre in inches.	Length of piece in calibres.	Weight of shell, lbs.	Muzzle velocity, f.s.	Approximate maximum vertical range in yards.	Weight.	Method of Transport.	Maximum rate of fire.	Remarks.
76-mm. anti-aircraft gun, 1923.	3	50	14·8	2,600	10,000	2¾ tons, plus lorry 5¾ tons.	Lorry, or alternatively mounted on a 4-wheel trailer and drawn by a tractor.	50 rounds per min.	150 of these guns were to have been made during 1926. In some cases they are fitted with the new "recoil check and silencer." Maximum elevation 85°. Said to resemble the U.S.A. and Bofors guns.
47-mm. anti-aircraft gun (Obukhov).	1·85	—	2½ lbs.	3,200	3,300	—	—	90 rounds per min.	A fully automatic weapon. It is thought that this very high muzzle velocity is likely to cause rapid "wear." It is considered that this is too small a calibre except against low-flying planes.
40-mm. anti-aircraft gun, Vickers.	1·59	40	2½ lbs.	2,000	8,300	—	—	300 rounds per min.	Fires a proportion of tracer ammunition. Also used on fixed mounting. Fully automatic weapon for use against low-flying aircraft.
105-mm. anti-aircraft gun.	4·2	60	33	—	14,300 (horizontal range, 19,800).	In action, 10⅜ tons.	—	20 rounds per min.	Angles of fire :—Elevation; 80°. Depression, 5°. Traverse, 360°. (*Vide* CX.9542I/0205, d.25.1.38).

Appendix "C"—*continued*

U.S.S.R. Characteristics of Artillery Weapons. Anti-Aircraft—*continued*

(ii) Non-mobile Guns (forming part of Coast Defence).

Type.	Calibre in inches.	Length of piece in calibres.	Weight of shell, lbs.	Muzzle velocity, f.s.	Approximate maximum vertical range in yards.	Approximate maximum range horizontal.	Maximum elevation.	Maximum rate of fire.	Remarks.
76-mm., adapted for anti-aircraft, 1900.	3	30	13	1,960	5,500	10,000	80°	—	These guns have a poor performance compared with a modern design of anti-aircraft gun by, say, Armstrong-Vickers.
76-mm. anti-aircraft, 1914.	3	30	13	1,960	5,500	10,000	65°	30 rounds per min.	
76-mm. anti-aircraft, 1915.	3	30	13	1,960	6,000	10,000	75	30 rounds per min.	
75-mm. naval gun, adapted for anti-aircraft.	3	50	13	2,490	(5,500) ?	11,000	60	15 rounds per min.	

APPENDIX "D"

TOOLS AND ENGINEER STORES CARRIED IN VARIOUS UNITS (APPROXIMATELY)

Equipment carried in:		Infantry company.	Infantry battalion (includes column 1).	Infantry regiment (includes columns 1 and 2).	Sapper and camouflage platoon.	Sapper troop (of cavalry regiment).	Sapper company.	Sapper squadron.	Divisional engineer park.
Entrenching tools (a).	Shovels (or spades)	14	54	300	150	150	100	100	1,500
	Hatchets	20	70	—	—	—	—	—	150
	Light axes	2	20	150	75	75	75	75	200
	Heavy axes	—	—	—	75	50	10	5	150
	Light picks	20	60	200	20	20	20	8	100
	Heavy picks	2	7	50	20	20	20	16	30
	Crowbars	—	2	20	15	15	20	16	20
	Chisels	—	—	—	5	4	20	8	20
	Cross-saws	—	1	14	20	6	20	8	150
Field fortification equipment (b).	Barbed wire, kg.	—	—	—	1,500	—	—	—	4,000
	Fasteners	—	—	—	?	—	—	—	250
	Sandbags	—	—	—	—	50	250	200	3,000
	Wire-cutters	—	—	—	50	70	20	8	50
	Ventilators (1)	—	—	—	—	—	—	—	—
Camouflage equipment (c).	No. 4 camouflage nets	—	—	—	150	40	40	40	60
	"Masks" for M.G.s and Bn. Art.	9	4	10	—	—	—	—	—
	Camouflage covers (U.Z.H.)	—	—	67	100 ?	22	12	4	12
	Camouflage clothing (summer)	—	20	67	200 ?	22	12	4	—
	Camouflage clothing (winter)	—	20	67	220	22	12	4	—
	Summer camouflage smocks	—	20	67	220	22	12	4	—
	Winter	—	—	—	—	—	12	4	—

240

Appendix "D"—continued
Tools and Engineer Stores carried in various Units (approximately)—continued

	Equipment carried in :	Infantry company.	Infantry battalion (includes column 1).	Infantry regiment (includes columns 1 and 2).	Sapper and camouflage platoon.	Sapper troop (of cavalry regiment).	Sapper company.	Sapper squadron.	Divisional engineer park.
Explosives	Contact fuzes	—	—	—	50	50	250	100	500
	1931 pattern exploders	—	—	—	—	—	2	—	2
	P.M.2 exploders	—	—	—	1	1	4	3	5
	Explosives (D.V.V.), Kg.	—	—	—	150	150	600	600	1,500
	Anti-tank land mines	—	—	—	150	100	500	250	1,500
Water equipment	Hand-pumps	—	—	—	—	3	—	—	—
	Norton tube-walls	—	—	—	—	1	3	—	—
	Reservoirs	—	—	—	—	3	—	1	—
	Pack-fitters	—	—	—	—	—	—	—	—
Mechanical equipment.	Motor saws	—	—	—	—	—	4	2	2
	Motor saw-mill	—	—	—	—	—	—	—	1
Bridging and ferrying equipment.	Polyanski floats	—	—	—	—	—	—	—	1,000
	T.Z.I. standard set	—	—	—	1	1	—	—	—
	Small pneumatic boats	—	—	—	3	3	—	—	—
	A-3 pneumatic boat, etc. (standard set).	—	—	—	—	—	—	—	1 set
	1931 pattern floating suits	—	—	—	3	—	4	—	4
	Compressor station	—	—	—	—	—	—	—	1
	Pneumatic apparatus, sets	—	—	—	—	—	—	—	2
	Folding pile driver	—	—	—	—	—	—	—	1

The road-building equipment carried in Divisional Engineer Park has been shown under paragraph 4 of this chapter.

Notes :— (1) For deep dugouts.
(2) Sufficient to build a footbridge 56 metres long.
(3) Sufficient to build 120 metres light bridge, 85 metres medium bridge or 70 metres of heavy bridge.

APPENDIX "E"

1. Infantry regiment chemical platoon

(*a*) Organization—
> Headquarters.
> Three chemical warfare sections.
> One transport section.

(*b*) Stores—
> 10 per cent. reserve gas masks for the regiment.
> Four decontamination sprayer outfits.
> 15 sirens for gas alarm.
> Chloride of lime.
> Toxic smoke candles.
> Smoke producing apparatus.
> 40 gasproof suits (war establishment).

The war strength of the platoon is about 45 men, 16 horses and eight vehicles.

2. Cavalry chemical troop

The chemical troop consists in peace of O.C., one chemical instructor and five other ranks.

The war establishment is reported to be 17 men, 19 horses and two carts.

3. Artillery chemical detachment

Details not available.

4. Sapper chemical section

Details not available.

242

APPENDIX "F"

SOVIET TANK TYPES

Type	Class	Crew	Engine	Transmission	Overall dimensions — Length	Breadth	Height	Width of track	Weight in tons	Max speed m.p.h. On roads	Across country	Obstacle crossing — Climbs	Crosses	Circuit of action in miles	Armour basis	Armament — Guns	A.T. guns	M.Gs.	Ammn. carried rds.	Remarks
T.27	Tankette	2	40 A.A. Ford	Ford planet differential steering	8' 2"	5' 8"	3' 6"	—	2	22	20	45° 1' 4" cert.	3' 6" Fords 2' 2"	120	8 mm.	—	—	One 7·6 mm.	—	An improved type (T.38) has lately been introduced. No details available but it is generally similar to T.37.
T.37	Light amphib.	2	Meadows 6 cyl. 56 H.P.	Differential	14' 3"	5' 10"	7' 2"	—	—	In water.	25	—	—	—	11 mm.	—	—	One 7·6 mm.	—	—
T.26	Light medium	3	Russian made engine, 90 h.p. (V) or 80 b.p.	4-speed and low reduction gear-reverse steering couplings, radius of turn 43'.	16' 4"	8' 0"	7' 2"	9·2"	8·5	26 22 ?	20	45° climbs 2' 6" vert.	6' 0" Fords 3' 0"	160	13–16 mm.	—	One 47 mm.	One 7·6 mm.	4,000 S.A.A. 30 shell.	This is a single turret model. The two-turret model carries 2 M.G.s and no gun.

Appendix "F"—*continued*

Soviet tank types—*continued*

Type.	Class.	Crew.	Engine.	Transmission.	Overall dimensions.			Width of track.	Weight in tons.	Maximum speed, m.p.h.		Obstacle crossing capacity.		Circuit of action in miles.	Armour basis.	Armament.			Ammn. carried. rds.	Remarks.
					Length.	Breadth.	Height.			On roads.	Across country.	Climbs.	Crosses.			Guns.	A.P. guns.	M.G.s		
B.T.	Light medium	3	Liberty V-12 350 h.p. or 280 h.p.	4-speed and reverse	19 2	7	2 7 8	—	11	On wheels 45.	On tracks at least 30.	40° 2' 6" vert.	6' 2"	100 248 (H) (V).	16 mm.	—	One 45 mm.	One 7·6 mm.	—	Front vertical plate, 20 mm.
T.28	Medium	8	Hispano-Suiza, 750 h.p.	—	—	—	—	—	27	—	25	—	—	100	Front and turret 26 mm. Side 16 mm. Deck and floor 10 mm.	One 76 mm.	—	Four 7·6 mm. One A.A. M.G. 7·6 mm.	—	—
M.I.	Heavy	6	250 h.p. (V) V.12 cyl.	—	24 0	9 9	9 10	—	33	29	—	43° 3' 3" vert.	7' 0" Fords 4' 0"	124 (H).	35 mm.	—	One 37 mm.	Three 7·6 mm.	—	Possibly experimental models of the T.32.

245

Appendix "F"—continued
Soviet tank types—continued

Type.	Class.	Crew.	Engine.	Trans-mission.	Overall dimensions.			Width of track.	Weight in tons.	Maximum speed, m.p.h.		Obstacle crossing capacity.		Circuit of action in miles.	Armour basis.	Armament.			Amm. carried. rds.	Remarks.
					Length.	Breadth.	Height.			On roads.	Across country.	Climbs.	Crosses.			Guns.	A.P. guns.	M.G.s		
M.2	Heavy	12	350 h.p. V.12 (V) cyl.	Hydraulic	31' 0"	9' 10"	9' 2"	—	36	19	—	40° 3' 0" vert.	15' Hand V Fords 4' 0"	186 (H).	25 mm.	One 76 mm.	Two 37 mm.	Two 7·6 mm.	—	Replica Vickers Independent 36-ton tank? One main, two forward and one rear turret.
T.32 T.35	Heavy tanks.	—	—	—	30' 6"	6' 0"	9' 0"	—	30 to 36	30 to 36	18	—	—	—	44 mm. to 16 mm.	One 76·2 mm. gun. One 76·2 mm. gun.	One 45 mm. gun.	Five 7·62 mm. M.G.s One 7·62 mm. A.A. M.G. or Six 7·62 mm. M.G.s One 7·62 mm. A.A. M.G.	—	There are numerous variations in the armament and equipment of these tanks.

APPENDIX "G"

METHOD OF COMMUNICATION BETWEEN GROUND AND AIR

Army co-operation

1. Army co-operation machines, which maintain liaison between units and headquarters, bear the following distinguishing mark :—

2. Co-operation machines communicate with ground units by means of klaxon horns and lamps. Ground units signal their positions by means of smoke, white flags, or tin reflectors measuring 15 cms. in diameter.

3. According to general instructions, infantry units should be able to signal to planes at any time. In practice, however, serious difficulties have been encountered, and it is now laid down that time and/or position from which infantry intend to communicate must be determined beforehand.

4. On the approach of the co-operation plane, a piece of dark blue cloth measuring $7 \cdot 75 \times 9 \cdot 25$ metres and bearing the number of the regiment in white is spread out on the ground. In the case of a battalion, the same sign is used, but with the addition of the battalion's number in smaller figures underneath the regimental number.

5. As soon as the plane has identified the unit, signalling commences by means of a form of Popham panel, which consists of white strips on a dark blue square measuring $7 \cdot 5 \times 9$ metres. The horizontal bar of the T always placed nearest the enemy.

6. The panel is numbered as shown in the accompanying sketch, page 248.

7. The code used in the Polish campaign was compromised by deserters and a new code, as given below, has been adopted for the Finnish campaign.

8. It should be noted that each sentence commences with the sign I and ends with the sign T.

APPENDIX "G"—*continued*

Method of communication between ground and air—*continued*

9. The Air Force observer records the various positions of the panel on special forms on which the T frame-work is printed. Messages are subsequently decoded at headquarters.

Code

	67	Signal received.
	6789	Message ended.
	136	First objective reached.
	145	Second objective reached.
	245	Third objective reached.
	246	Final objective reached.
	247	Am preparing to advance.
	248	Our troops are proceeding to ——.
	567	We have no news of our advanced units.
	256	I am held up by enemy fire from ——.
	257	I am held up by wire at ——.
	578	Advance of left flank has been checked.
	389	Advance of right flank has been checked.
	678	Counter attack successful.
	679	Counter attack repulsed.
	134	I am moving my headquarters to ——.
	135	I am in touch with my left flank.
	137	I am in touch with my right flank.
(?)	145	I am in touch with both flanks.
	156	Our forces are near ——.
	235	Am out of touch with right flank.
	236	Am out of touch with left flank.
	234	No messages received from advanced troops.
	258	I am sending report by pigeon.
	259	I am sending report by orderly.
	267	Heavy losses.
	167	Enemy is located ——.
	168	Enemy is concentrating at ——.
	456	Our troops are retiring ——.
	467	Enemy has penetrated my centre.
	468	Enemy has penetrated my left flank.
	469	Enemy has penetrated my right flank.
	456	Enemy advancing.
	457	Enemy commencing counter attack.
	458	Enemy counter attack repulsed.

APPENDIX "G"—*continued*

Method of communication between ground and air—*continued*

Code.

345	Barrage not required.
346	Shorten barrage.
347	Lengthen barrage.
459	Concentrated gunfire.
478	Artillery fire still required.
579	A.T. guns in action near ——.
123	Require reinforcements.
124	Stretcher bearers required.
125	Rations running short.
126	Carrier pigeons required.
127	Shortage of ammunition.
128	Shortage of S.A.A.
129	Shortage of hand grenades.
157	Shortage of water.
158	Shortage of Verey lights.
1234	Westerly direction.
1235	Northerly direction.
1246	Southerly direction.
1247	Easterly direction.
1258	North-westerly direction.
1259	South-westerly direction.
1345	North-easterly direction.
1346	South-easterly direction.

APPENDIX "G"—*continued*

Method of communication between ground and air—*continued*

Code for use by Artillery in Communication with Planes equipped with W/T

2345	Yes.
2346	No.
2347	Am repeating last signal.
2348	Please repeat.
2349	I understand.
2356	I do not understand.
2357	Communication established.
2358	I am not in communication.
2359	Your signals weak.
2367	Your signals are stronger.
2368	Your signals good strength.
2369	Repeat call sign.
2378	Change to wavelength ——.
2379	Battery No. ——.
2389	Battery has fired one round.
2456	Battery not yet ready.
2457	Battery is ready.
2458	Ranging concluded.
2459	Please correct target No.
2467	I am correcting fire by means of my observer.
2468	Wait. The battery has ceased fire for a short period only.
2469	Land. The battery has ceased fire.
2478	Change over to dispersed fire.
2489	Land. All over.
2567	Action broken off.

APPENDIX "G"—*continued*

Method of communication between ground and air—*continued*

1	1
2	2
3	3
4	4
5	5
6	6
7	7
8	8
9	9
123456789	0
12	B
13	W
14	A
15	W
16	W
17	W
18	W
19	E
23	W
24	W
25	M
26	H
27	K
28	W
29	O
34	C
35	W
36	P
37	W
38	y
39	T
45	W
46	X
47	W
48	W
68	W
69	W
79	—

APPENDIX "H"
CONVENTIONAL SIGNS USED IN THE RUSSIAN ARMY AND ON RUSSIAN MAPS

Headquarters

H.Q., Front (South-Western)
Штаб фронта (юго-западного)

H.Q., 5th Army
Штаб 5-й армии

H.Q., 2nd Corps
Штаб 2-го стрелкового корпуса

H.Q., 10th Division
Штаб 10-й стрелковой дивизии

H.Q., 15th Regiment
Штаб 15-го стрелкового полка

H.Q., 7th Reserve Regiment
Штаб 7-го запасного полка

H.Q., 1st Battalion, 5th Regiment
Штаб 1-го батальона 5-го стрелкового полка

Infantry

5th Division
5-я стрелковая дивизия

15th Regiment
15-и стрелковый полк

1st Battalion, 3rd Regiment
1-й батальон 3-го стрелкового полка

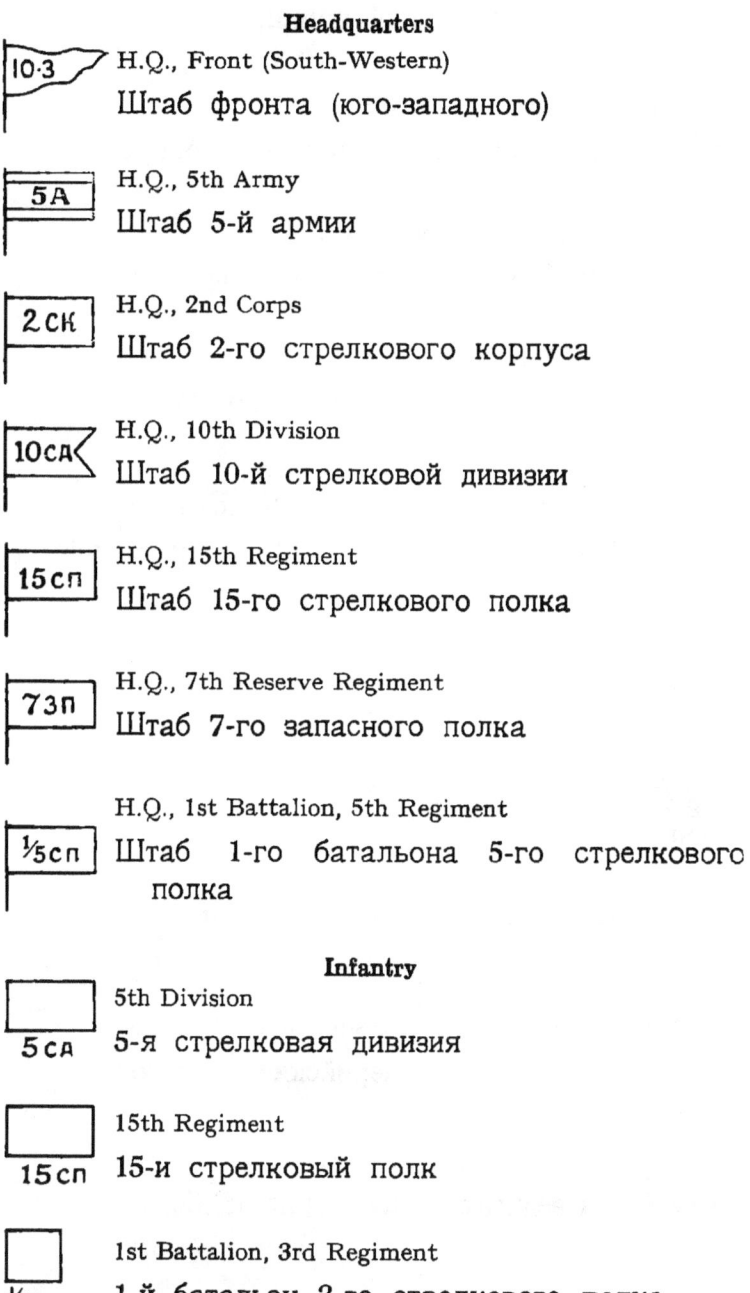

Cavalry

H.Q., 1st Cavalry Army
Штаб 1-й конной армии

H.Q., 3rd Cavalry Corps
Штаб 3-го кавалерийского корпуса

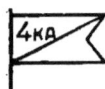
H.Q., 4th Cavalry Division
Штаб 4-й кавалерийской дивизии

H.Q., 9th Cavalry Regiment
Штаб 9-го кавалерийского полка

H.Q., 1st Squadron, 1st Cavalry Regiment
Штаб 1-го эскадрона 1-го кавалерийского полка

1st Cavalry Division

1st Cavalry Regiment

1st Squadron, 1st Cavalry Regiment

Independent Cavalry Squadron
Отделный кавалерийский эскадрон

Recce. Detachment (on the move)
Разведивательный отряд (Р.О.)

Artillery

H.Q., 8th Artillery Regiment
Штаб 8-го артиллерийского полка

H.Q., 3rd Artillery Group
Штаб 3-го артиллерийского дивизиона

8th Artillery Regiment
8-ой артиллерийский полк

1st Group, 5th Artillery Regiment
1-й дивизион 5-го артиллерийского полка

45th Regiment, A.R.G.K.

1st Group, 8th Corps Artillery Group

Sapper

H.Q., 5th Pontoon Regiment
Штаб 5-го понтонного полка

H.Q., 1st Sapper Battalion
Штаб 1-го саперного батальоня

2nd Sapper Battalion
2-ой саперный батальон

Sapper—*continued*

✖ 2CP	2nd Sapper Company
▬ 2ПОНТ Б	2nd Pontoon Battalion
☐ TEX Б·Н	Technical Battalion
☐ TEX POT	Technical Company

Signals

2CBП	Signal H.Q., 2nd Regiment
3CBБ	Signal H.Q., 3rd Battalion
1CBБ	1st Signal Battalion
2CBP	Signal Company Рота связи

 Advanced signal post
Головной пост связи

 Report centre
Пункт сбора донесений

Mechanised Troops

H.Q., 45th Mechanised Corps

5th Armoured Division

133rd Mechanised Brigade

2nd Mechanised Regiment

1st Battalion, 2nd Tank Regiment

4th Tank Battalion, Type T-28

135th Motorised M.G. Battalion

Independent Motorised Battalion

Air Force

H.Q., 12th Air Brigade
Штаб 12-й авиационной бригады

Air Force—*continued*

| 9 ↑ И | H.Q., 9th Fighter Squadron |

| 2 Р. | H.Q., 2nd Reconnaissance Squadron |

| 3 ↓ Ш | H.Q., 3rd Storm Squadron |

| 1 ↓ Б | H.Q., 1st Bomber Squadron |

Note.—Fighter : Истребитель
Storm : Штурмовик

Rifle Units

)╫ Rifle company in defence

)╫╫ Rifle battalion in defence

)╫► Rifle company in the attack

)╫╫► Rifle battalion in attack

(4) Battery of heavy machine guns (4 guns)

)—• Section of grenade throwers

Artillery Units

 Anti-aircraft battery

 Battery in fire position

 Howitzer battery in position

 Artillery fire concentration

Armoured Units

 Tank platoon in reserve position

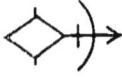 Tank platoon on the starting line

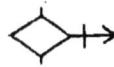 Tank platoon in the attack

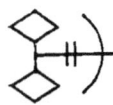 Tank company in reserve

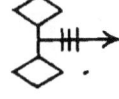 Tank battalion in the attack

 Platoon of armoured cars

Armoured Units—*continued*

Company of armoured cars

Light armoured train

Heavy armoured train

Company of motorised infantry

Motorised gun (76 mm.)

Obstacles through which tanks can go

Wireless

Field receiving and transmitting station

Mobile radio station, 6 receiving sets

Central telegraph office

Post for communication with the air

Engineering Constructions

　　　　　Barbed wire, three aprons

　　　　　Mine field—two rows of mines

　　　　　Anti-tank ditch

　　　　　Unfinished portion of road

　　　　　Sector of road in bad state

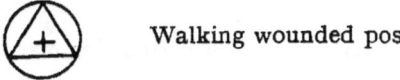 Destroyed portion of road

 Pit well

　　　　　Pipe well

Medical

　　　　　Divisional hospital

　　　　　Walking wounded post

　　　　　Divisional aid post

Medical—*continued*

 Veterinary hospital of division

 Regimental aid post

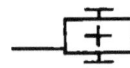 Two-wheeled ambulance

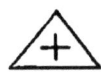 Battalion aid post

Supply

 Baggage train of 103rd Regiment

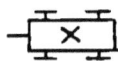 Regimental chemical stores

 Regimental ammunition supply point

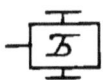 Battalion ammunition supply point

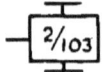 Baggage train, 2nd Battalion, 103rd Rifle Regiment

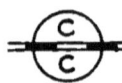 Supply railhead

Supply—*continued*.

✕   Refilling point

▭   Advanced depôt

⊙   Fuel depôt

RUSSIAN CONVENTIONAL SIGNS

Roads	
1ST Class, asphalt or concrete — Kilometre Post	
With, without trees, width in metres	
" paved	
In good, bad condition	
Gravel or mud, 1ST Grade	
Easy, difficult progression	
Country, mud, with ditches	
Country, without ditches	
In good, bad condition	
Brushwood	
" through swamp	
Fenced	
Lane through forest	
Tracks, cross country, forest	
Caravan route	
Railways	
Three lines	
Two lines	
Single line	
Narrow gauge	
Under construction	
Electric	
Station	
" , large and depot	
Boundaries	
International, state	
Inter-Union	
Autonomous Unions and Oblasts	
Kpaus and Oblasts	
National districts and regions	
Regional	
Wall	
Hedge	
Wooden fence	
Customs house	
Aerodrome	

Rivers Perennial, showing speed, direction of flow, navigable limit ← —03—	
Non-perennial	
Stream	
Canals Broad — Towpath	
Narrow	
Locks Iron — Жe
Stone — Кat
Wood — Дер
Weir	
Rapids	
Bridges Iron	
Stone	
Wooden on piles	
Wood	
On boats	
On rafts	
Drawbridges Iron	
Stone	
Wood	
Ferries Rope — Па
Paddle, carrying up to 8 tons — Па
Small boat — Пе
Raft at anchor — Пi
Ford, depth in metres, firm bottom — Бр
Water conduits Above ground	
Below ground	
Wells Ordinary, dry OK OK(су
Artesian, crane, wind pump OApnk
Quay — Sea/Land	
Anchorage	

The above signs are representative only and **not** drawn to scale.

(PART APPENDIX H)

...le	▵▵▵▵▵▵▵▵▵
...ghthouse, lightship, buoy	⚓ ⚓ △
...iding mark on shore	⊤
...ck, above, below water	Ⓛ Ⓣ
...urch and monastery	✠
...apel, mosque, buddist monastery	♦ ♦ ♠
...metery, Christian, non-Christian	[+ + +] [· · ·]
...ouse, barn, inn	▫ ▪ ◢
...indmill, stone, wood	✗ ✗
...ctory, with, without chimney	⌂ ▬
...ine shaft, working, disused	✕ ✕
...ine, goldfield	⚲ Kel Nedu ⚲ Jol Col
...il well, tower	○ Heqm. △
...bservation tower	♠
...re watch tower and water point	●
...ilo	⓪ Culoc
...ost Office with telegraph	✉
...elephone and telegraph lines	•—•—•—•
...adio station	♂
...lectrical station	✕
...lectric cable (high tension)	•—•—•—•
...orest, mixed	🌳
...ndergrowth, bushes etc	° ° ° ° °
...undra	♣ ♣ ♣
...wamp, impassable, passable	≡ ≡
...and	▨▨▨
...oles, mounds	○ ⬭
Points { Astronomical	☆ 82·1
Points { Trigonometrical	△ 79·3
Points { Spot height	⊙ 91·5

War Office, 1940.

APPENDIX "I"

RUSSIAN MILITARY AND OTHER ABBREVIATIONS

The Russian Alphabet

а	=	a	р = r
б	=	b	с = s
в	=	v	т = t
г	=	g	у = u
д	=	d	ф = f
е	=	e	х = kh
ж	=	j	ц = ts
з	=	z	ч = ch
и	=	i	ш = sh
й	=	i (soft)	щ = shch
к	=	k	ъ = (hard sign) or '
л	=	l	ы = i
м	=	m	ь = (soft sign)
н	=	n	э = e
о	=	o	ю = yu
п	=	p	я = ya

Abbreviation transliterated.	Russian in full.	English translation.
	А	
2 А	2-я армия	2nd Army.
11 Аб	11-я абиационная бригада	11th Aviation Brigade.
Абд	Авто-броневой дивизион	Armoured Detachment.
4 Абп	4-ый автомобильный полк	4th Motorised Regiment.
Абр	Авто-броневая рота	Armoured Car Company.
Авиабаза	Авиационная база	Air Base.
Авиот	Авиационный отряд	Air Detachment.
А.В.П.	Авиационный парк	Aviation Park.
Автобаза	Автомобильная база	Mechanical Vehicles Base.
Автомотополк	Автомоторный полк	Motorised Regiment.
Аг	Авиационная группа	Aviation Group.
Агк	Авиационная группа корпуса	Corps Aviation Group.
Аго	Автомобилвные группы обоза	Mechanical Transport.
5 Агр	5-я авто-грузовая рота	5th Lorry Loading Company.
Адд	Артиллерия дальнего действия	Long Range Artillery.
А.Н.П.	Артиллерийский наблюдательный пункт	Artillery O.P.
Аон	Артиллерия особого назначения	Artillery detached for special duty.
Аоо	Аэродромное осветительное оборудование	Aerodrome illumination equipment.

35 Ап	Артиллерийский полк 35-ой стрелковой дивизии	Artillery Regiment of the 35th Infantry Brigade.
А.Р.	Артиллерия разрушения	Artillery for destructive shoots.
А.Р.Г.К.	Артиллерия резерва главного командования	Army Artillery (General Reserve).
А.р.м.	Авторемонтная мастерская	Motor Repair Workshop.
Артиллерия П. К.	Артиллерия поддержки конницы	Cavalry Support Artillery.
Артиллерия П. П.	Артиллерия поддержки пехоты	Infantry Support Artillery.
Артполк	Артиллерийский полк	Artillery Regiment.
Артприм	Приморская артиллерия	Coast Defence Artillery.
Артсклад	Артиллерийский склад	Artillery Depôt.
Артснаб	Снабжение артиллерии	Artillery Supply.
Артсух	Сухопутная артиллерия	Land Artillery.
Арту (артуп)	Артиллерийское управление	Artillery control.
Архозком		All Russia War Supply Committee.
А.С.Р.	Авиасигнальный пост	Air Signals Point.
А.С.Т.	Артиллерия сопровождения танков	Tank Close Support Artillery.
А.Т.Р.	Автотранспортная рота	M.T. Company.
А.Э.Р.	Аэродром	Aerodrome.
А.Э.Р.	Аэродромная рота	Aerodrome Company.

Abbreviation transliterated.	Russian in full.	English translation.
	Б	
Б (or Бел) Prefix	Белорусский	White Russian.
6.Б.	6-ая батарея	No. 6 Battery.
Б.А.	Батальонная атриллерия	Battalion Artillery.
Б.В.О.	Белорусский военный округ	White Russian Military District.
Бепо	Бронепоезд	Armoured Train.
Б.К.П.	Батареиный командный пункт	Battery Command Point.
Б-н	Батальон	Battalion.
Бн		Mark of Soviet Gas Mask.
Бо	Баталионный обоз	Battalion transport.
Б.О.	Береговая оборона	Coast Defence.
Б.П.В.	База питания и востановления	Reorganising and Feeding Depôt.
Б.П.О.	Банно-прачечный отряд	Hygiene Section (baths and laundry).
Б.П.П.	Баталионный патронный пункт	Battalion Ammunition Point.
Б.П.Т.	Батарея поддержки танков	Tank Support Battery.
Б-рея	Батарея	Battery.

Б.С.С.Р.	Белорусская социалистическая советская республика	White Russian Soviet Socialist Republic.
Б.Х.В.	Боевые химические вещества	War Chemicals (Gas, etc.).
	В	
В	Восток	East.
3.В	3-ий взвод	No. 3 Platoon.
В.А.О.	Всесоюзное авиационное обединение	Union of Aviation.
В.А.Т.О.	Всесоюзное авто-тракторное обединение	Union of Motor-Tractor Industry.
В.В.	Взрывчатое вещество	High explosive material.
В.В.С.	Военные воздушные силы	Air Force.
В.Д.О.	Военнодорожный отряд	Military Road Detachment.
Взв	Взвод	Platoon.
В.И.К.	Волостной исполнительный комитет	District or Area Executive Committee.
В.К.П. (б)	Всесоюзная коммунистическая партия (большевиков)	All-Union Communist Party (Bolsheviks).
В.К.С.	Войска конвойного сопровождения	Escort Troops.
В.М.С.	Военные морские силы	Navy.
В.Н.О.С.	Воздушное наблюдение оповещение и связь	Air Observation, Report and Liaison.

Abbreviation transliterated.	Russian in full.	English translation.
	B—*continued.*	
В.О.	Военный округ	Military District.
В.О.	Вычислительное отделение	Survey Section.
Военком	Военный комиссариат	Military Commissariat.
Военкор	Военный корреспондент	Military Correspondent.
Вокр	Войска окранения хозяйственных предприятий	Troops for protection of Civil Undertakings.
В.О.С.О.	Военное сообщение	Military Communication.
В.П.У.	Военное промышленное управление	War Industry Administration.
Врвос	Воздушноплавательная бригада	Air Brigade.
В.С.П.	Взвод связи с пехотой	Platoon for communication with Infantry.
В.Т.	Воздушная тревога	Air Alarm.
В.Т.С.	Военно-топографическая служба	Military Topographical Service.
В.Ф.О.	Военно-финансовый отдел	Military Finance Department.
В.Х.О.	Военно-химический отдел	War Chemical Department.
В.Х.О.	Военно-хозяйственный отдел	Military Supply Department.
В.Х.П.	Всесоюзная химическая промышленность	All-Union Chemical Industry Combine.

В.Х.С.	Военно-хозяйственное снабжение	Military Supply.
В.Х.У.	Военно-хозяйственное управление	Military Supply Administration of the Red Army.
В.Ц.И.К.	Всесоюзный центральный исполнительный комитет Р.К.К.А.	All-Union Central Executive Committee.

Г

Г.В.С.У.	Главное военно-санитарное управление	Chief Administrative Department of Army Medical Services.
Г.О.	Головной отряд	Vanguard.
Горем	Головной ремонтный поезд	Advanced Repair Train.
Госплан	Государственная плановая комиссия	State Planning Committee.
Г.П.З.	Головная походная застава	Forward Protective Piquet on the march.
Г.П.М.П.	Главный пункт медицинской помощи	Main Medical Aid Point.
Гр.	Граната	Grenade.
Г.Р.Б.	Головная ремонтная бригада	Forward Repair Brigade.
Г.С.Д.	Горная стрелковая дивизия	Mountain Infantry Division.
Г.У.Г.Б.	Главное управление государственной безопасности	Chief Directorate of State Security.

Abbreviation transliterated.	Russian in full.	English translation.
	Г—*continued*.	
Г.У.Р.К.К.А.	Главное управление Р.К.К.А.	Central Administration of the Red Army.
Гутап	Главное управление тракторной и автомобильной промышленности	Central Department of the Tractor and Motor Industry.
Г.Э.М.Б.	Головной эшелон мотопарка батальона	Forward Echelon of Battalion Motor Park.
Г.Э.П.	Головной эшелонный парк	
	Д	
Д.А.	Дивизионная артиллерия	Divisional Artillery.
Д.А.О.П.	Дивизионный артиллерийский обменный пункт	Divisional Artillery: Delivery Point.
Д.А.Р.М.	Дивизионная артиллерийская мастерская	Divisional Artillery Workshop.
Д.В.	Дымообразовывающее вещество / Дымовое	Smoke substance,

Д.В.Л.	Дивизионный ветеринарный лазарет	Divisional Veterinary Hospital.
Д.Г.	Дивизионный госпиталь	Divisional Hospital.
Д.Д.	Дальнего действия	Long distance (Artillery, etc.).
Див.	Дивизия	Division.
Дивинж	Дивизионный инженер	Divisional Engineer.
Д.К.П.	Дополнительный командный пункт	Additional Command Point.
Д.О.	Дивизионный обоз	Divisional Transport.
Д.О.Н.	Дальнее огневое нападение	Long range fire.
Донбасс	Донецкий угольный бассейн	Don Coal Basin.
Д.О.П.	Дивизионный обменный пункт	Divisional Delivery Point.
Д.П.	Дегазационный пункт	Decontamination Point.
	Ж	
Ж-д	Железная дорога	Railway.
	З	
З	Запад	West.
З	Заместитель	Deputy.
З.А.	Зенитная артиллерия	Anti-aircraft Artillery.
9 Зад	9-ый зенитный дивизион	9th A.A. Artillery Group.

Abbreviation transliterated.	Russian in full.	English translation.
	3—*continued.*	
Зак	Закавказский	Trans-Caucasian.
З.А.О.П.	За активну оборонительную работу	"For Active Defence Work" (an order).
З.А.Э.Р.	Запасной аэродром	Reserve Aerodrome.
5 36	5-ая зенитная батарея	5th Anti-aircraft Battery.
З.В.	Зажигательные вещества	Incendiary substances.
Зевод	Заместитель коменданта воды	Deputy Water Transport Commandant.
З.К.	Заместитель коменданта железнодорожного узла и станции	Deputy Commandant of Railway Junctions and Stations.
З.К.	Защитная комната	{ Gas-proof Room. Splinter-proof Room.
З.К.С.	Заместитель коменданта станции	Deputy Station Commandant.
З.К.У.	Заместитель коменданта уезда	Deputy District Commandant.
Зкувод	Заместитель коменданта уезда воды	Deputy River District Commandant.

З.Н.П.	Запасной наблюдательный пункт	Reserve O.P.
З.П.	Запасной полк	Reserve Regiment.
З.П.	Зенитный пулемёт	Anti-aircraft Machine Gun.
З.П.Р.	Зенитные проекторы	Anti-aircraft Searchlights.
	И	
И.А.	Истребительная авиация	Fighting planes.
И.К.К.И.	Исполнительный комитет коммунистического интернационала	Executive Committee of Communist International.
Инж П.35 сд	Инженерный парк 35-ой стрелковой дивизии	Engineer Park of the 35th Infantry Division.
2 Иэ	2-ая истребительная эскадрилья	2nd Fighter Squadron.
	К	
К.А.	Корпусная артиллерия	Corps Artillery.
К.А.	Конная армия	Cavalry Army.
К.А.Д.	Конно-артиллерийский дивизион	Horsed Artillery Detachment.
3 Као	3-ий корпусный авиационный отряд	3rd Corps Aviation Detachment.
4 К.А.П.	Артиллерийский полк 4-го стрелкового корпуса	Artillery Regiment of the 4th Infantry Corps.

Abbreviation transliterated.	Russian in full.	English translation.
	K—*continued*.	
К.В.	Конный взвод	Cavalry Troop.
Кв-м.	Квадратный метр	Square metre.
К.В.П.	Команды ветеринарной помощи	Veterinary Aid Detachments.
К.Г.	Корпусной госпиталь	Corps Hospital.
К.Д.	Кавалерийская дивизия	Cavalry Division.
К.И.М.	Коммунистический интернационал молодёжи	Communist International of Youth.
К.К.	Кавалерийский корпус	Cavalry Corps.
К.К.А.	Кавказская красная армия	Caucasian Red Army.
4 Кнап	Конноартиллерийский полк 4-ой кавалерийской дивизии	Horsed Artillery Regiment of the 4th Cavalry Division.
К.Н.П.	Командирский наблюдательный пункт	Commander's O.P.
Колхоз	Колективное хозяйство	Collective Farm.
Комсомол	Коммунистический союз молодёжи	Communist League of Youth.
Комсостав	Командующий состав	Commanding Personnel.
К.О.П.	Корпусной обменный пункт	Corps Delivery Point.
22 Кп.	22-ой кавалерийский полк	22nd Cavalry Regiment.

К.П.	Командный пункт	Headquarters (Operations).
К.П.П.	Контрольный пункт на путях подвоза	Control Point on Supply Routes.
К-р.	Командир	Commander.
Кузбасс		The Kuznets Basin.

Л

1-Л.А.Ш.	1-ая ленинградская артиллерийская школа	1st Leningrad Artillery School.
8-Л.А.Э.	8-ая легко-бомбардировочная эскадрилья	8th Light Bombing Squadron.
Л.В.О.	Ленинградский военный округ	Leningrad Military District.
Летнаб	Лётчик наблюдатель	Air Observer.
		Person Deprived of Civil Rights.
Л.С.	Лошадинная сила	Horse-power.

М

Маскр	Маскировочная рота	Camouflage Company.
М.Б.	Мостовой батальон	Bridging Battalion.
М.В.В.	Метательное взрывчатое вещество	High explosive (shell filling).
М.Д.З	Маскирующая дымовая завеса	Camouflaging smoke screen.
М.О.	Местная оборона	Local Defence.
М.О	Мото-отряд	Motor Detachment.

278

Abbreviation transliterated.	Russian in full.	English translation.
	M—*continued.*	
М.О.П.Р.	Международная организация помощи бойцам революций	International Aid Organization for Revolutionary Fighters.
Мотомеханчаст Мотмехчаст	Мото-механические части	Motorised and Mechanised Units.
Мп.5.Понтб	Мостовой парк 5-ого понтонного батальона	Bridge Park of 5th Pontoon Battalion.
М.Р.	Механизированные разезды	Mechanised Patrols.
М.С.К.	Медико-санитарная команда	Medical Sanitary Squad.
М.С.Т.	Метеорологическая станция	Meteorological Station.
М.С.Ч.М.	Морские силы черного моря	Black Sea Naval Forces.
	Н	
Наморси	Начальник морских сил	Chief of Naval Forces.
Нарком	Народный комиссар	Peoples' Commissar.
Нач	Начальник	Chief.
Начарт	Начальник артиллерии	Chief of Artillery.

Начхим	Начальник химической службы	Head of Chemical Service.
Начштадив	Начальник штаба дивизии	Chief of Staff of a Division.
Н.В.Д.	Начальник военных дорог	O.C., Military Roads.
Н.В. Р.К.К.А.	Народный комиссариат военных дел Р.К.К.А.	War Commissariat of the Red Army.
Н.З.О.	Неподвижный заградительный огон	Stationary Barrage.
Н.З.О.	Непосредственная зенитная оборона	Direct or Independent Anti-Aircraft Defence.
Н.К.В.Д.	Народный комиссариат внутренних дел	Peoples' Commissariat for Internal Affairs.
Н.К. Внешторг	Народный комиссариат внешней торговли	Peoples' Commissariat for Foreign Trade.
Н.К. Внуторг	Народный комиссариат внутреной торговли	Peoples' Commissariat for Home Trade.
Н.К. Вод	Народный комиссариат воды	Peoples' Commissariat for Water Transport.
Н.К. Здрав	Народный комиссариат здравоохранения	Peoples' Commissariat for Health.
Н.К. Зем	Народный комиссариат земледелия	Peoples' Commissariat for Agriculture.
Н.К.	Народный комиссариат	Peoples' Commissariat.
Н.К.И.Д.	Народный комиссариат иностранных дел	Peoples' Commissariat for Foreign Affairs.

Abbreviation transliterated.	Russian in full.	English translation.
	H—*continued.*	
Н.К. Лес	Народный комиссариат лесов	Peoples' Commissariat for Forests and Timber.
Н.К.Л.П.	Народный комиссариат легкий промышленности	Peoples' Commissariat for Light Industry.
Н.К.О.	Народный комиссариат обороны	Peoples' Commissariat for Defence.
Н.К. Пищ	Народный комиссариат пищи	Peoples' Commissariat for Food Industry.
Н.К.П.С.	Народный комиссариат путей сообщения	Peoples' Commissariat for Communications (Railways).
Н.К.Т.П.	Народный комиссариат тяжелой промышленности	Peoples' Commissariat for Heavy Industries.
Н.К. Совхоз	Народный комиссариат совхозов	Peoples' Commissariat for State Farms.
Н.К.Ф.	Народный комиссариат финансов	Peoples' Commissariat for Finance.
Н.П.П.	Непосредственная поддержка пехоты	Close Infantry Support.
Н.П.Ф.С.	Начальник продфуражного снабжения	Chief of Forage Supply ("Q" appointment in Cavalry Regiment).

Н.Ш.	Начальник штаба	Chief of Staff.
Н.Э.Т.С.	Начальник этапо-транспортной службы	Chief of Transport Service.
	О	
Обл.	Областной	District (adjec).
О.В.	Отравляющие вещества	Toxic Gases.
О.Д.З.	Ослепительная дымовая завеса	Blinding Smoke Screen.
О.З.	Огневое заграждение	Fire Barrage.
О.З.	Отравленная зона	Contaminated Area.
О.З.Е.Т.		Society for the Settlement of Jewish Workers.
1. О.К.Б.	1-ая Отдельная кавалерийская бригада	1st Independent Cavalry Brigade.
О.О.Д.	Отряды обеспечения движения	Details for Securing Movement (Provost details or Advance Guard of mechanical formation).
О.П.	Огневая позиция	Fire position.
О.Р.Б.	Отдельный разведывательный батальон	Independent Reconnaissance Battalion (in a Division).
О.Р.Г.	Охранительная разведывательная группа	Protective Reconnaissance Group.
Орудие Г.П.	Орудие танковой поддержки	Tank Support Gun.

Abbreviation transliterated.	Russian in full.	English translation.
	O—*continued.*	
Осоавиахим	Общество друзей обороны и авиахимического строительства	Society for Aviation and Chemical Defence.
О.Т.Б.	Отдельный танковый батальон	Independent Tank Battalion.
О.Т.Д.	Отдел	Department.
О.Т.С.Р.	Отдельная телеграфно строительная рота	Independent Telegraph Construction Company.
О.Т.Э.Р.	Отдельная телеграфно эксплоатационная рота	Independent Telegraph Operating Company.
	П	
П.А.	Полковая артиллерия	Regimental Artillery.
П.А. 105	Полковая артиллерия 105-ого стрелкового полка	Regimental Artillery of the 105th Infantry Regiment.
П.Б.	Полковая батарея	Regimental Battery.
П.Б.	Передовой батальон	Forward Battalion.

П.Б.О.	Противоброневая оборона	Anti-A.F.V. Defence.
П.В.О.	Противовоздушная оборона	Anti-aircraft Defence.
П.В.Х.О.	Противовоздушная и противохимическая оборона	Anti-aircraft and Anti-gas Defence.
П.Г.	Полевой госпиталь	Field Hospital.
П.Е.Р.П.	Перегрузочный пункт	Reloading Point (Railway).
Пер	Переулок	Side Street.
П.З.О.	Переносный заградительный огонь	Creeping Barrage.
П.З.Р.	Полевой записный рекорд	Field Note Book.
П.К.	Поддержка кавалерии	Cavalry Support.
П.М.	Пункт медицинской помощи	Medical Aid Post.
П.Н.П.	Передовой наблюдательный пункт / Подвижный наблюдательный пункт	Forward O.P. / Mobile O.P. (for mechanical column on the march).
П.Н.С.	Пост наблюдения и связи	Observation and Intercommunication Post (generally in Tank and Infantry attack).
П.О.	Передовой } отряд / Прикрывающий } отряд	Advanced } Detachment. / Covering } Detachment.
П.О.	Полковой обоз	Regimental Baggage.
П.О.Д	Перевязочный отряд дивизии	Divisional Dressing Station Detachment.

Abbreviation transliterated.	Russian in full.	English translation.
	П—*continued*	
Подив	Политбюро дивизии	Political Department of a Division.
Подрем	Поезд по ремонтированию подвижного состава	Repair Train for Vehicles.
Полит	(Prefix only)	Political.
Политбюро		Political Bureau.
Политпросвет		Board of Political Education.
Политрук	Полит-руководитель	Political Leader.
Полпред	Полномочный представитель	Plenipotentiary Representative (Ambassador).
Полпредство	Полномочное представительство	Embassy.
Помполит	Помощник политруководителя	Assistant Political Leader.
Понтб	Понтонный батальон	Bridging Battalion.
Понтп	Понтонный полк	Bridging Regiment.
Понтр	Понтонная рота	Bridging Company.
П.П.	Перевязочный пункт	Dressing Station.
П.П. 105	Артиллерийская группа поддержки 105-ого стрелкового полка	Artillery Support Group of the 105th Infantry Regiment.

П.П.В.	Передовой пункт ветпомощи	Forward Veterinary Aid Post.
П.П.З.О.	Переносный противотанковый заградительный огонь	Creeping Anti-tank Barrage.
П.П.Л.	Посадочная площадка	Landing Ground.
П.П.М.	Полковой пункт медпомощи	R.A.P.
	Передовой пункт медпомощи	Forward Medical Aid Post.
П.П.П.	Полковой патронный пункт	Regimental Ammunition Point.
П.П.П.	Пункт первой помощи	First Aid Post.
П.П.С.	Полевая почтовая станция	Field Post Office.
Пр.-к	Противник	Enemy.
Профинтерн	Профессиональный интернационал	Communist International Trades Unions.
Профсоюз	Профессиональный союз	Trade Union.
П.Р. 108 С.П.	Пулемётная рота 108-ого стрелкового полка	Machine Gun Company of the 108th Infantry Regiment.
П.С.	Пункт сбора	Collecting Point.
П.С.Д.	Пункт сбора донесения	Message Collecting Point.
П.С.М.	Подвижные средства медпомощи	Mobile Medical Unit.
П.С.О.	Пункт санитарной обработки	Medical Aid Post.
П.С.Т.	Пункт санитарного транспорта	Medical Transport Point.
П.Т.	Поддержка танков	Tank Support.

Abbreviation transliterated.	Russian in full.	English translation.
	П—*continued*.	
П.Т.Б.	Противотанковая батарея	Anti-tank Battery.
П.Т.О.	Противотанковая оборона	Anti-tank Defence.
П.У.	Полевой устав Р.К.К.А.	Field Service Regulations (Manual) of the Red Army.
П.У.А.З.О.	Прибор управленая артиллерийским зенитным огнём	Device for controlling anti-aircraft Artillery fire.
П.У.Р.К.К.А.	Политическое управление Р.К.К.А.	Political Administration of the Red Army.
П.Х.О.	Противохимическая оборона	Anti-chemical Defence.
П.Х.З.	Противохимическая защита	Anti-chemical Defence.
П.Ш.	Помощик штаба	1st Assistant Chief of Staff.
П.Э. 24 К.П.	Пулемётный эскадрон 24-ого кавалерийского полка	Machine Gun Squadron of the 24th Cavalry Regiment.
П.Э.С. 8 К.П.	Полуэскадрон связи 8-ого кавалерийского полка	A Half-squadron of Signals of the 8th Cavalry Regiment.

Р

Р. 1	Разъезд но. 1	No. 1 Mounted Patrol.
3 Р.	3-я рота	No. 3 Company.
Р.А.Д. 2 А.	Отдельный радио дивизион 2-ой армии	Independent Radio Unit of the 2nd Army.
Раз	Разведывательный	Reconnaissance (adjec.).
Р.Б.	Разведывательный баталион	Reconnaissance Battalion.
Р.Б.	Рабочий баталон	Labour Battalion.
Р.В.О.	Разведывательные войска охранения	Protective Reconnaissance Troops.
Р.В.С.	Революционный военный совет	Revolutionary Military Council.
Р.Г.	Разведывательная группа	Reconnaissance Group.
Р.Д.	Разведывательный дозор	Reconnoitring Patrol (dismounted).
Р.Д.	Разведывательный дивизион	Reconnaissance Party (of an Artillery Regiment).
Р.К.И.	Рабоче-крестьянская инспекция	Workers' and Peasants' Inspectorate.
Р.К.К.А.	Рабоче-крестьянская красная армия	Workers' and Peasants' Red Army.
Р.К.К.Ф.	Рабоче-крестьянский красный флот	Workers' and Peasants' Red Fleet.
Р.О.	Разведывательный отряд	Reconnaissance Detachment.
Р.О.К.К.	Российское общество красного креста	Russian Society of the Red Cross.

Abbreviation transliterated.	Russian in full.	English translation.
	Р—*continued.*	
Рот	Рота	Company.
Р.П.П.	Ротный патронный пункт	Company Ammunition Point.
Р.Р.	Рабочая рота	Labour Company.
Р.Р.Д.	Рота регулирования движения	Movement Regulating (Provost) Company.
Р.С.Ф.С.Р.	Российская социалистическая федеративная советская республика	Russian Socialist Federal Soviet Republic.
10 Р.Э.	10-ая разведывательная эскадрилья	10th Air Reconnaissance Squadron.
	С	
С.	Север	North.
С.А.	Самоходная артиллерия	Mechanised Artillery.
35 С.А.П.Б.	Сапёрный батальон 35-ого стрелкового корпуса	Sapper Battalion of the 35th Infantry Corps.

15 С.А.П.Р.	Сапёрная рота 15-ой стрелковой дивизии	Sapper Company of the 15th Infantry Division.
С.А.П.Э. 3 К.Д.	Сапёрный эскадрон 3-ой кавалерийской дивизии	Sapper Squadron of the 3rd Cavalry Division.
2 С.В.Б.	2-ой батальон связи	2nd Signal Battalion.
С В.В.	Взвод связи	Signal Platoon.
4 С.В.П.	4-ий полк связи	4th Signal Regiment.
1 С.В.Р.	1-ая рота связи	1st Signal Company.
С.В.Э.	Советская военная энциклопедия	Soviet Military Encyclopaedia.
С.В. Я. Зрем	Поезд для ремонта железнодорожной связи	Railway Line Repair Train.
5 С.Д.	5-ая стрелковая дивизия	5th Infantry Division.
Севзап	Северо-западный	North Western (adj.).
4 С.К.	4-ий стрелковый корпус	4th Infantry Corps.
Скадив	Сигнальные коммуникации артиллерийского дивизиона	Signal Communications of an Artillery Group.
Скарм	Сигнальные коммуникации армии	Army Signals.
С.К.В.О.	Северо-кавказский военный округ	North Caucausus Military District.
Снар	Снаряд	Shell.
С.Н.Д.		Survey Section.

L

Abbreviation transliterated.	Russian in full.	English translation.
	C—*continued.*	
С.Н.И.С.	Служба наблюдения и связи	Observation and Communication Service.
С.Н.К.	*See* Совнарком	
С.О.В.	Стойкие отравляющие вещества	Persistent Gases.
Совнарком	Совет народных комиссаров	Council of Peoples' Commissars.
Совхоз	Советское хозяйство	State Farm.
С.О.П.	Стационарный обмывочный пункт	Stationary Washing Point.
2 С.П.	2-ой стрелковый полк	2nd Infantry Regiment.
С.П.А.М.	Сборный пункт аварийных машин	Collecting Point for Damaged Machines.
С.П.М.	Стационарный пункт медпомощи	Stationary Medical Aid Post.
С.С.	Станция снабжения	Supply Station.
С.С.М.	Стационарные средства медпомощи	Stationary Medical Aid Posts or Appliances.
С.С.С.Р.	Союз советских социалистических республик	Union of Soviet Socialist Republics (U.S.S.R.).

Станк пул	Станковый пулемёт	Heavy Machine Gun.
Стахановизм		Movement for increasing Productivity of Labour.
С.Т.О.	Совет труда и обороны	Council of Labour and Defence.
Стр.	Стрелковый	Rifle (adjec.).
С.Т.Т.	Средняя точка попадения	Mean Point of Impact.
С.Э.	Санитарно-эпидемический отряд	Epidemic Fighting Detachment.

Т

2 Т.А.Н.Б.	2-ой танковый батальон	2nd Tank Battalion.
2 Т.А.Н.Р.	2-ая танковая рота	2nd Tank Company.
7 Т.А.Э.	7-ая тяжело-бомбардировочная эскадрилья	7th Heavy Bombing Squadron (Aircraft).
Т.Б.Е.П.О.	Тяжёлый бронепоезд	Heavy Armoured Train.
Т.Д.Д.	Танки дальнего действия	Long-distance Tanks.
Тер.	Территориальный	Territorial.
Техр.	Техническая рота	Technical Company.
Т.З.И.	Трудно-затопляемое имущество	Non-sinkable Material.
Т.Н.К.	Танкетка	Tankette.
Т.Н.К.Р.	Танкетная рота	Tankette Company.
Т.О.	Тылный отряд	Rear Detachment.

Abbreviation transliterated.	Russian in full.	English translation.
	T—*continued*.	
Т.П.	Танковая поддержка	Support by Tanks.
Т.П.П.	Танки поддержки пехоты	Infantry Support Tanks.
Т.Р.	Транспортная рота	Transport Company.
Т.Р.В.И.	1-ый танковый курс вождения	1st Tank Driving Course.
Т.Р.Г.К.	Танки резерва главного командования	Army Tanks (General Reserve).
Т/С.	Телеграфно-строительный	Telegraph Construction (adjec.).
Т/Т.	Телеграфно-телефонный	Telegraph-telephone (adjec.).
Турксиб.		Turkistan-Siberian Railway.
Т.Э.М.П.	Тыловой эшелон мотор-парка	Motor-parks Rear Echelon.
Т.Э.П.	Тыловой эшелон парка	Parks Rear Echelon.
	У	
У.	Управление	Administration.
У.Б.П. Р.К.К.А.	Управление боевой подготовки Р.К.К.А.	Directorate of Military Training of the Red Army.
У.В.В.С.	Управление военно-воздушных сил	Air Ministry.

У.В.И.	Управление военных изобретений	Administrative Body for Military Inventions.
У.В.М.С.	Управление военно-морских сил	Admiralty.
У.З.	Участок заражения	Contaminated Area.
Ул	Улица	Street.
У.М.М.	Управление механазации и моторизации	Administrative Body for Mechanisation and Motorisation.
У.Н.И. Р.К.К.А.	Управление научного института Р.К.К.А.	Directorate of the Red Army Scientific Institute.
У.П.В.О. С.О.	Управление военного сообщения	Directorate of Military Communications.
2 Химб	2-ой химический батальон	2nd Chemical Battalion.
Химв	Химический взвод	Chemical Platoon.
Химр	Химическая рота	Chemical Company.
Х.Н.О.С.	Химические наблюдение, оповещение и связв	Gas Observation, Report, and Liaison.
Х.С.	Ход сообщения	Communication Trench.
Х.Т.	Химическая тревога	Gas Alarm.

Ц

Ц	Центральный	Central.
Ц.А.В.О.	Центрально-азиатский военный округ	Central Asian Military District.

Abbreviation transliterated.	Russian in full.	English translation.
	Ц—*continued.*	
Ц.А.Г.И.	Центральный аэро-гидродинамический институт	Central Aero-Hydrodynamic Institute.
Ц.Д.К.А.	Центральный дом красной армии	Central Red Army House.
Ц.И.А.М.	Центральный Институт авиомоторстроения	Central Institute for Aircraft Engine Construction.
Ц.И.К. (СССР.)	Центральный исполнительный комитет (С.С.С.Р.)	Central Executive Committee of U.S.S.R.
Ц.К.	Центральный комитет	Central Committee.
Ц.К.К.	Центральная контрольная комиссия	Central Control Commission.
Ц.ЧО.	Центрально-черно зёмная область	Central Black Earth Region.
	Ч	
Ч.О.Н.	Части особого назначения	Special Duty Units.

	Ш	
З. Шэ.	3-ая Штурмовая эскадрилья	3rd Fighter Squadron.
Шр.	Шрапнель	Shrapnel.
	Э	
Э	Эскадрон	Squadron (Cavalry).
Э	Этап	Halting Place.
Э.О.	Эвакуационный отряд	Evacuation Detachment.
	Ю	
Ю.В.	Юго-восток	South-East.
Ю.З.	Юго-запад	South-West.

APPENDIX "J"

GLOSSARY OF CERTAIN COMMON MILITARY TERMS

(Russian)

А

Авангард	advance guard.
Административные приказы	administrative orders.
Анфиладный огонь	enfilade fire.
Арьергард	rearguard.
Атаковать с тыла	to attack from the rear.
Атаковать с фланга	to attack from a flank.
Аэроплан	aeroplane.
Аэродром	aerodrome.

Б

Беглый огонь	rapid fire.
Бензин	petrol.
Бивак	bivouac.
Близкая поддержка	close support.
Блиндаж	dug-out.
Боевой порядок	disposition, order of battle.
Боковой авангард	flank guard.
Больница	hospital.
Бомбовоз	bomber aeroplane.
Брать на себя инициативу	to take the initiative.
Бризантный снаряд	high explosive shell.
Брод	ford.
Бронеавтомобиль	armoured car.

Б—contd.

Броневик	armoured vehicle.
Бруствер	parapet.
Быть на страже	to be on guard.

В

В глубину	in depth.
Велосипед	bicycle.
Верховой	despatch rider.
Вестовой	orderly.
Веха	landmark.
Взаймодействовать	to co-operate.
Винтовка	rifle.
Внезапная атака	surprise attack.
Внутреннее сообщение	inter-communication.
Водопой	watering point.
Военная хитрость	ruse of war.
Военно-полицейская служба	Provost Service.
Войнская повинность	Conscription.
Войнский устав	military regulations.
Войсковая эскадрилья	army co-op squadrons.
Вооружение	armament.
Врасплох	by surprise.
Встречный бой	encounter, battle.
Вступать в бой	to come into action.
В ударном порядке	with concentration of all forces.
Входящий угол	re-entrant.
Выполнять	to execute, fulfil.
Высаживать из грузовиков	to debuss.
Выставлять часового	to post a sentry.
Вьючное животное	pack animal.

Г

Главнокомандующий	Commander-in-Chief.
Главные силы	main body.
Головная ж-д станция	railhead.
Головной отряд	vanguard.
Грузовик	lorry.
Групировка	disposition, grouping
Гусеница	caterpillar track.

Д

Дальность	range.
Дальность действия	range of action.
Дать залп } Дать очередь }	to fire a salvo.
Двигаться { скачками перекатами }	to move by bounds.
Действительность огня	fire effect.
Делать привал	to make a halt.
Денщик	batman.
Десант	landing, disembarkation of troops.
Десантный отряд	landing force.
Дозор	patrol.
Донесение	report, message.
Дымовая завеса	smoke screen.

Ж

Железная дорога	railway.
Житель	inhabitant.

З

Загродительный огонь	covering fire.
Задержка	delay.
Закреплять	to consolidate.
Занимать ⎫ позицию Занять ⎭	to occupy a position.
Запас	reserve of any kind, including men.
Запасная часть	spare part.
Заряд	charge.
Застава	outpost, picket.
Заставлять Замолчать батарею	to silence a battery.
Захватывать	to capture, occupy.
Защищать	to defend.
Земляные работы	earth works, field works.
Зенитный	anti-aircraft.
Значёк	badge.
Зрительная сигнализация	visual signalling.

И

Изнурительный огонь	harassing fire.
Инженер	engineer.
Интендантство	R.A.S.C.
Истребитель	fighter aeroplane — destroyer (ship).
Исходная позиция	forming-up position.
Исходная точка	starting point.
Исходящий угол	salient.

К

Казарма	barrack.
Карта	map.
Колючая проволока	barbed wire.
Команда	word of command—small detachment.
Команда связи	signal section.
Контр-разведка	intelligence service.
Корректирование артиллерийской стрельбы самолётом	aircraft spotting.

Л

Лазарет	hospital (mil.).
Лазаретная линейка	field ambulance.
Лазутчик	scout, look-out.
Личный знак	identity disc.
Ложная атака	feint attack.
Ложная тревога	false alarm.

М

Марш рут	route of march.
Мертвое пространство	dead ground.
Меры охранения	protective measures.
Место снижения	landing ground.
Меткий огонь	accurate fire.
Минировать	to lay mines.
Мишень	target.
Мундир	uniform.

Н

Наблюдение	observation.
Навесный огонь	plunging fire.
Наводить мост	to bridge.
Наподать	to attack.
Настильный огонь	grazing fire.
Натиск	rush, pressure.
Начальная скорость	muzzle velocity.
Нащупывать } Нащупать }	to search an area (arty.).
Непробиваемый пулей	bullet-proof.
Непромокаемое пальто	waterproof coat.
Нестоикий газ	non-persistent gas.
Новобранец	recruit.

О

Обеспечивать	to secure.
Обменный пункт	refilling point.
Обмундировывать } Обмундировать }	to equip.
Обоз	baggage train.
Обоз первого разряда	1st line transport.
Обоз второго разряда	2nd line transport.
Оборудование	equipment (technical).
Обход	turning movement.
Огневая мощь	fire power.
Огнестрельные припасы	ammunition.
Одерживать верх	to overcome.
Окапываться	to entrench oneself.
Окопная война	trench warfare.

O—contd.

Окружать / Окружить	to surround.
Оперативный приказ	operation order.
Орудие	gun.
Осветительная ракета	Very light.
Открывать огонь	to open fire.
Отменить приказание	to countermand an order.
Отодвигать / Отодвинуть назад	to push back.
Отрезать	to cut off (mil.).
Отстаять позицию	to hold ones ground.
Отстранять	to dismiss.
Отступление	retreat.
Отход	retirement.
Отхожие ровики	latrines.
Офщерское собрание	officers' mess.
Охват	flanking movement.
Оценка обстановки	appreciation of the situation.

П

Паром	ferry.
Пароль	pass-word.
Перебежки	short rushes (inf.).
Передача	transmission (radio).
Передовые части	leading units.
Передовой участок	forward area.
Перекидной огонь	plunging fire.

П—*contd.*

Перекрёстный огонь	cross fire.
Переносить огонь	to switch fire.
Переходить в наступление	to take the offensive.
План военных действий	military plan of action.
Плацдарм	parade ground.
Побатальонно	by battalions.
Повзводно	by platoons.
Погреб	cellar.
Подвижной состав	rolling stock.
Подкрепление	reinforcement.
Позиционная война	trench warfare.
Поле зрения	field of view.
Помещение	accommodation.
Понтон	pontoon.
Попадать	to hit (a target).
Поротно	by companies.
Поражение	a defeat.
Посадка на суда	embarkation.
Посадочная площадка	landing ground—place of disembarkation.
Поход	campaign.
Походная колонна	a column on the march.
Почётный караул	guard of honour.
Предмостное укрепление	bridge-head.
Прекращать огонь	to cease fire.
Привал	a halt.
Приказы	standing orders.
Прикрывающая часть	covering force.
Прикрытие	covering party or cover

П—contd.

Применение местности	use of ground.
Приступ	assault (on a position).
Проверять караул	to inspect the guard.
Проволочное заграждение	barbed wire entanglement.
Проделка	trick.
Продольный огонь	enfilade fire.
Производить атаку	to deliver an attack.
Производить разведку	to reconnoitre.
Проникновение	infiltration.
Пропуск	permit, pass.
Прорыв	gap, break-through.
Противогаз	gas mask.
Пуля	bullet.
Пушка	gun.

Р

Разбивать палатку	to pitch a tent.
Разбираться в обстаноьке	to estimate the situation.
Разведка	reconnaissance (tactical and strategical).
Разведывательная служба	intelligence service.
Разворачивать / Развёртывать / Развернуть	to deploy.
Разомкнутый строй	open formation.
Разрабатывать	to frame a plan.
Ранец	soldier's pack.

Р—contd.

Рапортовать	to report.
Расквартировывать-расквартировать	to billet.
Располагаться / Расположиться } на бивак	to go into bivouac.
Редкий огонь	slow fire.
Реляция	oral report.
Рекогноцировка	reconnaissance (strategical)
Ручной пулемёт	light M.G.

С

Сажать на самолёты	to emplane.
Самолёт	aeroplane.
Сапёр	sapper.
Сборный пункт	rendezvous.
Сверять / Сверить } часы	to synchronise watches.
Сдаваться / Сдаться	to surrender.
Седло	saddle.
Сила	the force.
Склад	store house, magazine.
Скопление войск	concentration.
Снаряд	shell, projectile.
Снаряжение	equipment.
Снять батарею с позиции	to withdraw a battery.
Согласованность	co-ordination.
Соединение	formation.

C—contd.

Сомкнутый строй	close formation.
Спешное донесение	priority message.
Станковый пулемёт	heavy M.G.
Стать под ружём	to be under arms.
Стойкий газ	persistent gas.
Сторожевое охранение	outpost system.
Стоять на биваке	to be in bivouac.
Стрельба ударными снарядами	percussion fire.
Строевой приказ	routine orders.
Схватка	skirmish, encounter.

Т

Тактический предмет	tactical feature.
Тесная связь	close touch.
Тет-де-пон	bridge-head.

У

Удар в штыки	bayonet attack.
Ударное действие	shock action.
Узел	railway junction, knot, meeting point.
Унтер офицер	N.C.O.

Ф

Форсированный марш	forced march.
Фронтальная атака	frontal attack.
Фураж	forage.

Ч

Часовой	sentry.
Частыи огонь	rapid fire.

Ш

Шанцевый инструмент	entrenching tool.
Шинель	greatcoat.
Шоссе	main road.
Штаб	staff.

Э

Эшелонами	in echelon.

Я

Ядовитый газ	poison gas.

APPENDIX "K"

WEIGHTS AND MEASURES

The metric system is now generally used in the U.S.S.R., though the old Russian measures sometimes occur.

1. Conversion Tables

(a) *Length*

Metric.	English.	Russian.
1 mm.	·0393 inch.	—
7·6 mm.	·299 inch.	—
8·3 mm.	·303 inch.	—
25 mm.	·9825 inch.	—
25·4 mm.	1 inch.	1 duim.
37 mm.	1·45 inches.	—
50 mm.	1·965 inches.	—
75 mm.	2·95 inches.	—
76·2 mm.	3 inches.	—
100 mm.	3·93 inches.	—
107 mm.	4·2 inches.	—
122 mm.	4·8 inches.	—
152 mm.	6 inches.	—
200 mm.	7·86 inches.	—
203 mm.	7·98 inches.	—
304·8 mm.	1 foot.	1 foot.
	2 feet 4 inches.	1 arshin.
1 metre.	3 feet 3 inches.	—
1 kilometre.	—	·9732 versts.
	·6628 mile.	1 verst.
	1 mile.	1·5088 versts.

(b) *Weight*

Metric.	English.	Russian.
1 gramme.	·035 oz.	—
28·34 grammes.	1 oz.	—
453·58 grammes.	1 lb.	1·1076 foont.
1 kg.	—	2·442 foont.
—	36·1128 lb.	1 pood.
50·802 kgs.	1 cwt.	3·1 poods.
1 metric ton.	·984 ton.	61 poods.
1,016·04 kgs.	1 ton.	62 poods.

(c) *Liquid*

Metric.		English.
1 litre	=	1·75 pints.
		·219 gallon.
4·58 litres	=	1 gallon.
5 litres	=	1·09 gallons.

(d) *Area.*

Metric.	English.	Russian.
—	2·7 acres.	1 desiatina.
1 hectare (10,000 sq. m.)	2·471 acres.	—
258 hectares or 2·58 sq. kms.	} 1 sq. mile.	—

(e) *Coinage.*—It is almost impossible to give table of the comparative values of Soviet and English money, as the official exchange rate of 25 roubles to £1 is purely arbitrary.

The principal Soviet monetary units are—
  The kopek.
  The rouble (100 kopeks).

2. Convenient approximate Conversions for Metric System

Centimetres to inches : multiply by four and divide product by 10.

Metres to yards : add one-ninth of the number of metres (9 metres = 10 yards).

Kilometres to statute miles : multiply by five and divide by eight.

Litres to pints : multiply by seven and divide by four.

Kilogrammes to lbs. : multiply by two decimal two.

Kilogrammes to cwts. : divide by 50.

Centigrade to Fahrenheit : multiply by nine, divide by five, and add 32 to the answer.

Plate I

45-mm. Anti-Tank Gun.

76-mm. Field Gun, Short.

76-mm. Field Gun, Long.

122-mm. Field Howitzer.

107-mm. Gun.

152-mm. Howitzer.

Plate VII.

203-mm. Howitzer.

203-mm. Howitzer.

76-mm. Anti-Aircraft Gun.

Light Amphibian Tank (T.37).

Infantry Divisional Tank (T.26 Light-Medium).

B.T. Cruiser Tank.

Plate XII

T.28 Heavy Medium Tank.

T.32 Heavy Tank.

Plate XIV

B.A.27 Armoured Car.

Plate XV

B.A. Broniford Armoured Car.

B.A. Amphibian Armoured Car.

B.A. Ford Armoured Car.

PLATE XVIII.

GENERAL SERVICE UNIFORM
(Excluding Cossack Regiments)

Service Cap.

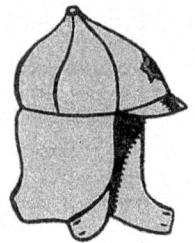

Shako (helmet).

Tunic

Great Coat.

(F.9883). Wt. 13485. 2500 5/40. Gp.961. FOSH & CROSS LTD.

COSSACK UNIFORMS

Don Cossacks.

Tall fur hat, soft cap, greatcoat, grey hood with long ends, khaki-coloured tunic shirt, dark blue full knee breeches with red side-strips and knee boots.

Terek and Kuban Cossacks.

Kubanka, soft cap, greatcoat, coloured hood, khaki-coloured tunic, blue full knee breeches with light blue piping down the side for Terek Cossacks and red piping for Kuban Cossacks, and army boots.

HOW TO DISTINGUISH ARMS OF THE SERVICE

(a) Head-dress.

When not equipped with steel helmets, all arms of the Service (with the exception of Cossack formations) wear either a General Service cap or a shako helmet.

The metal General Service badge is worn in front of vertical band of cap or (on shako) fastened over cloth star.

The coloured cloth stars are sewn onto shako (helmet).

PLATE XIX.

GENERAL SERVICE (CAP) BADGE (OF METAL)

Infantry.　　　　　Cavalry.　　　　　Air Force.

Artillery and　　　Administrative and
Technical Troops.　Supply Personnel.

HOW TO DISTINGUISH ARMS OF THE SERVICE

(*Continued*)

(b) **Tunics, Smocks and Greatcoats.**

The various arms of the Service are distinguished by (a) the colours of the gorget patches worn on the tunics, smocks and greatcoats, and (b) by crests worn on the gorget patches.

NOTE.

Administrative and supply personnel wear only badges of rank and no crest on the gorget patches.

PLATE XX A.

TUNIC PATCH   GREATCOAT PATCH   SPECIALISTS BADGES

INFANTRY

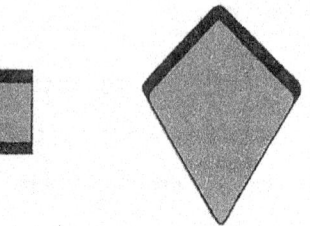

CAVALRY

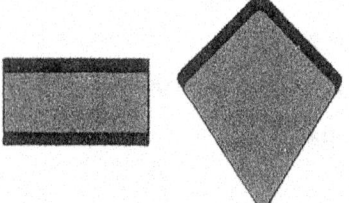   

Machine Guns.   Cav. Scouts.   Band.

ARTILLERY

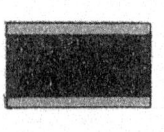  

Artillery.

AIR FORCE

Air Force.

PLATE XX B.
CHEMICAL TROOPS

Medical and Veterinary

Tunic Collar Patch. Greatcoat Patch.

 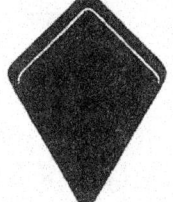 

Veterinary Personnel.   Medical Personnel.

RAILWAY TROOPS

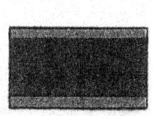  

Administrative and Supply Personnel

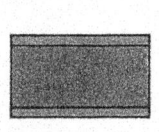 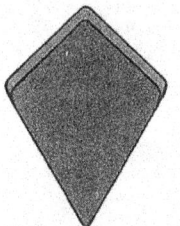 

Etappe and Transport Units.

CORPS AND RANK BADGES ARE WORN ON GORGET PATCHES AS SHOWN BELOW

 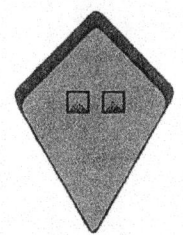  

HOW TO DISTINGUISH REGIMENTS

Regimental crests and badges are not worn in the Red Army.

Distinguishing badges of the various arms of the Service should not be mistaken for Regimental crests.

There are, therefore, so far as is known, no visual means of identifying the unit or formation to which a Red Army soldier belongs.

HOW TO DISTINGUISH BADGES OF RANK

Badges of rank are in red enamel or red cloth and are worn on the gorget patches of the tunic, smock and greatcoat and on the sleeves.

PLATE XX C.
TECHNICAL TROOPS

Tunic Collar Patch

Greatcoat Patch

Electro-Technical (and Search-Light) Units.

Pontoon Units.

W/T. Units.

Mechanised Units (Motorised Units).

Mounted Sapper Units.

Inspectorate of Signals.

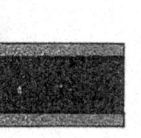

Chemical Troops.

Inspectorate of Engineers.

Mining Units.

Signals.

Sapper Units.

Carrier Pigeon Units.

Armoured Trains.

Armoured Cars.

Tanks.

Camouflage Units.

PLATE XXI.

BADGES OF RANK

RANK	GORGET PATCHES		DESCRIPTION	SLEEVE BADGES	DESCRIPTION
	TUNIC	GREATCOAT			
Marshal of the Soviet Union			Large gold star on red cloth, gold piping.		A large gold star over broad gold braid on red cloth.
Army Commander 1st rank	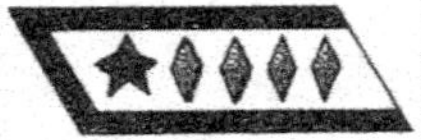		Gold star, 4 rhomboids, gold piping.		Gold star, gold braid stripe.
Army Commander 2nd rank	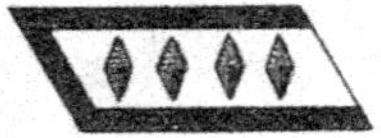		4 rhomboids (no star).		4 gold braid stripes of medium width.
Corps Commander	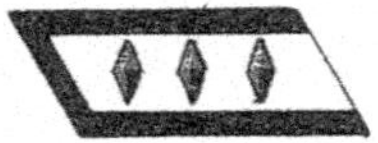		3 rhomboids, gold piping.		3 gold braid stripes of medium width.
Divisional Commander	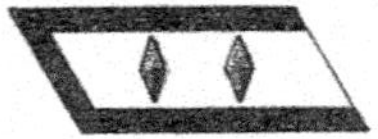		2 rhomboids, gold piping.		2 gold braid stripes of medium width.
Brigade Commander			1 rhomboid, gold piping.		1 gold braid stripe of medium width.

Rank				Sleeve stripes
Colonel		3 rectangles.		with thin gold braid edges.
Major		2 rectangles.		2 medium red stripes.
Captain		1 rectangle.		1 medium red stripe.
Senior Lieutenant		3 squares.		3 narrow red stripes.
Lieutenant		2 squares.		2 narrow red stripes.
Junior Lieutenant		1 square.		1 narrow red stripe.

NOTES

1. The colour of the background of the gorget patches and colour of piping varies according to the arm of the service of the wearer. Reference should be made to App. A, and App. D, Plate I.

2. Political Commissars wear similar gorget patches to their corresponding combatant rank. On the sleeve, however, all ranks wear a sewn red star with a small metal hammer and sickle fixed in the centre.

New notes on the Red Army

No. 1 — Tactics and organization

Prepared under the direction of the Chief of the Imperial General Staff

The War Office
August 1944

CONTENTS
PART I

SEC	PAGE
1. General	2
2. Attack	4
3. Defence	7
4. Forcing of rivers	8
5. Tactics of particular arms—	
Infantry	10
Cavalry	12
Tanks	13
Motorized and mechanized troops	16
Ski troops	17
Airborne and parachute troops	18
Artillery	18
6. Assault of a town : street fighting	22
7. Partisan warfare	25
8. Conclusions	27

PART II

APPENDIX ON RED ARMY ORGANIZATION

CHARTS

A. (i) Infantry division, (ii) infantry regiment, and battalion	*facing* 28
B. Artillery division	29
C. Cavalry division	31
D. (i) Independent tank brigade	32
(ii) Independent assault tank regiment	33
(iii) The tank corps	34
E. Organization of supply and transport	*facing* 34
Illustrations	35

DISTRIBUTION

All arms	Scale A
OCTUs	Scale I

NEW NOTES ON THE RED ARMY
No. 1, PART I
TACTICS AND ORGANIZATION

Section 1.—GENERAL

1. The circumstances in which the Red Army has developed since it entered the war with Germany have been dominated by features which have left their imprint on the Army to-day. The main features were two. First, mobilization had to be completed, new classes called up speedily, and equipment and armament provided on a rapidly expanding scale: what is more, this task had to be accomplished with an army continuously engaged in fierce action. Secondly, the fact that this mobilization had to draw very largely on strata of the population only one generation removed from illiteracy necessarily meant that a considerable proportion of the growing army had to be composed of men who could absorb only a limited amount of training, and that of a simple kind. There was the further problem of providing quickly a large number of junior commanders: the Red Army had the advantage, however, of starting the campaign equipped with a considerable number of senior commanders who had a background of continuous experience and profound study of military science, many from the ranks or officer class of the Imperial Army. Nearly all of the senior commanders now proving their skill on the Eastern Front have had experience in every action in which the Red Army has been involved, from the Civil War onwards. Therefore, though commanders were few, there was a well of experience on which they could draw for training others.

2. Three basic principles can be discerned in the endeavours of the Russians to deal with their problems: simplicity, flexibility, improvisation. Simplicity both of organization and equipment was essential if large numbers of inexperienced officers and NCOs were to succeed in managing their material at all: it is probable that had the Red Army tried to elaborate establishments and weapons down to every detail, the result would have been chaos. Flexibility in organization is the corollary of simplicity. In many instances organization has grown out of developments in tactical doctrine, based on experience; nor has this growth necessarily been uniform in all formations or sectors. This system has had the further advantage of leaving a great deal of control over the mechanism of operations in the hands of the experienced higher commanders of whom the Red Army already disposed. Improvisation was and is a prominent feature: in combination with flexibility it has proved a powerful factor in training and tactics and has done much to make the Red Army as vigorous as it is.

3. The results in practice are, however, often bewildering: while basic units are fairly constant as well as simple in organization, they

are at all levels combined or varied to form a wide range of formations and units, some purely *ad hoc*, some surviving as permanent. Thus, to quote a few examples among many, army groups, armies, and above all corps, vary so much from one operation to another that no degree of uniformity can be laid down for them—a factor no doubt as confusing to the enemy, as it is convenient to the commander of the operation. It follows, however, that such a system required a correspondingly high degree of centralization of planning and tactics, and it is probably true to say that this centralization is indeed to be found in the Red Army to a higher degree than in any other. Not only are a preponderating number of troops (especially artillery) who would normally be found under army or even corps control retained under GHQ control, but the General Staff intervenes through a representative committee at the front in the planning and direction of co-ordinated operations by several neighbouring army groups, and the amount of discretion left to army or corps commanders is correspondingly reduced.

4. Russian corps organization, which is particularly puzzling, requires some explanation. The corps is a fighting, never an administrative, formation. Its organization is largely *ad hoc*, and therefore particularly flexible, though usually the particular formation is built up on a nucleus of a permanent staff and components. According as the components are mainly infantry, cavalry, tanks, armoured car borne or truck borne troops, the corps are called infantry, cavalry, tank, mechanized, or motorized respectively. No artillery corps organization is known to exist.

5. As with organization, so with training. The problem was always to exploit the main advantage and to deal with the main weakness. In training, the weak point was the large proportion of the armed forces whose capacity to absorb training of any complexity was limited—but this was counterbalanced by a developed political machine which for years past had been successfully grappling with the problem of turning a backward agricultural people into a highly industrialized state. A solid background of military science, evolved in experience and in the military schools and based on close study of the past, already existed : means had to be found not only of making every soldier aware of the basic elements of this experience, but of keeping the training alive and in step with the new experiences gained day by day. The hierarchy of Communist Party cells at all levels represents within the Army no less than in industry the fountainhead of exhortation, example, and instruction. It is true that some time after the German invasion the political commissar who had shared the command of units and formations with the military commander was abolished as such, and the unity of military control re-established. Nevertheless, the commissar in modified form reappeared and has remained ever since at all levels from army group to company as deputy commander for political affairs. He no longer has the power of interfering in purely military matters with the commander's decisions, but he plays in all aspects of morale, welfare, and above all training, a part in which he is

helped by the party organizations which are found at all levels down to platoon. In training he has the important duty of ensuring that lessons have been thoroughly learnt, a duty which he is expected to perform by example no less than by precept, since he is at the same time a combatant soldier. In addition to officially circulated directives, a daily Red Army newspaper "The Red Star" ventilates problems, explains elementary and occasionally more advanced problems of tactics, and lays down the answers to new enemy weapons and devices. A rapid and popular method is thereby provided of training by study and reiteration, under guidance of the political commanders who are helped by the party cells found in every unit throughout the army. Great stress is laid on morale, on the individual's responsibility in playing his own particular part in the common struggle, and, if a member of the Communist Party, of showing an example to the others. It is no exaggeration that the political system is the backbone of training and morale in the Red Army. The achievements of the Red Army are, in exactly the same way as the achievements of industry, the direct results of a totalitarian political system.

A short appendix on some of the basic organization of the Red Army will be found at page 28. The following sections deal in outline with the most characteristic doctrines as applied to the different aspects of warfare and arms of the service.

Section 2.—ATTACK

"An enemy caught off his guard is half beaten."

Suvorov.

6. From Suvorov onwards Russian doctrine, as every other military doctrine, has emphasized as the basic principle of the attack the ability to achieve a decisive superiority of striking forces where the enemy does not expect it—and the fullest exploitation of surprise before the enemy has had time to recover. Since on the Eastern Front, involving hundreds of divisions, the assembly of a force on the scale required for modern warfare is in general impossible to conceal, other means must be found to achieve surprise.

7. The solution has been found in the marked differentiation that exists in the Red Army between the élite shock troop formations—armoured, motorized, infantry and artillery, especially SP—and the general body of infantry and tanks. In the main, the initial task of forcing the break-through falls in an offensive to the élite shock troops, while the exploitation of success after break-through is the task of the main body of infantry. Now, while Russian superiority in numbers has generally been sufficient to enable them to maintain powerful concentrations of troops on more than one sector at a time, it is the movement of the shock troops that is most indicative of their intentions. This is particularly the fact since there exists a considerable difference in fighting quality between the élite shock troops, which are excellent, and the rank

and file which, though very numerous, are less intensively trained. The greatest attention has been paid to concealment in every form : camouflage, movement by night, and every form of military ruse have been studied and applied, as results show, with a considerable measure of success in the movement of these troops. On most occasions their mobility has enabled the final concentrations to take place within the space of the last nights preceding the offensive.

8. But camouflage and deception are not the only means relied on to achieve vital surprise. Every form of the unexpected is exploited to the full in planning—the choice of least favourable terrain, frequent attacks in the dead of moonless nights, the mounting of an offensive at the moment least favourable to the attacker from the point of view of climate—all these methods have been used with success to defeat the enemy's appreciation.

9. The next basic doctrine in attack is what the Russians call " The fist ", which means the co-ordinated and concentrated blow carried out as swiftly as possible. This is achieved in training by meticulously planned co-operation of all arms so as to avoid dissipation of fire power. Artillery, Air Force (which in the Red Army is a part of the Army), mortars, and small arms, must all play their own part in a carefully planned and timed assault, so that when the blow falls it can fall with crushing effect making possible the immediate exploitation of success before the enemy can recover from the first effects of surprise. The improving mastery of the problem of achieving co-operation of all arms was one of the most distinctive features of the campaign of 1943–44, while failure to achieve it was one of the factors that had prevented outstanding success in attack in 1942–43.

10. The rapid exploitation of success before the enemy has had time to recover from the initial blow has been the dominant feature of the campaigns of 1943–44. The rapid advance of the Red Army in the early stages of the attack has been due equally to simplicity of organization, making rapid movement easier, and the cutting down of establishments, especially HQ establishments, to the bare minimum, which has simplified the problem of supply, as to real service organization. The result is that the need for refitting and regrouping, and the consequent lull in the attacking impetus have been time after time postponed for just long enough to upset enemy appreciation and unhinge his defensive plan.

11. Methods of attack vary. Where they have the means to do it, the Russians prefer to mount a series of blows, simultaneously or in quick succession, so as to pin down enemy reserves and obstruct the switching of mobile reserves to meet the threat. In the tactical field this result has been achieved more than once. On the strategic scale, the Russians had not up till the summer of 1944 succeeded in maintaining two equally powerful major offensives at the same time. The reason may have been shortage of air, artillery, armour, and élite troops required, in view of the enormous scale on which

the Red Army builds up for break-through assaults: developments in training and industry have meant that they are able to do so now (July, 1944), and this may well prove the decisive factor.

12. Frontal assaults are made when necessary, but are always followed by outflanking movements or by sudden attacks from the rear by cavalry or motorized troops. When making a frontal assault the Russians have realized the importance of mounting it on a scale sufficient not only to breach the enemy defences, but to pin and hold the main enemy forces for long enough and in sufficient strength to prevent the enemy from switching reinforcements from his frontal positions to the threat created by the subsequent attack on the flank or rear.

13. In breaching the enemy defences after artillery preparation the troops most usually employed are the heaviest tanks, organized in special assault regiments, in closest co-operation with picked infantry. Since the object of this assault echelon is to penetrate deep into the enemy defences at the greatest possible speed, a second exploiting echelon follows on the first, with the task of wiping out points of resistance that have been by-passed. Great importance is attached at this stage to the task of this second echelon of immediately consolidating positions won and of making preparations for immediate counter-attacks. It is normally composed of medium tanks in co-operation with infantry. At the same time as this second echelon, mobile forces of cavalry, medium tanks, and motorized troops will pour in through the gap in the defences with the object of penetrating as deep as possible, to seize enemy airfields and supply centres in the rear and to cut off routes of retreat and reinforcements. These mobile troops relieve the heavy tanks that have effected the penetration, so that these can be withdrawn for refitting. A fourth element in the attack is the special reserve force. This preferably mobile body is kept in readiness to deal immediately with enemy counter-attacks, and for that reason invariably includes a high proportion of anti-tank guns and rifles and of infantrymen trained in tank destruction. The tasks of the GHQ artillery reserve will also include special counter battery, anti-personnel, and anti-tank tasks, in the event of an enemy counter-attack.

14. Mention must be made of the favourite Russian tactics of infiltration in the attack, designed to facilitate the task of the break-through force. Small shock groups of picked troops are formed some two or three days before an offensive. These groups, which are lightly armed and carry their own supplies, are used to slip through the front at night, penetrate some 15–20 miles into the enemy rear, and dig in. As soon as the main offensive is launched their task is to hold up all movement on roads in the rear areas and to hold out until relieved by the heavy tanks and picked infantry, and later by the mobile forces carrying out the attacks in depth on the flanks and rear. In winter ski troops have been used for this task of infiltration.

Section 3.—DEFENCE

15. The importance of defence in depth was realized by the Russians from the very outset of the war. The expanse of territory available for defence enabled them to exploit the advantage of depth on the strategic plane. On the tactical plane the pattern of defence is fairly constant at all levels. Its basic features are :

16. *First*, a system of strongly fortified mutually supporting defensive positions, with all-round interlocking fire; particular emphasis is laid in all teaching on the importance of all-round anti-tank fire ready to deal with an armoured threat wherever it may arise, and great care has been devoted to the study of anti-tank positions in this connection. The object aimed at is to achieve a plan of fire by means of which the whole weight of fire can be brought down with the minimum delay on the sector from which the enemy attack is anticipated. The anti-tank role is not confined to the specialized anti-tank weapons—guns and rifles. Infantrymen trained in tank destruction, and the rapid switching of artillery to an anti-tank role all form an important part of this defensive organization.

17. *Secondly*, in defence, as in attack, the greatest importance is attached to a mobile reserve, for which a considerable force is normally employed, ready to attack a successful enemy penetration from the flanks or rear. Such a reserve, the plan of which must be co-ordinated with the reserve tasks of the artillery, will always include considerable anti-tank forces.

18. Training and propaganda have played a considerable part in the successful development of defence in depth. One aspect of it, when forces are deployed on as wide a front as in Russia, is that forward groups encircled in the early stages of the attack are subsequently relieved by counter-attack. Troops are therefore ceaselessly instructed to fight to the last man and last round by all the force available in the political training machinery. Another aspect of defence in depth to which the Russians showed themselves particularly alive, notably in their defensive fighting in the Kursk bulge in July 1943, is that of ensuring the holding of the haunches of a sector which is attacked, especially from the point of view of anti-tank defence, so as to restore the situation by blows at the flanks and rear of the enemy thrust after penetration and, by closing in on the flanks of an armoured spearhead, to cut off the tanks from their supporting infantry. The Russian experience in defence has its reflection, incidentally, in the tactics of attacks : time and time again in the course of their advance the Russians have been able to consolidate their forces on the haunches of an enemy line before their main frontal assault on the line, thus forestalling enemy tactics in defence of a position.

19. Three main tactical forms of defence are recognized in teaching :—
    (a) Positional defence, where a comparatively narrow sector is held in the form of a series of interlocking and mutually supporting positions, with a powerful reserve in readiness.

(b) Defence on a wide front, where the frontage of the area held is considerably wider and defensive positions can no longer be mutually supporting. In this form of defence particular importance is always attached both to the strength and mobility of the reserve, to the artillery reserve tasks, and above all to the duty of every single position to fight stubbornly even when encircled.

(c) Mobile defence, which consists of gradual withdrawal from position to position without engaging the enemy, under rear guard cover. This presents no special features, but emphasis is laid in teaching on the need to go over to the counter-attack at the earliest moment.

Section 4.—FORCING OF RIVERS

" Forward, forward—the head cannot wait for the tail."
Suvorov.

20. The rapid forcing of rivers is an essential accomplishment for an army operating on the Eastern Front, where over large areas rivers form the only natural defence lines available to an enemy. Russian training has recognized that if bridgeheads can be secured rapidly the enemy's natural defence line is thereby disrupted before it has been consolidated. Experience during 1943–44 on the Eastern Front shows that this idea has dominated Russian tactics—notably on the Dnieper where bridgeheads were secured and consolidated immediately the river was reached, thereby gaining a valuable element of surprise against an enemy who had with some justification appreciated that some weeks' interval would be required for the necessary build-up before crossings could be attempted.

21. In considering the factors which contributed to this success, the following appear to predominate :—

First, training. The Russian soldier had been trained for some time to get across a river as soon as he got to it—not to wait for supplies, equipment, or weapons, but to get across.

22. Secondly, great emphasis had been laid on the need to exploit to the full material available locally, particularly timber. The Russian peasant has the advantage of being exceptionally skilled with an axe—this natural faculty made a sapper of every infantryman. Both underwater and overwater bridges were constructed rapidly, in the course of a few days, entirely of local timber, including pile railway bridges. There is little doubt but that, particularly in the crossing of the Dnieper, the independence of the forward troops of formal sapper equipment was one of the main factors of success in the Kiev offensive.

23. In general, the Russian soldier is trained to expect an enemy counter-attack immediately. To meet this, the following principles are taught :—

(a) All fire power must be co-ordinated and ready for instant action when the first crossings take place. If possible, guns should be mounted on ferry craft at an early stage.

(b) No attempt should be made in the early stages to achieve success in depth. The first object should be to organize as broad a front as possible, so as to dissipate the enemy forces. Particular attention must be paid to early organization of anti-tank defence. Experience shows that the Russians have been able to achieve in the initial stages numerous shallow, but firmly held, bridgeheads, and have subsequently exploited their success by the linking up of several of these bridgeheads to form a broad wedge for further advances.

(c) Above all, in the early stages, crossings must be kept mobile. For this end rafts and boats are used largely. Where bridges are constructed sappers are trained to move them frequently from one crossing place to another, so as to keep the front as broad as possible and to dissipate enemy fire power.

24. Emphasis is also laid in training on the need for careful reconnaissance, including the selection of localities that have a plentiful supply of timber; on the selection of bends in the river facing the advances, so that fire power can be concentrated to cover the crossings; on the frequent use of dummy crossings and multiple crossings—especially in the early stages when crossings are mainly by rafts. Little is known of the sapper equipment used—pontoons are certainly used extensively. In general, pontoon bridges are used for tanks, rapidly constructed timber pile bridges for loads up to 10 or 12 tons.

25. The last peculiar feature of Russian tactics in the forcing of rivers is the part played by partisans. The role of the partisans is difficult to estimate precisely. They can obviously provide a variety of services to advance troops operating in enemy held territory beyond their main forces and supplies. They have on occasions played an important part in the preparatory stages of crossings—by reconnaissance of enemy positions, by the selection of suitable sites, and by the preparation of timber and other equipment in advance to enable the forward troops to cross with the maximum speed. In many instances their knowledge both of the topography of the river and of enemy dispositions on the other side has proved invaluable in ensuring the success of a crossing.

26. There is no evidence that parachute troops or airborne troops have been used as yet on any large scale in forcing rivers. They have, however, been used on a small scale to ensure co-ordination with partisans behind the enemy lines and to help them in their preparatory tasks when operating in advance of the main forces during their approach to a river. The Russians at one time used amphibious tanks, but there is no known instance of their use in the recent campaigns.

Section 5.—TACTICS OF PARTICULAR ARMS

Infantry

"There is less danger from enemy guns the closer one gets to them."—*Peter the Great.*

27. Russian teaching stresses that infantry is the basic arm. Acting either independently, or in co-operation with tanks and artillery, it can destroy the enemy and can seize and hold ground when in the attack; while in the defence it alone can prepare and fortify defensive positions. This section is concerned only with heavy infantry, which is the arm used for winning and consolidating ground, in close co-operation with tanks. For this purpose it disposes of a considerable sapper establishment. (*See* Charts A (i) and A (ii)). The Russians also use light or motorized infantry for rapid mobile attacks on enemy flanks and rear.

28. A marked feature of the organization of the Russian infantry division in the present war has been its successive reduction in size. Its present strength is approximately 10,000 (*see* Chart A). This reduction in strength has, however, in part been compensated by a proportionate increase of fire power, especially of automatic weapons and mortars. The reasons for this reduction are no doubt bound up with development of tactical doctrines, but the following may have contributed to the change :—

   (*a*) The need for economy of manpower.

   (*b*) The increasing policy of the Red Army of withdrawing supporting arms, especially artillery, to the centralized control of GHQ.

   (*c*) A policy of increasing the firepower of the individual infantryman to a maximum by the lavish allocation of self-loading rifles and of sub-machine guns.

29. The significant increase in the use of the sub-machine gun, which is essentially a short range weapon, is fully in accord with the personal training of the infantryman, in which the strongest emphasis is constantly laid on the need to get to the closest grips with the enemy. In the same way, the modern maxim "First the grenade, then after it with your bayonet" is the modern equivalent of Suvorov's maxim "The bullet's a fool but the bayonet knows its job." Headlong and fearless attack is stressed at all times by the whole machine of training and propaganda of which the Red Army disposes. The soldier is further taught to keep as close as possible to the shell bursts of his own guns, so as to be ready to go in to the attack the moment the gunfire lifts. If tanks are co-operating with infantry, the infantryman must keep as close as possible to his own tanks. On the other hand, if enemy tanks are attacking, the greatest stress is laid on the infantryman's duty to attack them,

not only with anti-tank rifles but with grenades and incendiary bottles. It is, however, impossible to say whether the stress laid in training on the infantryman's anti-tank tasks is due to the success of these methods or to the value of such training for morale. Finally, the infantryman is enjoined not to go to the dressing station if wounded without his commander's permission. The frequent testimony of the Germans confirms that the Russian infantrymen will again and again continue in battle although wounded.

30. The tactics of infantry follow the main principles of Red Army doctrine. In attack, frontal assaults are, where possible, to be avoided, except in co-operation with heavy artillery support and with the heavy break-through tanks. However, attacks from the flanks and rear should be co-ordinated with a pinning down frontal attack, which must be strong enough to hold the enemy forces and prevent them from switching to the flank or rear to meet the attack. The infantry must at all times be on the alert for any soft spot in the enemy defences that may be disclosed during battle, and the commander must at all times maintain such control over his attacking force and reserve as will enable him at the decisive moment to throw all the weight of his fire power into the weak point. In defence, the greatest stress is laid on tenacity and the duty to fight to the last. Great stress is also laid on discipline in holding fire until the enemy has penetrated close enough for it to be effective. If encircled, an infantry position must fight its way out; as a last resort an encircled group must try to go into hiding and become a nucleus for partisan activities.

31. In the early part of the war Russian training manuals laid down the form of infantry attack in successive echelons; the first echelon, the assaulting force, had the task of penetrating the enemy defences with the utmost rapidity, while the second echelon followed to mop up and consolidate. This formation has been abandoned. The new regulations lay down that attack must, at all levels from platoon to division, be in such formation, whether extended, arrowhead, or inverted arrowhead, as will bring into the assault at one blow (and not successively) the full weight of the attacking force. The commander should only retain under his control as a reserve such a nucleus of forces, including especially the anti-tank guns and artillery under his command, as will enable him to throw in a decisive blow should emergency demand it. This change in infantry tactics is probably an outcome of the growing centralization and influence of GHQ over operations, since it is clear that the infantry commander's power of influencing the course of operations is considerably reduced. It is, however, consistent with the cardinal Red Army doctrine that fire power must be used as a " fist " and must on no account be weakened by being dissipated.

Cavalry

"Cavalry must go for the enemy flanks."
Suvorov.

32. The Red Army has not only retained a considerable proportion of cavalry, but also makes constant tactical use of this arm in all types of country, in main and not subsidiary roles, both alone and in co-operation with other troops. It is probably true that the Red Army has not yet solved the problem of the vulnerability of cavalry, especially to air attack, in defence against which cavalry largely relies on dispersal; it is, however, the case that the campaign in the East has proved that there is still in modern warfare a sufficient variety of circumstances and terrain in which the advantages of rapid mobility which cavalry troops provide outweigh this disadvantage. Moreover, as will be seen from Chart C, the arming of the cavalryman with tommy guns has concentrated a considerable automatic fire power in the sabre squadron.

33. The tactics of cavalry, whether alone or in co-operation, are always designed to exploit mobility to the fullest extent. "Swift and concealed manœuvres, powerful fire, sudden and headlong attack, must be the basic principles of cavalry in action," say the Russian FSR. Great stress is also laid in training on the need for constant readiness to resist an enemy attack from the air or from tanks, and the importance of bringing all fire power to this end into action immediately and forcibly. In the event of tank attacks, training aims at skilful diverting of enemy armour onto the anti-tank defences provided by supporting arms. Smoke is used in such diversionary manœuvres; it is also used in the attack, in order to achieve the necessary surprise in the approach. Every form of natural concealment must also be exploited to this end, such as that provided by forests, marshes, or mountains, or by the cover of darkness.

34. In general, cavalry attacks are aimed at the flanks or rear, well into the depth of the enemy defences. The normal practice in the attack is to develop the initial surprise achieved by the assault echelon by immediately following up the attack by a second echelon, which will include the greater part of the available heavier fire power (*see* Chart C). This is in effect the use of a feint frontal attack designed to draw enemy fire and expose his firing positions so as to make the real weight of the subsequent main attack the more effective. The rapid, bold cavalry thrust has been used with success in seizing in advance of the main forces suitable crossing places on rivers and making the preliminary crossings; it has also proved effective in the pursuit in disorganizing enemy defensive preparations before the main force can be brought up to deal with them or in seizing the enemy's defensive positions in his rear before he can consolidate them.

35. In defence, the aim of cavalry must be to exploit its own mobility by making the enemy fight on ground of its own choosing. Particular stress is laid in training on the need for co-ordinated

fire power by all arms ; and particular stress is laid in cavalry tactics on the need for a strong counter-attacking body which is kept in the rear to deal immediately with enemy penetrations, and which should be large, up to half of the available force. Great care must be devoted to the anti-tank defence. Cavalry is particularly adapted to mobile defence, since by its mobility it can often force the enemy to move his artillery up for each defence line on which the cavalry stands.

36. In practice, it is mostly in co-operation with tanks and SP guns that cavalry has been used, thus exploiting its mobility while at the same time giving adequate protection against extreme vulnerability. Great flexibility of organization is a marked feature of the tank-cavalry partnership. The tanks may be in support, or under command, or neighbouring formations may co-operate, or all three forms may be used in succession as the result of regrouping following on the changing course of a battle. Thus, to take the example of a cavalry corps and a tank corps in co-operation : in the approach to the objective the tanks will normally protect the flanks and rear of the cavalry divisions. A number of tanks may, however, be put under command of each cavalry division to act as a break-through force in the initial stages of the attack and thus enable the cavalry to get onto its objective, while the bulk of the armour attacks independently at other points of the enemy defences. If the enemy defence stiffens and the initial assault fails to disrupt it, the cavalry will normally fight dismounted, co-operating closely with the tanks in exactly the same way as infantry. Other circumstances may dictate other methods ; thus, if a powerful initial blow is required, the tank groups under command of the several cavalry divisions may be put under command of the leading cavalry division to strike the first blow, and enable the cavalry to get onto their objective in force. The Russians claim that this variety of systems of co-operation does not create any special difficulties of liaison that cannot be overcome by personal contact between commanders, and skilful use of wireless. This view may be correct, but a good part of the success is no doubt due to the great degree of centralized control from above over the course of operations that is practised in the Red Army.

Tanks

37. The Russians use three main types of tanks : a heavy breakthrough tank, of which the KV is the basic model, a medium tank for co-operation with infantry (basic model the T.34), and a light tank (T.70 and variants). The light tank is falling into disuse and is now used mainly for reconnaissance and liaison. Illustrations and some details on the KV and T.34 will be found on page 37.

38. The organization of armoured forces is subject to much variation, and has undergone changes since the outset of the war. There is no longer a divisional organization. The heavy tanks are now believed to be organized entirely in independent or special regiments.

They may sometimes be found under corps command, but since their tasks are largely of an independent nature they are usually kept under GHQ, or army group, control, and are allocated for special tasks. The medium tanks, with a decreasing proportion of light tanks, are organized in independent tank brigades, and in tank corps. A number of independent brigades will normally be allocated by GHQ to each army commander to use for reinforcement of infantry divisions, or for co-operation with cavalry divisions. The tank corps, which are used in bulk for particular tasks, are allocated by GHQ to army group commanders, sometimes to army commanders. (Corps in the Red Army are not administrative commands but are organized largely *ad hoc*, as and when required, see para 5.)

39. Basically tank corps are composed of three tank brigades, the organization of which is similar to that of the independent tank brigades, but includes additional motorized infantry and SP artillery. The composition of each corps is however very variable, and depends entirely on the task allotted to it. Thus, a corps will often include additional SP artillery, a mechanized brigade, and sometimes the assault regiments of heavy tanks also come under corps command. Thus, in effect, all Russian armour is under GHQ control, a factor which contributes considerably to the ease and speed with which armoured concentrations can be built up on any sector required.

40. The basic principles for the employment of armour in the offence and defence have been worked out by the Red Army in bitter experience. The following are the main principles, as they are now taught :—

   (a) Medium tanks, which are vulnerable to enemy anti-tank fire, must never be used for direct frontal assault on the enemy defences. This is primarily the task of the infantry, supported by artillery. When available, the special heavy tanks are used for forcing a break through, in close co-operation with infantry.

   (b) Tanks must primarily be used against enemy infantry, and in support of own infantry. It is the task of artillery to neutralize enemy tanks. Only in exceptional circumstances, such as most favourable ground or overwhelming superiority, will tanks engage tanks.

   (c) Tanks must at all times co-operate as closely as possible with the infantry, keeping within 200–400 yards of them. It is a very frequent practice for the infantry to ride right up to the objectives on the tanks, usually dropping off before going into action. While the tanks clear the way for the infantry by attacking the enemy infantry, guns, and strong points, the infantrymen in turn support the tanks by silencing enemy weapons with their anti-tank guns, by clearing minefields, protecting tanks when going over obstacles, and by supplying fuel and ammunition. Finally the infantry must consolidate ground, while the tanks speed on on their next bound, paving the way for the next wave of tanks which follows the first, and its supporting infantry. In general, while the timing of tanks and infantry in the original breakthrough must be carefully planned in advance so as to ensure that the full weight of the attack goes in in one strong blow, no such planning in advance is considered possible in the subsequent operations within the breached enemy defences : here co-ordination must be achieved by constant co-operation on the spot by visual signs and by wireless, so as to ensure that one arm does not hold up or impede the other.

(d) Tanks must never lose their mobility, since their main task is to find gaps in the flanks or rear of the enemy defences where they can penetrate. Therefore the commander must always be in a position to gather his entire tank strength into a single " fist " so as to strike a powerful blow at one of the gaps that the course of fighting has revealed.

(e) The most careful reconnaissance is needed before tanks go into action, since otherwise incomplete knowledge of any fire positions and defences will impede their advance.

(f) The closest co-operation is required between tanks and artillery and tanks and air force. Artillery must not only silence the enemy anti-tank fire in the main defence zone before the tank attack is put in, but must co-operate closely to deal with tasks as they arise in the course of the action. The artillery commander directs the fire of the weapons detailed for the support of tanks from a mobile observation tank equipped with radio. The same close and continuous control by radio is required for supporting aircraft.

(g) When on the defensive, tanks form the vital core of the counter-attacking force. In the event of an enemy armoured penetration, the task of engaging armour falls to anti-tank artillery and infantry. The armoured forces will strike at the enemy infantry following behind the attacking enemy tanks with the object of outflanking the attack and of cutting off the enemy infantry from their supporting armour.

(h) Finally, tanks must exploit every advantage of cover afforded by the ground, so as to ensure surprise. For the same reason, all movement of tank forces usually takes place by night. It is also known that the Russians have occasionally carried out tank attacks by night with success. There is not, however, sufficient detail available of these operations to show how they overcome the obvious difficulties which must arise.

41. The tactics of tanks in the attack have already been sketched in outline (*see* para 13), but something must be said of the battle formation adopted by tanks. This varies a great deal with the particular task, but will include the following elements :—

The first wave will normally consist of a fighting reconnaissance screen of tanks, followed by the main wave of tanks, keeping in visual touch with the screen. Infantry will follow in the spaces between the tanks (possibly 200–300 yards) and behind them. Anti-tank guns will be allocated to the infantry and SP guns will be used, if available, to guard the flanks of the main body of tanks.

42. The second, usually larger, wave nearly always consists of tanks with infantry mounted upon them. In some instances " suicide squads " of tank-borne infantry actually go into battle on the tanks, though usually they fight dismounted. The flat surfaces of Russian tanks, incidentally, are particularly adapted for tank-borne troops. Since the task of this second wave is mainly one of consolidation and of dealing with points of resistance that have been by-passed by the first wave, infantry can with safety co-operate more closely with the second wave.

43. Thirdly, the reserve wave follows closely behind : this must include both tanks for flanking attacks on enemy infantry attacks and a powerful fire group to deal with attacks by enemy armour.

Motorized and mechanized troops

44. The Red Army employs both motorized and mechanized troops, though there is no hard and fast distinction between them, either of tasks or organization. Both are in practice used as light infantry, for highly mobile tasks in the exploitation of success and in pursuit. Motorized infantry is truckborne infantry, which differs little from ordinary infantry except that it has transport allotted to it to increase its mobility and will tend to consist of higher grade picked troops employed for shock tasks. Mechanized troops, on the other hand, are combined into formations which include armoured cars for part, at least, of the infantry, and also supporting tanks. The basic mechanized formation is the brigade, consisting of (usually) three motorized battalions of infantry, some in armoured cars, and a regiment of tanks. These brigades may either be allotted as independent formations to army commanders, or may be combined into mechanized corps which are allotted for special tasks by GHQ to army group or army commanders. A mechanized corps may consist of three mechanized brigades, which include a tank regiment each, an extra tank brigade and reconnaissance, motor cyclist, sapper, anti-tank, and signals units ; the composition, however, is highly variable as in all Red Army corps organization, and is primarily compounded *ad hoc* for particular tasks. In particular, artillery, in addition to that found in the brigades, may be allotted to mechanized corps. (For the peculiar characteristics of Russian corps *see* para 4 above.)

45. Sudden, bold thrusts in attack, mobile reserve tasks in defence, occupation of key points in advance of the main forces in the pursuit—these are the main principles of the tactics of motorized and mechanized troops. The mechanized corps, with its own tanks, sappers, and artillery, is employed as a self-contained unit, capable of making independent attacks, well in advance of the main forces, on an enemy who has not yet organized his defences. In pursuit the mechanized corps can be employed to seize river crossings or important road junctions in the enemy rear, and, by holding them until the arrival of the main forces, contribute to the encirclement of the enemy. Two consequences follow : in the first place, the mechanized corps is only sent into action after the main enemy defences have been breached. Secondly, since it is operating ahead of the main supply organization, it can rely on its own resources only for a few days' fighting, and must then be allowed a two or three day period for refitting and bringing up supplies after action.

Ski troops

46. Ski troops have played a comparatively small, but important, part in winter warfare by the Red Army. While a number of more or less permanently organized brigades exist, the main employment of ski troops has been at all times in company or, occasionally, battalion strength. Moreover, there is no permanent establishment laid down : detachments are trained and composed for particular tasks by army and army group commanders. Skiers are all picked troops, highly trained, with excellent knowledge of the country in which they have to operate. Their armament is light—tommy guns, grenades, MG, and mortar. Their task is infiltration into the enemy lines under cover of darkness, fog, or snowstorm, for the carrying out of tasks of dislocation, reconnaissance, and capture of vital points, normally co-ordinated with the main offensive plan. Since they must be prepared at times to subsist for days without supplies they carry iron rations and ammunition with them.

47. For transport of their supplies and weapons ski troops use a particular type of sledge, of which several models exist. The usual model, which is drawn by two men on skis, has varied uses. It is in the first place suitable for use not only on firm snow and ice, but also over crumbly snow, marshes, and water as a boat ; moreover it is constructed either for the transport of ammunition, mortar, stores, and, if necessary, a wounded man, or it is designed for the transport of the heavy MG, for which it also acts as a firing platform. The Russians have also developed a larger motor-propelled aero-sleigh, which is now being used by ski troops. Communication between the ski detachment and the command from which it is detached is by aircraft and wireless : wireless, however, on grounds of security, is used only if the location of the detachment is immediately to be changed.

48. The tactics of ski troops are the general tactics of infiltrating troops (*see* para 14). Ambush, ground, weather, must all be

exploited in order to gain the objective in a swift, overwhelming, and, above all, surprise attack. When the objective has been seized it must be immediately consolidated and organized for all-round defence. Except as necessary for the attainment of the objective, engagement with the enemy must be avoided.

Airborne and parachute troops

49. Neither airborne nor parachute troops have as yet been used on a strategic scale by the Red Army. A number of Guards airborne divisions have, it is true, been in operation on the Eastern front, but there is no evidence that they have been used in an airborne role. On a smaller tactical scale parachute units are used. As described elsewhere they have been used for diversionary tasks behind the lines, sometimes alone, but usually in close co-operation with the partisan groups, with whom they make contact on landing. (*See* paras 26 and 72 (*d*)).

Artillery

" Artillery is the God of War."—*Stalin*.

50. There can be little doubt but that one of the main reasons for the successful survival of the Red Army, after the terrible punishment it received from the Germans in the two summer campaigns of 1941 and 1942, was the power and accuracy of Soviet artillery. The immense supply of guns at the disposal of the Red Army enabled the Russians to exact a heavy toll from the advancing German armies and repeatedly helped their own troops to fight their way out of encirclement.

51. This experience led to drastic changes in both the organization and the employment of artillery. The pre-war establishment of the divisional artillery was reduced from two regiments totalling 90 guns and howitzers to one regiment, and this one regiment reduced at first to 24 guns and howitzers, later increased to 32.

52. The Russians had discovered that the only effective means of using artillery was by massing fire power in vital sectors, which could be accomplished only by a highly centralized control of artillery. So immense were the battles fought that artillery had to be concentrated not merely on army or army group scale but even GHQ scale. Hence the doctrine of decentralization of artillery was abandoned in favour of concentration in accordance with the strategic plan and, therefore, under highly centralized control.

53. The infantry division now has what may be regarded as the minimum of artillery fire power under its immediate control, whereas the maximum available artillery of every calibre is concentrated under the direct control of GHQ, army group, and army commanders of artillery, to be employed as the strategy of the moment demands both in defence and offence.

54. It is apparent, even from German communiques, that the Russians have been able to make the successive break-throughs which have paved the way for each of their present offensive operations by their effective use of a surprising volume of fire-power. Their aim has been to concentrate guns and mortars of different calibres, to take on different tactical tasks simultaneously, and to produce overwhelming fire-power at the point of maximum effort.

55. Therefore the Red Army High Command organized a large proportion of the available artillery and mortar weapons into independent regiments, brigades, and later divisions which could be placed at the disposal of GHQ, army group, or army commands, and concentrated in any sector to support a given operation. To-day a great variety of organizations is to be found in the field of all types of artillery weapons. The artillery division, as will be seen from Chart B at page 30 does not include the heavier weapons, which are kept under GHQ control in independent brigades and regiments. (For a list of some of these see page 29.) The object of this form of organization is probably to ensure greater administrative ease in mobility and tactical employment: the Russians have concentrated, with success, on achieving surprise by rapid switching of artillery from one sector to another. Part of this success is doubtless due to the development of SP artillery, which industrial development made possible only at a later stage of the war.

56. According to the scale of the particular operation, the given artillery concentration may remain under the centralized control of GHQ, as apparently happened in the offensive for the relief of Stalingrad, where the artillery remained under the supreme direction of Army Artillery of the Red Army. On the other hand, the command of artillery for the given operation may be centralized in the hands of the commander of army group artillery or of army artillery. It is doubtful whether the control of artillery resources (other than divisional artillery) is decentralized to a lower level than army in any major operation.

57. The tactics and tactical control of the massed use of artillery and mortar fire in effecting a break-through are based on the following principles :—

   (a) The aim is to put down an artillery and mortar barrage which will suppress enemy fire-power and disorganize and destroy personnel throughout the depth of the enemy position virtually simultaneously.

   (b) Enemy defensive zones and strong points must be established by reconnaissance, so that definite fire tasks, suitable to the various weapons, may be allotted.

   (c) As, in practice, perfect knowledge of the enemy dispositions is impossible, the Russians insist on a highly flexible and mobile fire control based on the principle : " The artillery must lead the other arms through the enemy positions." This dictum means that artillery commanders must not wait to be asked for support or be content with laying down creeping or box barrages, which are considered a waste of ammunition. It is the duty of the gunners to use the maximum initiative in finding and taking on targets in such a way as to enable the other arms to get through with the minimum of delay and casualties. This result is accomplished partly by having FOOs well up in the forefront of the battle, partly by having artillery staff officers who observe from the air and give appropriate directions by means of visual signals and messages, though it must be admitted that Russian WT and RT communications are not particularly good. It is, however, abundantly established that their accuracy in shooting is of a very high standard. After the enemy front line defences have been breached, it is usual to decentralize the artillery, to the extent that only a part of the heavy weapons are retained to advance with and support the mobile groups operating within the breakthrough. The remainder, possibly the bulk, is withdrawn for refitting, if necessary, or for rapid switching to another sector. Divisional artillery, of course, accompanies the attack.

(d) As soon as the enemy positions are breached, the gunner must anticipate and smash up enemy preparations and concentrations for counter attacks and prevent reserves from being brought up.

(e) Although in the progress of the offensive the employment of artillery may be decentralized to the extent that a whole battery or group may be supporting a company of infantry or tanks, yet the aim is not to subordinate the artillery arm in small packets to the other arms, but, on the contrary, to preserve the independence of the arm under the general control of the army or army group artillery commander, while insisting on the closest form of co-operation with the other arms. The emphasis, in other words, is on agreement and mutual support between commanders of the different arms in a given operation rather than subordination of one arm to another.

(f) Emphasis is laid throughout on the need for obtaining surprise. Skilful movement of guns and effective camouflage is one method, but not the only one. Considerable effect has been obtained on occasions by lavish use of direct fire over open sights. By this method it is possible, for example, for divisional artillery and mortars only to register targets. While the divisional artillery is firing, the bulk of the heavier artillery is moved into position and then opens fire at point blank range, while divisional artillery and mortars lift their fire forward on to targets registered in the depth of the enemy defences.

58. Thus, the central emphasis in Russian teaching on the employment of artillery both in offence and in defence is laid on the need for concentrating fire rapidly on the required sector. Hence a high

degree of co-operation is required with other arms. In co-operating with the Air Force the need for joint planning of the operation to a careful time plan is stressed. Since an artillery shoot may last anything up to three hours, during which time the guns fire at varied rates, joint timing must ensure that during intervals when the gun fire is less intense the blows from the air must be reinforced. During the attack the main task of the air force is to discover the position of batteries that the enemy is bringing up for counter-attack, while after the break-through, when the artillery is usually considerably reduced, the Air Force takes on targets in depth outside artillery range. For purposes of co-operation in battle, an Air Force officer is attached to the artillery commander, from whom he receives concrete tasks.

59. An important step in the development of artillery co-operation with tanks has been the extensive use of SP guns. Thanks to their armour they can accompany tanks into the attack and thus fill a gap which formerly tended to arise in action between tanks and guns. SP artillery, which is under GHQ control, is believed to be organized in regiments of some 25 or 30 guns of various calibres; the types chiefly used are the 76·2 mm A tk gun on a light tank chassis and the 122 mm how and 152 mm how on medium and heavy tank chassis. SP guns are used in mass for the support of break-through attacks and for exploitation in depth. Their main tactics are to move rapidly from cover to cover, halting for a few minutes at a time, on the flanks of and in between the advancing tanks, at a distance of 250–500 yds. Their main task is to draw the fire from enemy anti-tank gun batteries and then engage and annihilate these targets, and in principle no other tasks should be allotted to them. In defence they should form part of the counter-attacking reserve force.

60. Skilful anti-tank defence played a decisive part in the first stages of the war. The nucleus of anti-tank defence is the independent anti-tank regiment, of some 48 guns of various calibres, of which the Russians are believed to have a very large number. The crews are picked troops who are trained to fire to the last gun, and to hold their fire until the enemy is within the most effective range. Troops are sited in depth, within effective range of one another and mutually supporting, and a reserve is kept: the object is rapid concentration of fire on any sector where a penetration is threatened. This reserve must be mobile, as indeed must all anti-tank artillery. It is stressed in training, however, that when tank battles are in progress every type of artillery must be prepared to fight in an anti-tank role, if necessary firing AP shot over open sights. The rapid change-over from firing HE to AP for unexpected anti-tank tasks at point blank range does not present Russian artillery supply with additional problems, since at least some and possibly all of their heavy howitzers fire a shell with a double action fuze. With normal, that is, instantaneous, setting the shell acts as an HE shell; with a delayed setting as AP shell.

Section 6.—ASSAULT OF A TOWN: STREET FIGHTING

61. There have been three phases in the war during which the Russians have learnt fully the importance of fighting for and inside towns and villages, and as the result of which a doctrine with definite principles can be said to have grown up. The first phase was the Russian offensive of 1941–42 when the Germans stemmed the Russian advance by determined defence of key towns along the whole front; the second was the Russian retreat in the summer and autumn of 1942. At first the Russians adopted, though without substantial success, the tactics of getting off the main routes of the German advance and striking at their lines of communication. When these failed to stem the advance these tactics were completely changed; every town and village was henceforth to be defended street by street and house by house, whether it was surrounded or not. The new policy was put into effect with determination and ruthlessness, and during the period of August–November achieved stabilization.

62. The third phase, in which the Russians were able to study and apply all the lessons they had already learned, and to perfect the principles that they had evolved, was the defence of Stalingrad. The principles followed by the Red Army in assaulting and defending towns and villages, and in fighting street by street, are considered shortly in the following sections. Three main conclusions can, however, be drawn from the Russian experience on the East front :—

 (a) The determined defence of all key inhabited points on main lines of communication in depth makes a sustained offensive by the enemy very difficult.

 (b) Determined street fighting inside a large and unfortified city had enabled the Russians to deny to the enemy one of the principal strategic goals of his summer campaign.

 (c) The buildings of a city ruined by air and artillery bombardment provide the best form of strong points for the defender. Hence, determined defence of a town can succeed even against air and artillery superiority, such as the Germans disposed of during part, at any rate, of the siege of Stalingrad. The Germans found, moreover, that tank attacks proved too costly, and the fate of the city was eventually decided by the hand-to-hand conflicts of small groups.

63. In assaulting a town the Russians learned that it is the surprise nature of enemy fire in street fighting that has the deadliest effect. The greatest care is, therefore, needed in reconnaissance preliminary to the attack so that the enemy defences can be established in detail, and a completely co-ordinated plan prepared down to the last detail. If necessary, armed reconnaissance to draw enemy fire is used. Surprise is the basis of the actual assault. Therefore an artillery or air preparation is unusual; the tasks of artillery are to give close support when the attack is already in progress.

64. The assault is carried out by two forces. The enveloping force isolates the town from the rest of the enemy defences, and severs communications. However, the Russians have found that the German fights desperately when cornered, and therefore it is their frequent practice in enveloping a town to leave at least one road of retreat open. The probable line of retreat is of course ambushed. Part of the enveloping force, which should include both tanks and artillery, is kept back as a reserve ; the task of this reserve is to deal immediately with counter-attacks by relieving enemy forces. The second force, which carries out the actual assault on the town, consists of a number of assault groups, usually composed of infantry, MGs, anti-tank rifles, sappers, mortars, and infantry close-support guns ; a reserve is also kept for emergency, to reinforce the assaulting troops, and to deal with counter-attacks. The assault invariably consists of simultaneous attacks from several directions, in order to disperse enemy fire power. Tanks are sometimes used in order to draw off the main enemy fire from the infantry groups attacking separately from the tanks and from different directions. On the basis of the plan of assault each group is allocated its particular task, which must be very definite, for example, the capture of a particular block.

65. The principal object is to get to grips with the enemy at the largest number of places in the shortest possible time. For this reason, while the bulk of available artillery is usually centralized and used for counter-battery tasks and for fire on enemy communications, and lines of withdrawal and counter-attacks, a part of the artillery, the heavy mortars, and sometimes tanks, are used at point blank range for " cut off " fire—that is, to isolate one strong point from the support of a neighbouring point. A FOO is attached to each assault group in order to control fire, and OPs are kept well forward, in view of the difficulty of observation. Communication with artillery and tanks is by wireless ; line communication is unreliable because of demolitions, fire, and falling buildings ; while runners are liable to be picked off by enemy snipers.

66. Assault groups should be flexible in composition, according to the task allotted to each. They are formed *ad hoc* from the troops available to the commander. The group will, however, always consist of three elements :—

    (a) The storm group. This body of 6–8 men armed with grenades, tommy gun, and dagger, is the key to the whole assault. Its task is to penetrate by rushing the enemy strong point, usually from several directions. " First the grenade, then after it yourself " is the rule. Since the storm group is something in the nature of a suicide squad, it is usual for all its members to be selected from the same unit.

    (b) The reinforcement group. This will normally consist of several sections of infantry armed with MG, anti-tank rifles, mortars, close support guns for point blank fire, and

sappers both for demolition and for clearing of mines.
Flamethrowers are used, but they do not appear to be used
very extensively. The task of the reinforcement group is
to rush in immediately after the storm group has effected
entry, occupy the enemy firing point, and create their own
fire system. This group is under command of the commander of the storm group spearhead commander and
rushes in on his success signal.

(c) A reserve, used to reinforce and to deal with counter attacks.

67. Speed and surprise in getting to grips with the enemy are un-
derlined in all Red Army training in street fighting, which is rigorous,
meticulous, and specialized. Both smoke and night attacks are used
to achieve these objects. Once in the town, assault troops are taught
to avoid advancing along streets or across squares. They must find
their way to the objective by using back yards, fences, lanes, sewers,
and even making their way from house to house, breaking through
walls, or moving from roof to roof, if necessary.

68. Great attention is paid not only to rushing and seizing a particular building, but also to the importance of consolidating immediately, so as to prevent the enemy from reinforcing. The task of
artillery and tanks in this connection has been mentioned. It is the
immediate task of the infantry to seize the middle and upper floors of
buildings so as to be able to control the approaches to the building.
Supplementary firing points must be established outside the building
without delay as soon as they have been set up inside the building.
Since some time may elapse before the entire town has been cleared,
Nos. 2 on the anti-tank rifles and MGs carry enough ammunition
and food for 24 hours when storming their objective.

69. In defence of a city the following are the main lessons of
Russian experience :—

(a) A belt of defence in depth outside the town is essential to
prevent the enemy from rushing the town with his tanks.

(b) Inside the town houses are reinforced and organized for
defence in groups, with artillery sited in barns, squares,
parks, and ground floors. Particular attention must be
paid to anti-tank defences; the Russians insist that a tank
barrier covered by fire is of little effect, and that to achieve
success ingenuity and cunning are needed. The object is
to force the tanks to hesitate or turn or be taken by
surprise. A good example is the placing of sufficient
obstacles to form a maze : concealed anti-tank guns, rifles,
grenades, and bottles, are then used to deal with the tanks
which are turning to find their way through the maze.

(c) A town largely burnt down or destroyed by air attack was
found to be even more suited to prolonged and stubborn
defence than one with all its buildings intact. Troops are
taught to improvise fortified nests among the ruins of
houses as quickly as possible, and to fix up a number of

alternative sites, all interconnected by a system of deep trenches. The debris has been found to offer greater opportunities for camouflage, surprise, and ambush than standing buildings and is not as likely to be affected by subsequent bombardment nor so vulnerable to incendiary attack.

(d) When the enemy has penetrated, the importance of surprise counter-attacks is stressed. It is therefore important not to give away one's position or fire plan by desultory movement or firing, and hence practically all movement in a prolonged defence is restricted to night time.

(e) In preparing fortified positions, all dead ground must be eliminated. This result can be achieved either by enfilade fire or by using mobile groups of tommy gunners making use of all available or improvised cover to attack enemy assault groups in the flanks or rear. Snipers can also play an important part, especially if they concentrate on officers and NCOs.

(f) Never erect a tank obstacle in front of a firing point : the enemy expects it, and it will therefore only draw his fire.

Section 7.—PARTISAN WARFARE

" A peoples' war should, like a mist of nebulous, vapoury essence, nowhere condense into a solid body. On the other hand, it is necessary that this mist should gather at some points into denser masses and form threatening clouds from which now and again a formidable flash of lightning may burst forth. . . . The easiest way for a general to produce this more effective form of a natural rising is to support the movement by small detachments sent from the Army. The peoples' war and the war of the regular Army must both be carried on according to a plan embracing the operations as a whole." *Clausewitz.*

70. The above quotation is an accurate description of the nature of guerilla warfare in Russia. It is probably true that the influence and control by the regular Army have increased considerably as the war has progressed, though there has been no attempt, until the actual re-occupation of territory, to incorporate partisans in the Red Army or to put them in uniform. What is clear is that partisan activity is neither sporadic nor spontaneous, but organized, calculated, and a part of the plan of the General Staff.

71. Three main objects can be discerned in the employment of partisans :—

(a) A partisan unit is primarily a unit for political propaganda. Organized by local party officials, it in turn becomes a centre for disseminating leaflets and underground newspapers and for maintaining solidarity of opposition to the occupying troops. There is no doubt but that this aim has been largely achieved and that the danger of political apathy under occupation, which in the rural districts of the USSR might be very considerable, has thereby been largely obviated.

(b) Secondly, the attack by numerous small units on vital points in enemy lines of communication, HQ, supply dumps, etc., These attacks are usually carried out by bands varying from 15 to 50 men. Bands of 100 to 300 are, however, not uncommon and bands of several thousands are known to exist. Their armament is mostly captured German small arms, though light artillery pieces are used and, on occasions, aircraft. The bands are known frequently to be led by Red Army officers, either sent over by air from the Russian side, or who have escaped the enemy net when territory has been occupied.

(c) The third function of partisan groups is reconnaissance behind the enemy lines. Sometimes this reconnaissance is directed by units of the Red Army. The information is sent back to the Red Army by aircraft and wireless, and on some occasions by runners, who penetrate the enemy lines.

72. The following methods of co-operation are used by the Red Army :—

(a) Direct contact, either by aircraft or, where the partisans are operating close to the front, by direct penetration of enemy lines, either by partisan scouts or by Red Army men.

(b) Wireless. In addition to the military radio, the Soviet broadcast system has, since May, 1942, maintained a regular system of daily broadcasts to partisans. This includes the broadcast at slow speed of communiques and news items, intended for dissemination among the population of occupied territory. Definite instructions on fighting were also given, including methods of reconnaissance. (A handbook on partisan warfare has also been published by the General Staff.)

(c) Partisans are mainly supplied by the civil population of the occupied territory, by captured weapons and ammunition, and by dumps established by the Red Army before withdrawal. With the growth of production they have, however, been increasingly supplied by air by the regular Army.

(d) Co-operation with partisans has hitherto been the main function of Red Army parachute troops. Dropping behind the lines some time before an intended operation they make contact with the partisans, and direct and co-ordinate their activities in the rear so as to maintain maximum effect at such points in the enemy rear as will most assist the tasks of the advancing army.

73. The partisans have proved of particular value to the advancing Army in difficult country—marshes, rivers, and forests ; for example, they have acted as guides, have stored materials

to help the advance element of the Army, and have played an important part in pinning down substantial enemy forces at the decisive moment. In the crossing of the Dnieper the combined activities of parachute troops and partisans on the right bank were, in at least one instance, decisive in ensuring the success of crossings by diverting forces which should have been employed against advance Russian elements on the left bank, and by cutting off rail routes vital for reinforcements.

74. The following conclusions can be drawn from the Red Army's partisan experience :—
   (a) Partisan activity is of considerable, at times even decisive, value, provided it is co-ordinated.
   (b) Partisans should operate mainly in small, scattered bands ; organization should aim, however, at being able to mass these bands together into a larger force at the decisive moment.
   (c) The morale of the partisan movement, especially in territory remote from the regular Army, cannot be left to look after itself. It must be kept alive by political instruction and the dissemination of news. In territories that have been occupied for a long time it may prove necessary to " restock " the partisan movement, by transfer from other districts, or by regular Army detachments.

Section 8.—CONCLUSIONS

75. Certain broad conclusions emerge from study of the Red Army in action in the war with Germany :—
   (a) At the very outset the Russians had to choose between a highly organized and equipped Army, and simplicity and improvisation ; they unhesitatingly chose the latter. The result has been an organism which has learned to make up for its lack of military refinement by numbers and weight of metal, intensity of training of shock troops, and by a highly centralized command. Only a vast reserve of manpower could have been able to pay the price in losses that this policy must have entailed.
   (b) Totalitarian control by the political machine is the king-pin of the whole Army. It pervades training, command, and supply. In other words, it was the existence of a system of ruthless party discipline and dictatorship and of a people habituated to unquestioning obedience that made possible both the rapid expansion of an enormous army in face of a powerful invasion, and the corresponding industrial expansion to maintain it.
   (c) A widespread partisan movement can be of considerable importance, both in defence and in attack, provided that it is highly organized and that the tasks of the partisans are co-ordinated with the plan of the regular army.

CHART A (ii) — PART II—APPENDIX ON RED ARMY ORGANIZATION

INFANTRY REGIMENT AND BATTALION

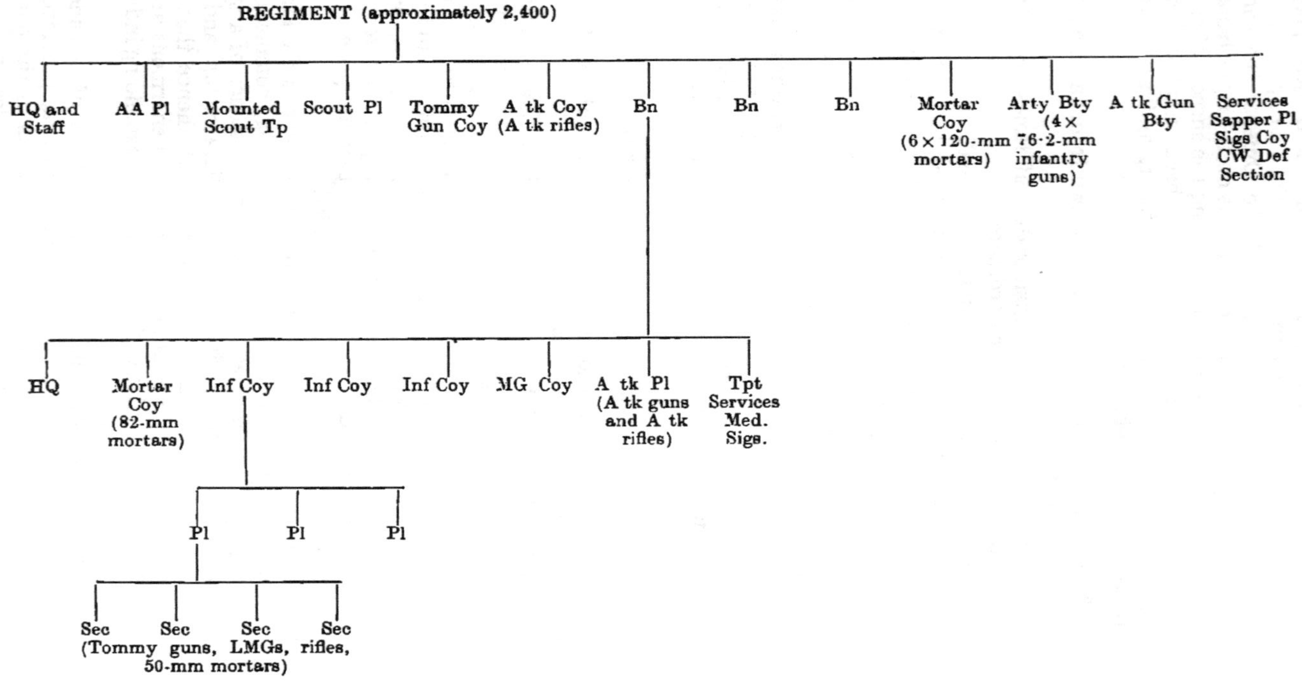

REGIMENT (approximately 2,400)

- HQ and Staff
- AA Pl
- Mounted Scout Tp
- Scout Pl
- Tommy Gun Coy
- A tk Coy (A tk rifles)
- Bn
- Bn
- Bn
- Bn
  - Mortar Coy (6 × 120-mm mortars)
  - Arty Bty (4 × 76·2-mm infantry guns)
  - A tk Gun Bty
  - Services
    - Sapper Pl
    - Sigs Coy
    - CW Def Section

BATTALION

- HQ
- Mortar Coy (82-mm mortars)
- Inf Coy
- Inf Coy
- Inf Coy
- MG Coy
- A tk Pl (A tk guns and A tk rifles)
- Tpt Services
- Med.
- Sigs.

Inf Coy:
- Pl
- Pl
- Pl
  - Sec (Tommy guns, LMGs, rifles, 50-mm mortars)
  - Sec
  - Sec
  - Sec

28

CHART A (1)

INFANTRY DIV

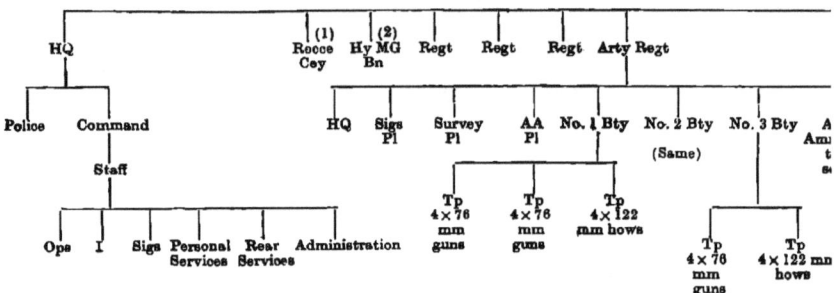

NOTES :—
(1) Usually 150 riflemen, but varies in composition.
(2) Only found in some divisions.
(3) This may be equipped with anti-tank guns of heavier calibre; it may also include anti-tank riflemen.
(4) In many divisions the allocation of tommy guns is much higher.

Divisional Fire Power
(Totals for small arms are very approximate, since they are subject to much variation, especially as regards the proportion of automatic and semi-automatic weapons.)

To face page 28

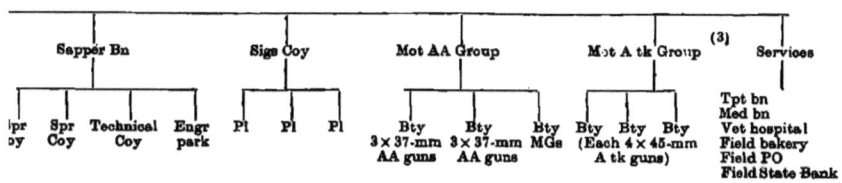

```
; 10,000 all ranks)

        Sapper Bn          Sigs Coy         Mot AA Group              Mot A tk Group    (3)    Services
                                                                                                |
  pr   Spr  Technical  Engr   Pl  Pl  Pl    Bty      Bty      Bty    Bty  Bty  Bty       Tpt bn
  oy   Coy    Coy      park                3×37-mm  3×37-mm   MGs   (Each 4×45-mm         Med bn
                                           AA guns  AA guns           A tk guns)         Vet hospital
                                                                                         Field bakery
                                                                                         Field PO
                                                                                         Field State Bank
```

m hows ... 12	A tk rifles	200 or more
mm fd guns ... 20	Hy MGs	100 or more
mm inf guns... 12	LMGs	350–500
m A tk guns... 48	Tommy guns ...	1,500 (4)
m AA guns ... 6	Rifles, incl	
m mortars ... 18	self loading ...	5,500
m ,, ... 81		
m ,, ... 54		

21047

CHART B.—ARTILLERY

NOTE

The attached chart shows the approximate organization of the artillery division, broken down into brigades and regiments. Artillery divisions, like the bulk of Red Army artillery are under GHQ control. (For the divisional field regiment, *see* Chart A.) In addition GHQ artillery is organized in a great variety of divisions, independent brigades, regiments, and groups, of which the organization is variable and flexible, including the following :—

AA division.
Mortar division.
Heavy artillery brigade.
Howitzer brigade.
Light artillery brigade.
Howitzer regiment.
Heavy artillery regiment.
SP artillery regiment.
Anti-tank artillery brigade.
Anti-tank artillery regiment.
Mortar brigade.
Mortar regiment.

CHART B

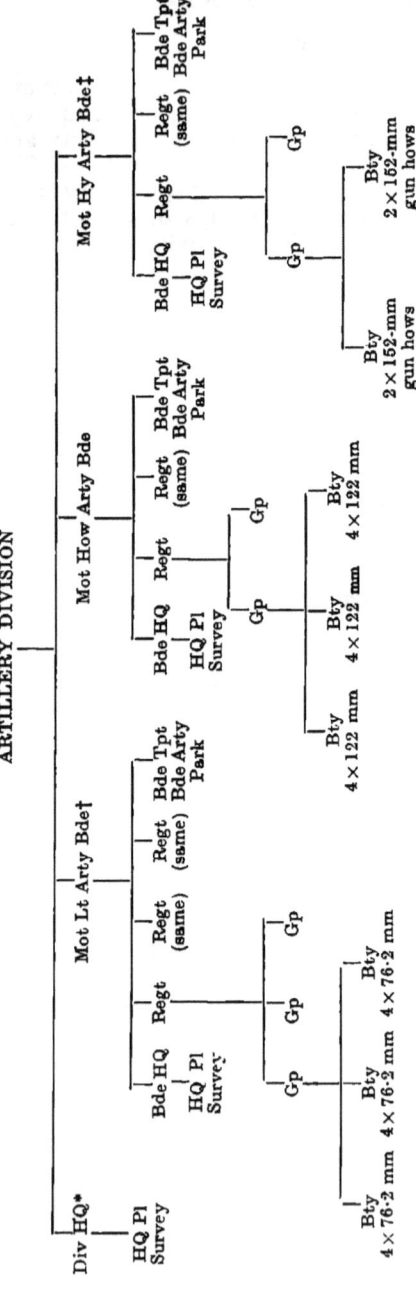

* Some divisions include a divisional aviation squadron of 9 artillery observation aircraft.
† The organization of the Independent Lt Arty Bde is similar. The 76·2-mm guns are used both with HE and AP.
‡ The organization of the Independent Hy Arty Bde is similar.

Total number of guns in the Division ... 108 × 76·2-mm guns (A tk or HE)
48 × 122-mm hows.
16 × 152-mm gun-hows.
———
172
———

CHART C

CAVALRY DIVISION (4,000–5,000) (1)

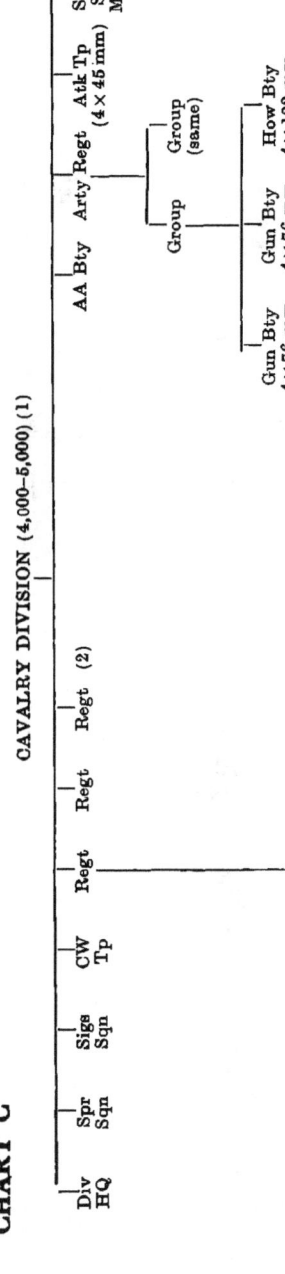
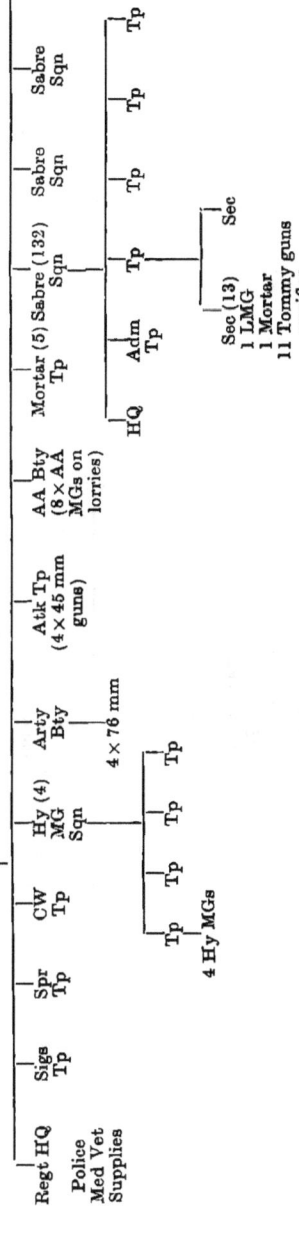

NOTES: (1) This approximate establishment is in practice usually lower.
(2) Light tanks or armoured cars may be found attached to Div and Regt HQs in some cases.
(3) The Atk strength is unknown; in all probability this varies considerably with particular tasks. Hy MGs with AP shot and Atk rifles are also used.
(4) The Hy MGs are conveyed on horse drawn carts and can be fired either from these carts or from the ground.
(5) Not found in all regiments, since in some cases mortars are sub-allotted from GHQ reserve.

CHART D (i)

INDEPENDENT TANK BRIGADE

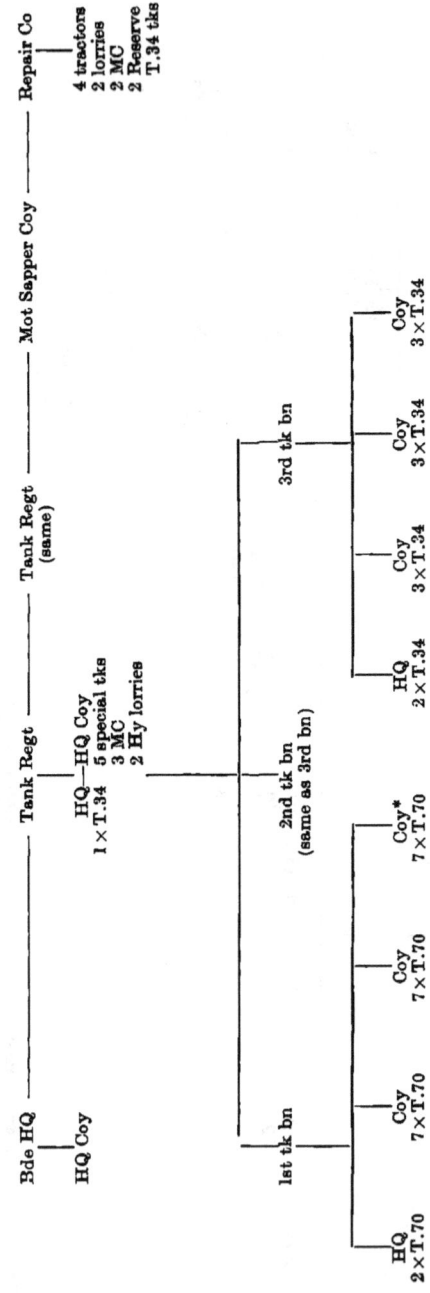

* The third coys are not usually found, as the T.70 is being used to a decreasing extent.

CHART D (ii)

INDEPENDENT ASSAULT TANK REGIMENT

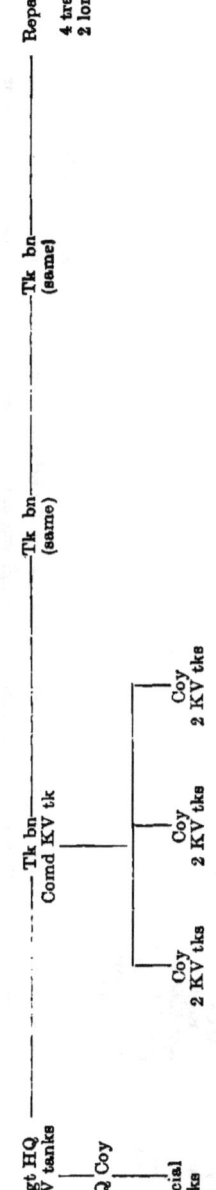

Regt HQ — 2 KV tanks

HQ Coy
- 5 special tanks
- 3 MC
- 2 hy lorries

Tk bn — Comd KV tk
- Coy — 2 KV tks
- Coy — 2 KV tks
- Coy — 2 KV tks

Tk bn (same)

Tk bn (same)

Repair coy
- 4 tractors
- 2 lorries

Total: 5 special tanks
23 KV tanks

CHART D (iii)

THE TANK CORPS

NOTE.—The Tank Corps is very largely an *ad hoc* organization and its composition therefore varies considerably. The following are believed to be the main features of Corps employed in the present offensive.

Corps HQ*	Tk bde	Tk bde (same)	Tk bde (same)	Special tk regt‡	Special tk regt‡	Spr coy	Repair coy	Tpt coy
HQ Coy	HQ Coy							
Police Section	Tk Regt							
Sigs Coy	Mot Rifle Bn							
Recce Group	Mot A tk Coy							
AA platoon	Mot AA Coy							
	SP Arty Bty							
	Adm Coy							

* Some corps include a motorized rifle regiment, others a mechanized brigade. Additional SP artillery is also usual.

‡ It is believed that KV tanks are now most usually employed in independent assault regiments under army or GHQ command; if under command of the corps, this would mean a further 46 KV tanks.

Total: About 180 T.70 and T.34 tanks.‡

CHART E

ORGANIZATI(

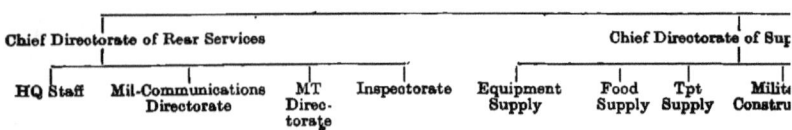

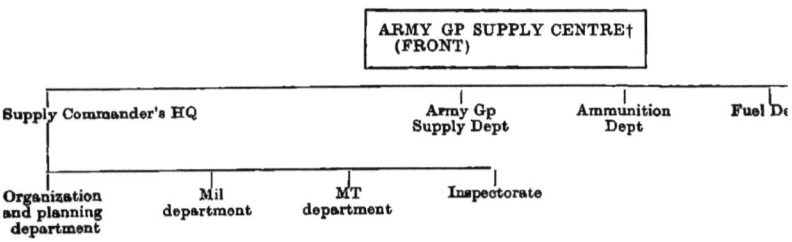

* In some cases railhead is as far forward as division.
† Army Group Supply Commander has a wide range of powers in obtaining supplies direct within his area of operations.
‡ The duty of these attached Commanders is to look after the interests of their own front line troops.
§ Where Army, or Divisional transport is inadequate, transport can be attached from Army Group or Army pool.

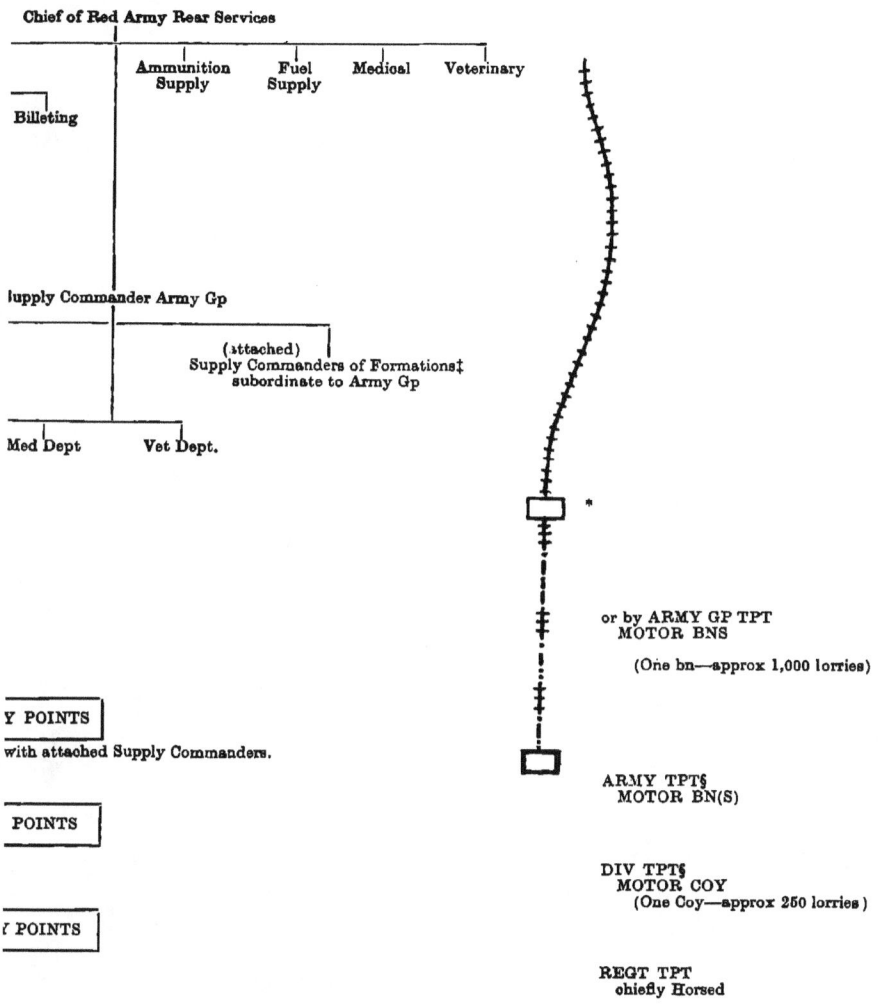

MOTOR AIR SLEIGHS

MEDIUM MG (1910 MODEL) ON SLEDGE

Details of MG :—Calibre, 7·62 mm (·300 ins)
   Water cooled : recoil operated.
   Weight of gun, 39½ lbs.
   Rate of fire, 300 rpm
   Maximum range direct fire, 1,500 metres
   Maximum range indirect fire, 3,000 metres.

HEAVY SP GUN
152 mm howitzer mounted on a KV chassis

203 mm Howitzer

Details:
MV	1,320 fs
Maximum range	18,700 yds
Weight in action	17·4 tons
Weight of shell	220 lbs

Tank Borne Infantry Riding on T34 Tanks

Heavy KV Tank

Details :—Weight	...	48 tons
Crew	...	5
Dimensions	...	22 ft 0 ins × 11 ft 0 ins × 9 ft 6 ins
Armament	...	1 × 76 mm long gun ; 1 MG co-axial in turret ; 1 MG in rear of turret ; 1 MG in hull ; 1 MG for dismounted action
Engine	...	600 hp water cooled diesel
Speed	...	22 mph maximum
Drive	...	Rear sprocket

Medium Cruiser T34 Tank

Details :—Weight	...	27½ tons
Crew	...	4
Dimensions	...	19 ft 11 ins × 9 ft 10 ins × 7 ft 10 ins
Armament	...	1 × 76 mm gun ; 1 MG Co-axial in turret ; 1 MG in hull ; 1 MG for dismounted action
Engine	...	500 hp water-cooled diesel
Speed	...	34 mph maximum
Drive	...	Rear sprocket

ANTI-TANK RIFLE WITH MACHINE CARBINE IN REAR

Details :
  (a) Anti-tank rifle " Degtyarev." Calibre, 14·5 mm (·57 ins). Weight, 35 lbs. Overall length, 6 ft 6¾ ins. Type of feed, single loading. Rate of fire, 8–10 rpm. Ammunition, AP/Incendiary.
  (b) Machine carbine model 1941. Calibre, 7·62 mm (·300 in). Weight (with filled magazine), 11·9 lbs. Overall length, 33·15 ins. Feed, 71 rd drum magazine. Single shot or automatic fire.

PONTOON BRIDGE

ROCKET PROJECTOR

Rocket projectors are mounted either on 3 ton trucks or on light tanks. Salvos of up to 38 shots can be fired by the largest models. The range of the shell is from 5,000 to 10,000 yards, according to the type used.

New notes on the Red Army

No.2 Uniforms and Insignia . . . .

Prepared under the direction of the Chief of the Imperial General Staff

The War Office
August 1944

New notes on the Red Army

No. 2. Uniforms and Insignia

Contents:

A. Uniforms
1. General
2. Shoulder-straps
3. Tunics and breeches
4. Greatcoats
5. Headgear
6. N.K.V.D. Troops

B. Insignia
1. Marshal's Star
2. Orders
3. Medals
4. Badges
5. Honorary Arms and Standards

Red Army Winter Uniforms

A Marshal of the Soviet Union wearing insignia

Red Army Summer Uniforms

A Marshall of Artillery wearing insignia

A. Uniforms

1. General

On the 6th January, 1943, a Decree of the Praesidium of the Supreme Soviet of the U.S.S.R. introduced new insignia for the personnel of the Red Army.

This Decree stated that the introduction of shoulder-straps, in lieu of the former badges of rank worn on the gorget patch, was made at the request of the People's Commissariat of Defence. These are to be entirely superseded, and in future no chevrons of rank are to be worn on the sleeve (officers). Other ranks are now to wear the number of their unit on their shoulder-straps.

The introduction of this change of uniform was to take place during the period 1-15 February, 1943. It is interesting to note that these shoulder-straps are very similar to the pre-revolutionary Russian uniform, and the "Red Star," in an article describing the details of this re-introduction of shoulder-straps, went as far as to explain that while the Tsarist officers were enemies of the people and that therefore the Red Army at first refused to wear the pre-revolutionary shoulder-straps, the country can now trust her soldiers to wear the traditional uniform of the Russian people. (Another significant departure from the Red Army's principles is the re-introduction of the words "officer" and "soldier," which have hitherto been scrupulously replaced by "commanders" and "fighting men." This change is not yet fully accepted, but is evidently intended to be encouraged).

Until this recent reform there were no visual means of identifying the unit to which a Red Army soldier belonged. The new decree states that shoulder-straps on walking-out dress will identify the unit of the wearer; this is a further step towards building up regimental tradition.

NOTE: The Red Army is divided up for all purposes into five categories referring to the various grades of personnel. Categories are composed as follows :—

Generals	Marshals and generals
Senior Officers	Colonels, lieutenant colonels and majors
Junior Officers	Captains, senior lieutenants, lieutenants and junior lieutenants
Serjeants	All non-commissioned officers
Privates	Red Army men

2. Shoulder-straps

These Short Notes do not include descriptions and details of the newly-established full dress, which were laid down by the above-mentioned decree. Owing to the exigencies of the present situation, full dress has so far had only a very limited issue.

All shoulder-straps are of two kinds:—

(a) **Walking-out dress** (for everyday use). These are of gold or silver silk-braid according to the particular arm of the service, for officers; and of coloured cloth, also according to the service arm for other ranks.

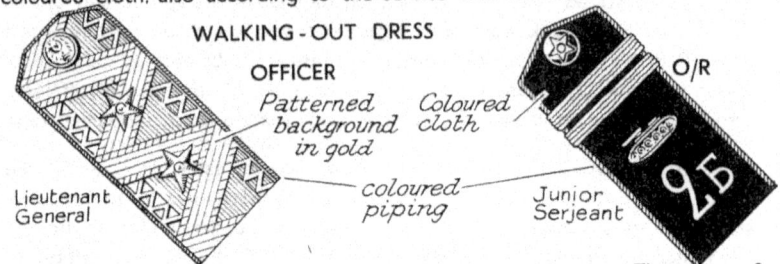

WALKING-OUT DRESS

OFFICER — Patterned background in gold, Coloured cloth, coloured piping

Lieutenant General

O/R — Junior Serjeant

(b) **Field dress** (for use in active operations or in training). These are of khaki coloured cloth for all ranks.

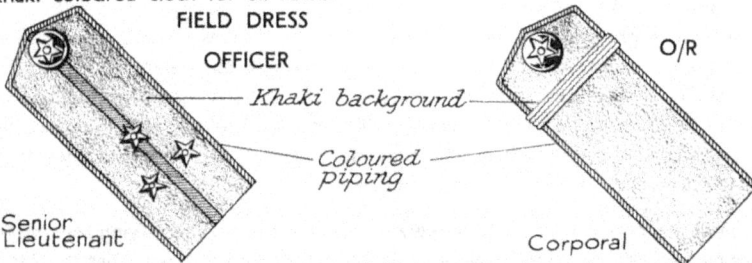

FIELD DRESS

OFFICER — Khaki background, Coloured piping

Senior Lieutenant

O/R — Corporal

All shoulder-straps, walking-out or field, are edged on three sides with coloured piping, according to the arm of the service so that even when field dress shoulder-straps are worn they give some indication of the branch to which the wearer belongs.

Officers' badges of rank are stars which vary in size with each successive category. The largest is that of a Marshal of the Soviet Union — diam. 50 mm. — which is decreased to 40 mm. for other marshals (of armoured troops, artillery, signals, etc.). Stars worn by the senior officers are again smaller, and those of the junior officers smaller still. Except for generals and marshals, all stars for officers of the same category are of identical size, irrespective of the service arm of the wearer. When gold shoulder-straps are worn, the badges of rank are coloured silver, and when the shoulder-straps are silver, the badges of rank are coloured gold.

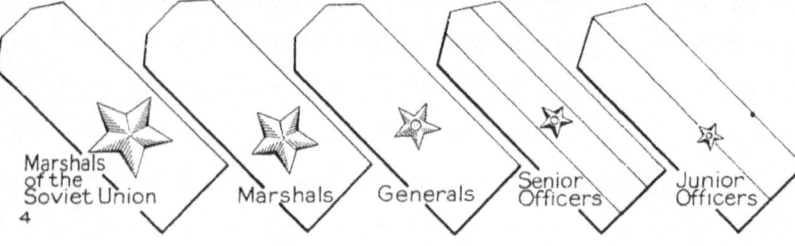

Marshals of the Soviet Union | Marshals | Generals | Senior Officers | Junior Officers

N.C.O's badges of rank are transverse cloth bars worn across the upper half of the shoulder-strap.

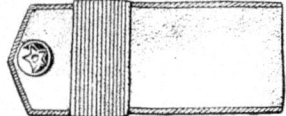 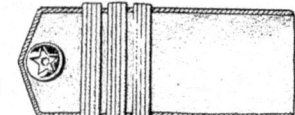

N.C.O. RANK BADGES

Senior Serjeant   Serjeant

Service emblems are in the shape of small badges coloured gold (combatant troops) or silver (administrative troops) and worn on the upper half of the shoulder strap below the button. Infantry and administrative troops do not wear any distinguishing emblem.

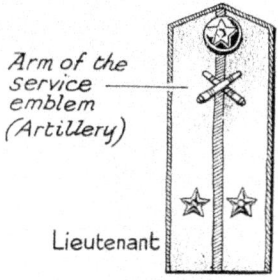

Arm of the service emblem (Artillery)

Lieutenant

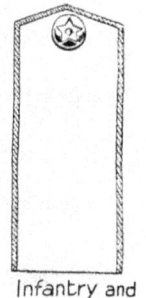
Infantry and Administrative troops
No emblem

Artillery

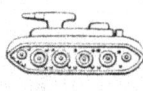
Armoured troops

Chemical troops

Signals

Drivers

Cavalry

Sappers

Railway troops

Commissariat

Pioneers

Survey troops

Electrical and Technical troops

Bridging troops

Gold
Medical

Silver
Veterinary

Justice

Military Bands

Air Force

Marshals and Generals — Shoulder-straps

Shoulder-straps of marshals and generals are larger than those worn by other officers. They are from 5 to 6 inches in length and 2½ inches in breadth.

MARSHALS AND GENERALS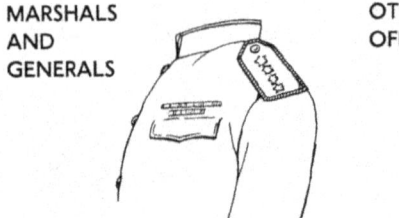

OTHER OFFICERS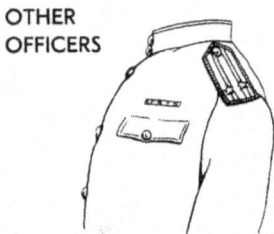

They are of a special interwoven pattern for all marshals and generals. Walking-out dress shoulder-straps are made of gold silk braid, with the exception of those worn by generals of the medical, veterinary, and judicial services, which are narrower and made of silver silk braid.

The piping varies as follows :—

All marshals and generals			...	...	...	crimson
except ,, ,, ,,	the Air Force		...	...		sky blue
and ,, ,, ,,	technical troops (engineers, signals chemical, etc.), and commissariat					magenta

Embroidered emblems are worn to denote arms of the service.

NOTE: By the new decree, a major general now wears one star, as opposed to the two stars formerly worn on the gorget patch.

MARSHALS   WALKING OUT DRESS

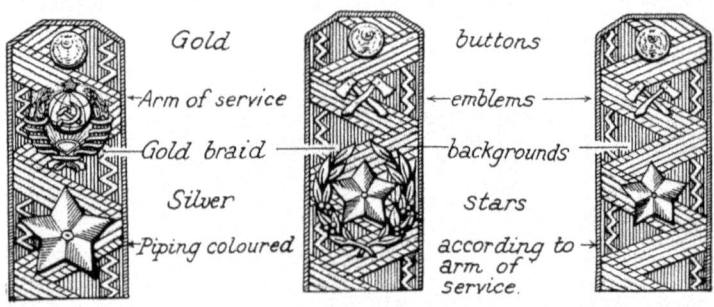

Marshal of the Soviet Union

Chief Marshal of Engineers

Marshal of Engineers

GENERALS

WALKING-OUT DRESS

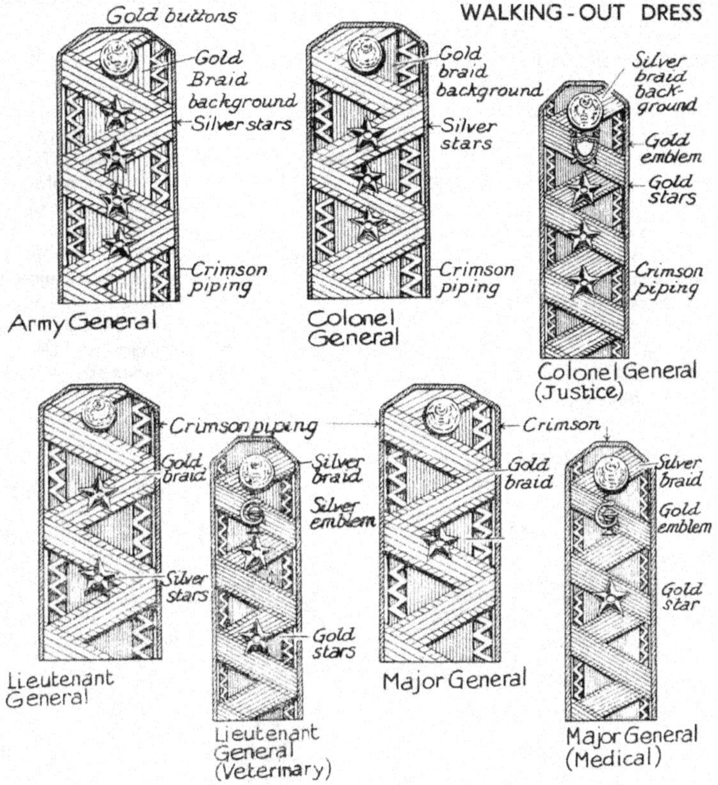

Field-dress shoulder-straps are of khaki colouring with embroidered stars.

MARSHALS AND GENERALS

FIELD DRESS

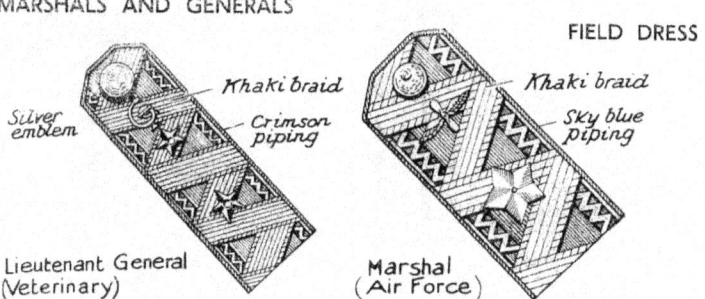

Senior and Junior Officers — Shoulder-straps

(Including all officers from the rank of Colonel to Junior Lieutenant).

Shoulder-straps of senior officers are distinguishable by the two centre stripes which run down the entire length of the shoulder-straps from the top button to the shoulder edge: the shoulder strap of junior officers has one centre stripe. Walking-out dress shoulder-straps are of gold silk braid with the exception of those of the following arms, which are of silver silk braid:—Technical troops, commissariat, medical, veterinary, judicial and administrative. (The four last mentioned are of the narrow type). Emblems showing service arms are worn by all senior and junior officers, except infantry and administrative: Emblems and stars are coloured silver, with the exception of those of the technical troops, commissariat, medical and judicial services, which are coloured gold. The veterinary emblem is coloured silver, and the stars are gold. Field dress shoulder straps have khaki background.

SENIOR OFFICERS

WALKING-OUT DRESS

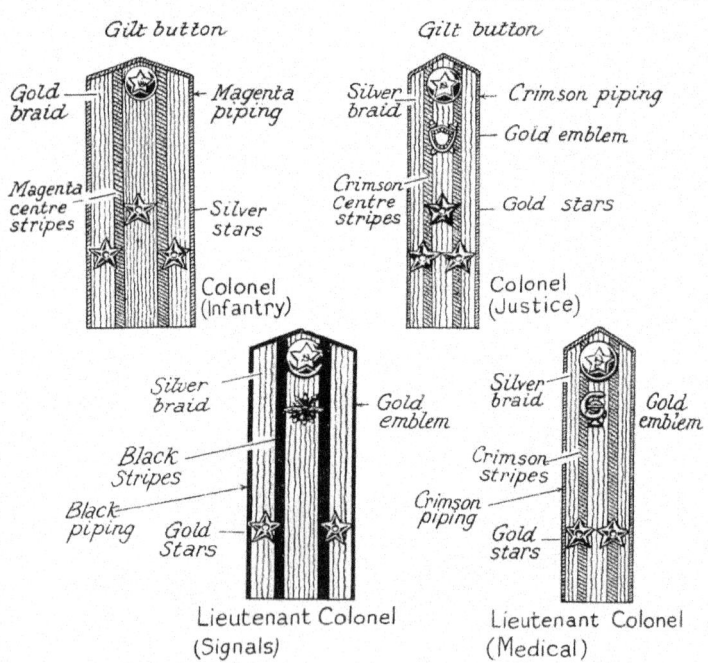

Senior officers — Walking-out dress (Contd.)

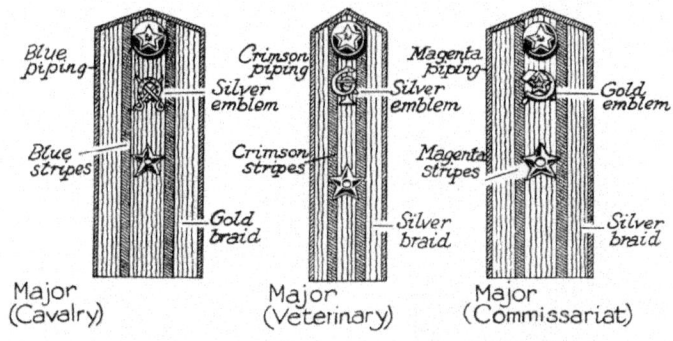

SENIOR OFFICERS — FIELD DRESS

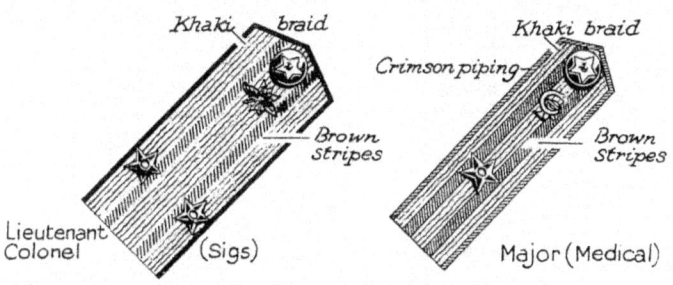

Significance of colours

ARM OF SERVICE	WALKING-OUT DRESS SHOULDER-STRAPS			FIELD-DRESS SHOULDER-STRAPS		
	Background	Colour of Piping (round edges)	Colour of Stripe(s) (down centre)	Background	Colour of Piping (round edges)	Colour of Stripe(s) (down centre)
Infantry	Gold	Magenta	Magenta		Magenta	Claret
Artillery	Gold	Crimson	Crimson		Crimson	Claret
Armoured troops	Gold	Crimson	Crimson	K	Crimson	Claret
Air Force	Gold	Sky blue	Sky blue	A	Sky blue	Claret
Cavalry	Gold	Blue	Blue	H	Blue	Claret
Sappers	Gold	Black	Black	K	Black	Claret
Commissariat	Silver	Magenta	Magenta		Magenta	Brown
Technical services	Silver	According to arm of service			According to arm of service	Brown
Medical, Judicial and Veterinary services and Administrative service	Silver (narrow)	Crimson	Crimson	(narrow)	Crimson	Brown

Junior officers   Shoulder-straps

The junior officer's shoulder-strap, as before mentioned, carries one centre stripe as distinct from the senior officer's two stripes.

JUNIOR OFFICERS

WALKING - OUT DRESS

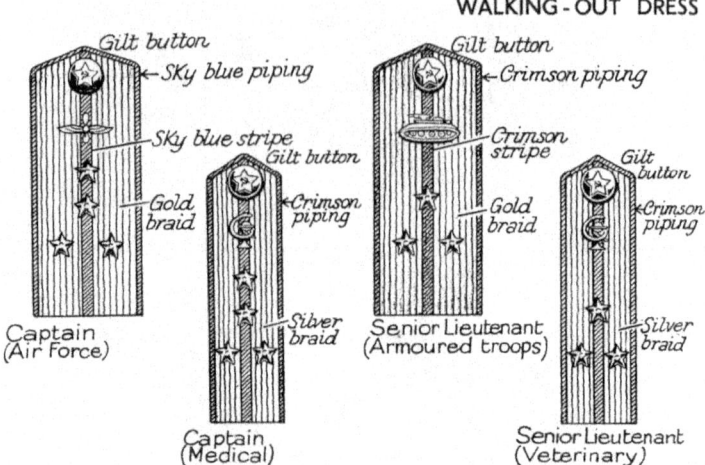

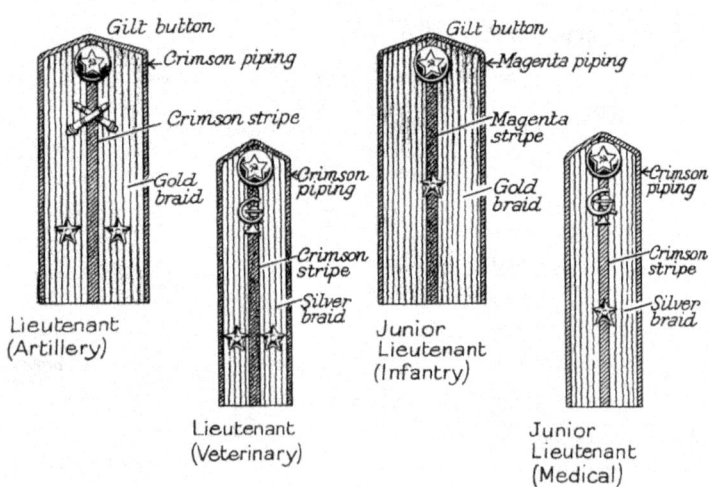

Junior officers

FIELD DRESS

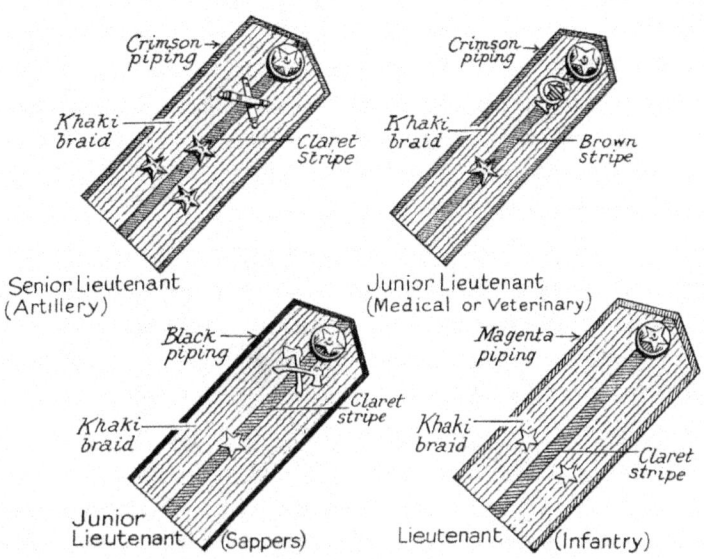

Significance of colours

ARM OF SERVICE	WALKING-OUT DRESS SHOULDER-STRAPS			FIELD-DRESS SHOULDER-STRAPS		
	Background	Colour of Piping (round edges)	Colour of Stripe(s) (down centre)	Background	Colour of Piping (round edges)	Colour of Stripe(s) (down centre)
Infantry	Gold	Magenta	Magenta	K H A K I	Magenta	Claret
Artillery	Gold	Crimson	Crimson		Crimson	Claret
Armoured troops	Gold	Crimson	Crimson		Crimson	Claret
Air Force	Gold	Sky blue	Sky blue		Sky blue	Claret
Cavalry	Gold	Blue	Blue		Blue	Claret
Sappers	Gold	Black	Black		Black	Claret
Commissariat	Silver	Magenta	Magenta		Magenta	Brown
Technical services	Silver	According to arm of service			According to arm of service	Brown
Medical, Judicial and Veterinary services and Administrative service	Silver (narrow)	Crimson	Crimson	(narrow)	Crimson	Brown

Serjeants

Shoulder-straps

(including Officer-Cadets Serjeant Majors, Serjeants and Corporals).

(a) Walking-out dress: Shoulder-straps — are made of coloured cloth, the colour depending on the arm of service of the wearer. Rank is determined by transverse cloth bars worn across the top of the shoulder-strap; and, in the case of officer-cadets and serjeant-majors, by longitudinal strips also. These bars and stripes are gold, for combatant, and silver, for non-combatant troops. Service emblems are worn by all arms except infantry and administrative service. The number, and sometimes also the designation, of the wearer's unit is worn on the lower half of the shoulder-strap. Officer-cadets wear walking-out dress shoulder-straps only.

(b) Field dress: Shoulder-straps are all of a khaki colour without indications of the wearer's unit. The transverse cloth bars determining rank are of coloured cloth, the colour depending on the arm of service. The piping round the three edges of the shoulder-strap also varies in colour according to the arm of service. See table opposite.

Officer-cadets wear walking-out dress shoulder-straps only.

SERJEANTS CATEGORY

WALKING - OUT DRESS

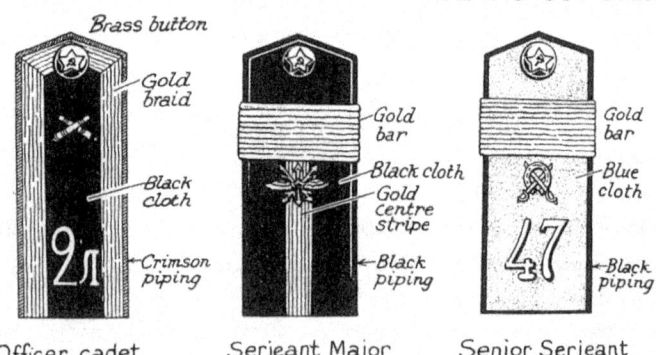

Officer cadet
(2nd Leningrad OCTU)

Serjeant Major
(Sigs.)

Senior Serjeant
(47 Cavalry Regt.)

Serjeants' Category—Walking-out dress—(Contd.)

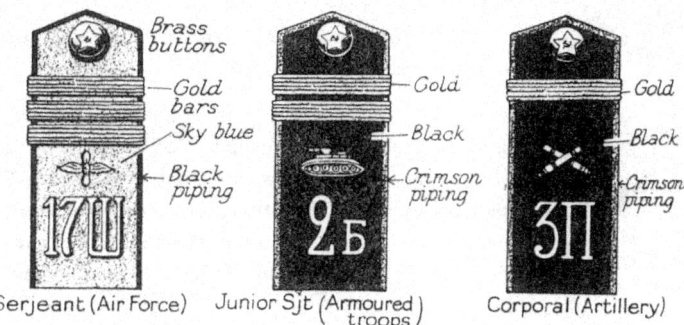

Serjeant (Air Force)   Junior Sjt (Armoured troops)   Corporal (Artillery)

SERJEANTS' CATEGORY

FIELD DRESS

Corporal (Infantry)   Serjeant (Administrative)

Significance of colours

ARM OF SERVICE	WALKING-OUT DRESS SHOULDER-STRAPS			FIELD-DRESS SHOULDER-STRAPS		
	Background	Colour of piping (round edges)	Colour of transverse bars indicating rank	Background	Colour of piping (round edges)	Colour of transverse bars indicating rank
Infantry	Magenta	Black	Gold		Magenta	Claret
Artillery	Black	Crimson	Gold		Crimson	Claret
Armoured troops	Black	Crimson	Gold	K	Crimson	Claret
Air Force	Sky blue	Black	Gold	H	Sky blue	Claret
Cavalry	Blue	Black	Gold	A	Blue	Claret
Technical troops	Black	Black	Gold	K	Black	Claret
Medical and Veterinary Services	Dark green	Black	Silver	I	Dark green	Brown
Non-Combatant Services	According to arm of the service		Silver		According to arm of the service	Brown
Officer-cadets	According to arm of the service		Gold or silver		-	-

Privates' (or "Red Army men") Shoulder-straps

Red Army Man (Infantry)

(Our rank of private is "Krasnoarmyeyets"= Red Army Man — in Russian).

Walking-out dress and field dress shoulder-straps are in accordance with the colour diagram for Serjeants but the shoulder-strap naturally has no transverse bars. The walking-out dress shoulder-strap carries a service emblem below the button for all arms of the service except infantry, and the number, etc. of his unit as worn by all ranks.

WALKING-OUT DRESS

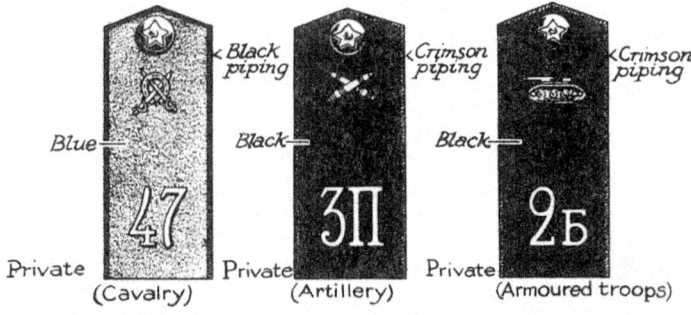

Private (Cavalry)   Private (Artillery)   Private (Armoured troops)

The field dress shoulder-strap is of khaki colouring with piping coloured according to the individual arm of the service.

Piping colours for field dress

FIELD DRESS

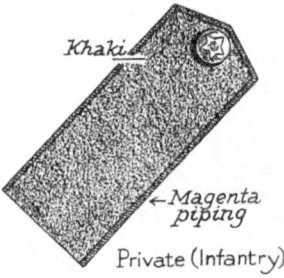

Private (Infantry)

Infantry	-	Magenta
Artillery	-	Crimson
Armoured troops	-	Crimson
Air force	-	Sky blue
Cavalry	-	Blue
Technical troops	-	Black
Medical and Veterinary	-	Dark green

Shoulder-straps — Quizz

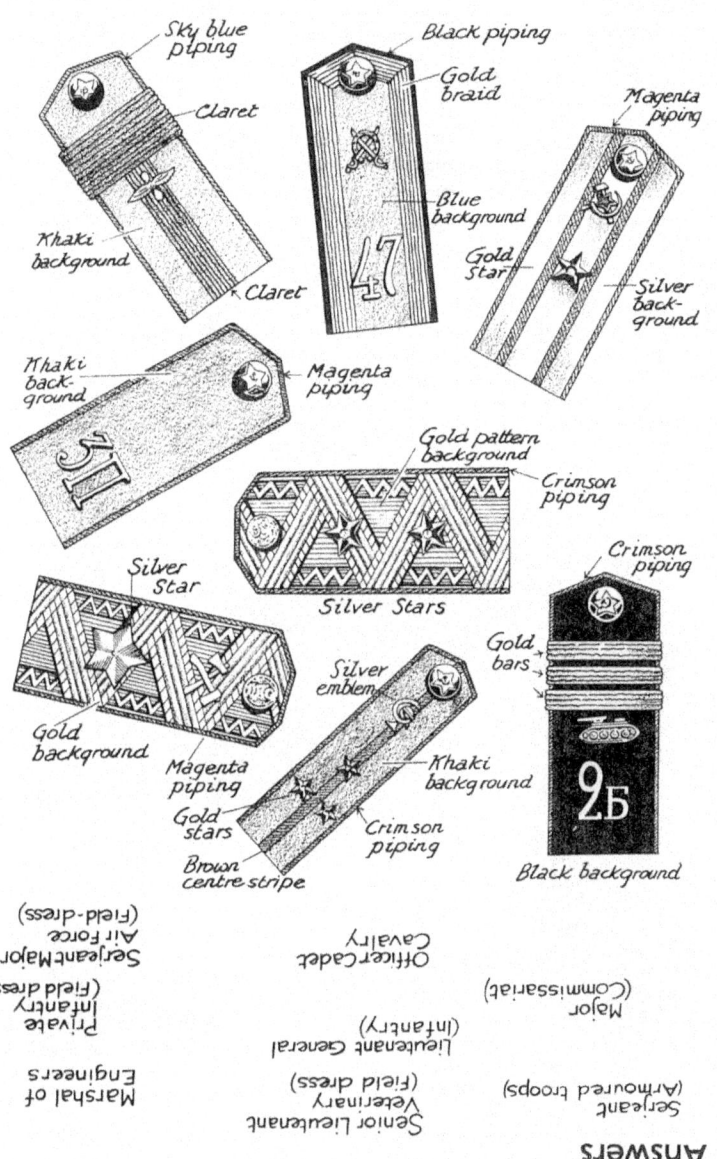

Answers

Marshal of Engineers

Private Infantry (Field dress)

Serjeant Major Air Force (Field-dress)

Senior Lieutenant Veterinary (Field dress)

Lieutenant General (Infantry)

Officer Cadet Cavalry

Serjeant (Armoured troops)

Major (Commissariat)

3. Tunics and breeches

The uniform for all ranks has undergone the following main change:

The collar is now of a close-fitting stand-up pattern, instead of the turned-down kind previously worn. Generally speaking the jacket is of two types, the tunic and the blouse. In the field the blouse is normally worn. The tunic is worn mainly by higher ranks and on the more formal occasions. A complete issue has not yet been made to all ranks. The blouse is fashioned according to the traditional Russian blouse fastened at the neck by two small buttons. It is a loose garment of khaki colour worn outside the breeches and caught in at the waist by a belt. Except on certain parade occasions breeches are worn by all ranks of the Red Army. Marshals and Generals wear two wide coloured stripes down the sides.

TUNIC, HIGHER RANKS

FORMAL OCCASIONS

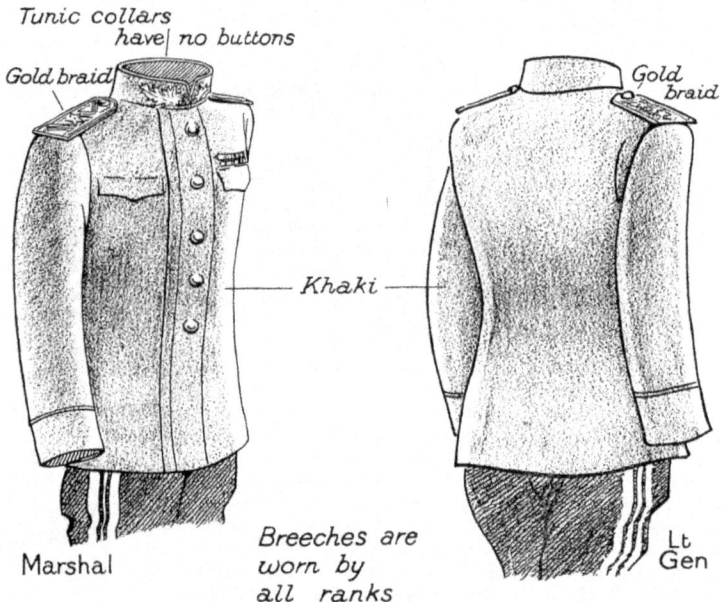

Two wide stripes indicate Marshal or General

Senior and Junior officers wear a blouse with a Sam Browne belt both for walking out and in the field.

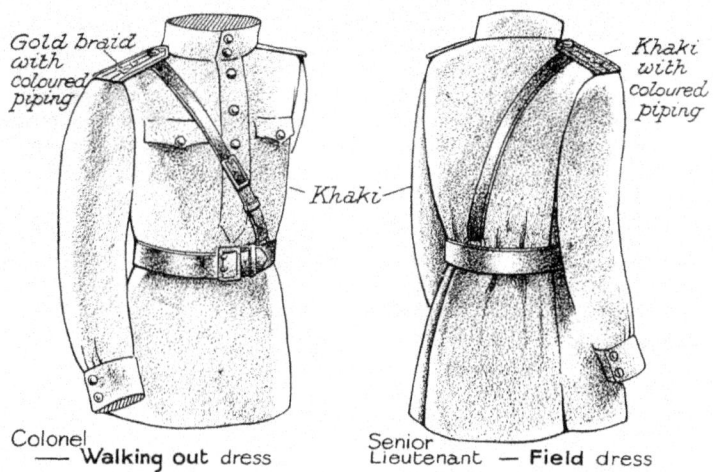

Colonel — **Walking out** dress

Senior Lieutenant — **Field** dress

The serjeant and private categories likewise wear the blouse but do not wear the Sam Browne.

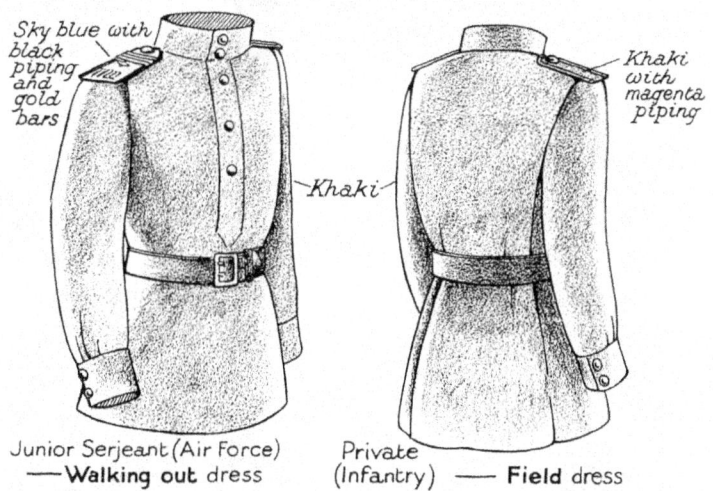

Junior Serjeant (Air Force) — **Walking out** dress

Private (Infantry) — **Field** dress

Note:
Eventually all the above will be equipped with tunics for walking out as worn by higher ranks.

4. Greatcoats

(a) Walking-out dress

These carry the same shoulder-strap as on the walking-out dress uniform, and have large buttons of gold with the national crest for marshals and generals, gold-plated with the star and hammer and sickle for other officers, and of brass with the star and hammer and sickle for other ranks. Tabs are worn on the collar-flaps with a large button on the top end. They are coloured and piped according to the arm of service of the wearer.

(b) Field dress

Shoulder-straps as on the field dress uniform. All buttons are of khaki colouring. The tabs are khaki-coloured, piped according to the coloured piping on the shoulder-strap, except for marshals and generals, where the piping is silver or gold thread.

ALL RANKS   WALKING-OUT DRESS

ALL RANKS   FIELD DRESS

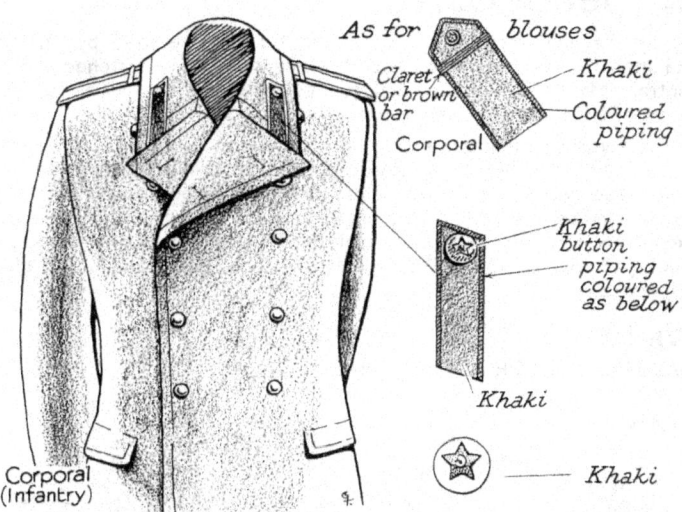

Significance of colours on greatcoat tabs

RANK	ARM OF SERVICE	COLOUR OF BACKGROUND	COLOUR OF PIPING
All Marshals and Generals		Crimson	Gold thread
Except	Artillery and armoured troops	Black	Gold thread
	Aviation	Sky blue	Gold thread
	Technical & commissariat	Magenta	Gold thread
	Medical and veterinary	Dark green	Silver thread
All Ranks — Colonel to Red Army Man	Infantry	Magenta	Black
	Artillery	Black velvet	Crimson
	Armoured troops	Black velvet	Crimson
	Air Force	Sky blue	Black
	Cavalry	Blue	Black
	Engineer & technical	Black	Black
	Commissariat	Magenta	Black
	Medical & veterinary	Dark green	Crimson
	Judicial service	Magenta	Black

Note: In the field the background is Khaki for all ranks

5. Headgear

During the winter months, a variety of fur hats are worn by officers and men of the Red Army, with the red star badge fastened in the centre. Marshals, generals, and full colonels wear a special tall hat made of light grey astrakhan fur.

In the summer months service caps are worn. They are somewhat smaller than the British service-cap with a small black patent leather peak. The colours of the covering, band and piping all vary with the arms of the service. Most caps are of either a brown or a grey colour, except for those worn by troops of the Frontier Guard and the home security troops of the NKVD, which are bright green and bright blue respectively.

Winter
MARSHALS, GENERALS AND FULL COLONELS

ALL RANKS BELOW THIS

Summer
WORN BY ALL RANKS

Service Cap

The Red Army Steel Helmet

Marshals and Generals — Service caps

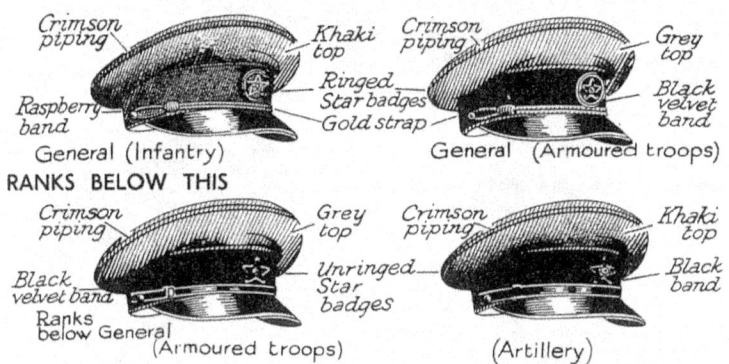

General (Infantry) General (Armoured troops)
RANKS BELOW THIS

(Armoured troops) (Artillery)

Significance of colours

Arm of service	Band	Piping	Material
Infantry	Raspberry	Raspberry	Khaki
Armoured troops	Black velvet	Crimson	Grey
Artillery	Black	Crimson	Khaki
Engineers	Black	Blue	Khaki
Cavalry	Blue	Black	Khaki
Don Cossacks	Crimson	Crimson	Blue-grey
Kuban and Terek Cossacks	Blue	Crimson	Khaki

Sidecap made on the lines of our service forage cap

Khaki

Worn mainly by lower ranks

6. N.K.V.D. Troops

(a) Home Security troops

In general these troops wear Red Army uniform and badges of rank, but with distinctions as described below.

SHOULDER - STRAPS:

(Generals) The gold criss-cross pattern is picked out in blue. Blue piping.

(Officers) Both centre stripes and piping are blue. It should be noted that neither change according to the service-arm of the wearer, which is shown only by the service emblem. Emblems are the same as those of Red Army, except that the old infantry emblem (crossed rifles on a target), which the Red Army no longer wears, has been conserved by home security troops.

(Other ranks) The background colour is red with blue piping. The transverse bars for N.C.O's are gold or silver.

GREATCOAT TABS:

(Generals) Blue with gold piping.

(Officers and other ranks) Blue with red piping.

Home security troops are easily distinguished by their bright blue service cap with a red band.

(b) Frontier guards

These troops are distinguished by the bright green hats, and the green piping and green centre stripes to the shoulder-straps of officers. Other ranks have green shoulder-straps, and N.C.O's wear gold or silver cross bars. Greatcoat tabs are green. Emblems are similar to those worn by home security troops.

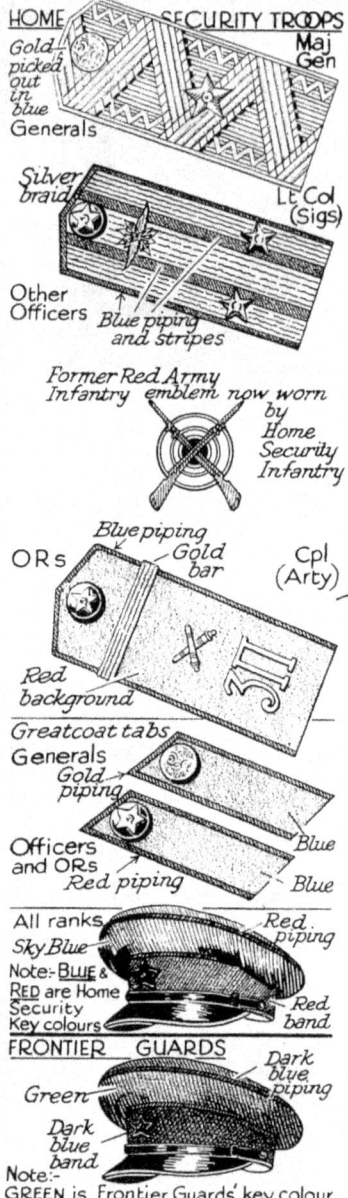

B. INSIGNIA

1. Marshal's Star

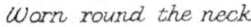
Worn round the neck

This decoration was instituted in September 1940. It consists of a 5 pointed gold star, inset with a platinum star, and mounted with diamonds totalling 6·9 carats in weight. Diameter of gold star — 44·5 mm. This decoration is worn round the neck, and is mounted on red moiré ribbon. (For chief marshals and service marshals the colour of the ribbon varies according to their particular service colour).

Note to following 2 paras:—

On 20 Jun 43 the Soviet press published the particulars of a new decree dated 19 Jun 43 confirming the future wearing of order and medal ribbons, as practised by other armies. The decree also established the order of precedence for all decorations, and gave full descriptions of all the new ribbons. Formerly all orders and medals were worn under all conditions on all types of uniform excluding greatcoats, winter fur coats etc etc.

Descriptions of all Soviet decorations are given below—the more recently-created ones in detail—in what is believed to be the accepted order of precedence.

2. Orders
"Gold Star" Medal

This is awarded with the title HERO OF THE SOVIET UNION, together with the Order of Lenin which is awarded automatically. It is the equivalent of our V.C. and has no separate ribbon, both star and ribbon being worn on all occasions on the left breast above all other decorations. It is awarded to all ranks. It carries with it a small life pension and the wearer is entitled to free transport by tram and underground throughout the country. 3,617 officers and men have received this award during the present war.

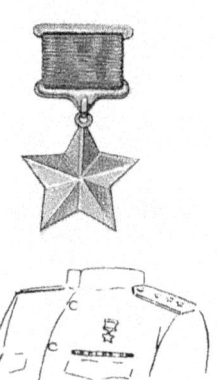

23

Orders — continued
"Hammer and Sickle" Medal

This is awarded with the title HERO OF SOCIALIST LABOUR, and ranks in precedence with the above medal and fulfils the same conditions as above. It is, however, a civil rather than a military decoration. N.B. Both the above Medals rank as Orders.

Worn on left breast

Order of "Victory" Medal

This Order was created during the present war by a decree dated 8 Nov 43. It is the highest military decoration for members of the higher commanding personnel of the Red Army, for successful execution of such military operations on the scale of one or several fronts as result in a radical change of the situation to the enemy's disadvantage. The Order consists of a five-pointed ruby star inset with 91 diamonds. In the centre is a circle of blue enamel bordered with a wreath of laurel and oak leaves. In the centre of the circle is the image of the Kremlin Wall with the Lenin Mausoleum and the Spasskaya Tower. The Order is made of platinum — total weight of diamonds —16 carats. A Roll of Honour inscribed with the names of the recipients is to be set up in the Grand Kremlin Palace. The Order is worn on the left breast 12-14 cms. above the belt. There is no ribbon.

Order of Lenin

This Order corresponds to our D.S.O. but is awarded to bodies and associations as well as to individuals, for notable achievements in any spheres of national activity. It is awarded automatically to recipients of the "Gold Star" and "Hammer and Sickle" Medals. Its ribbon colours are red and gold.

Worn on left breast

Order of the Red Banner

One of the oldest Soviet decorations. It is awarded as above to individuals and associations, and also, in recent months, to units in the field which have distinguished themselves in the capture of more than one important town. Ribbon colours — red and white.

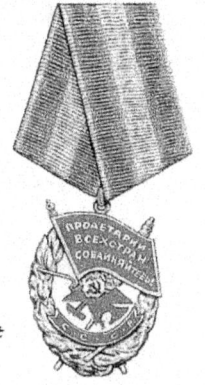

Worn on left breast

Orders of Suvorov

Worn on breast *right*

Class I

These orders were created during the present war by Decree dated 29 Jul 42. They are awarded in three classes, for the direction of successful operations in the field.

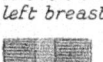

Ribbon on left breast

Class I

Class I. in platinum — to commanders of fronts and armies, their deputies and chiefs of staff.

Class II. in gold — to commanders of corps, divisions and brigades, their deputies and chiefs of staff.

Class II

Class III. in silver — to commanders of regiments, battalions and regimental chiefs of staff.

Class II

The orders themselves are worn on the right breast: the ribbons in order of precedence on the left breast. Ribbon colours — green and orange.

Class III

(Note: General Suvorov distinguished himself in the reign of Catherine the Great in wars against Turkey and Prussia and later against the French. One of his outstanding achievements was the crossing of the Alps by his army in 1799).

Class III

Orders of Kutuzov

Orders on

Class I

right breast

Class II

Created by the same decree as above in two classes—Class I. in gold, Class II. in silver with gilded centre (Class III. in silver was created by decree dated 8 Feb 43). Conditions and wearing of award exactly as those of Suvorov. Ribbon colours — dark blue and orange. (See Diagram B).

(Note: General Kutuzov commanded the Russian Armies in the Napoleonic Campaign of 1812).

Ribbons on

Class I
left breast

Class II

Class III

Orders of Bogdan Khmelnitsky

Class I

Class II

Class III

These Orders were also created during the present war by a decree dated 10 Oct 43. There are three classes distributed as follows:

Class I. — in gold — awarded to front, fleet (Red Navy), army, and flotilla (Red Navy), commanders. Their deputies, chief of staff and operational staff officers, and to partisan formation commanders.

Class II. — in silver — awarded to corps, divisional, brigade, and regimental commanders. Their deputies and chiefs of staff; and to partisan formation commanders and their chiefs of staff, and to partisan leaders.

Class III. — in silver — awarded to (Separate Order) all non-commissioned ranks and officers up to and including battalion commanders and their subordinates; and to leaders of small partisan units and to partisans.

These orders are worn on the right breast. The ribbons on the left breast. Ribbon colours — light blue and white.

(Note: Bogdan Khmelnitsky was a Ukrainian who, in 1648, led a series of successful revolts against Polish domination).

N.B. In the order of precedence for the Orders of Suvorov, Kutuzov, and Bogdan Khmelnitsky, Kutuzov Class I. ranks above Suvorov Class II. Bogdan Khmelnitsky Class I. above Kutuzov Class II. etc.

Class I

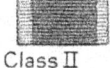

Class II

Class III

Order of Alexander Nevsky

This order was also created by the Decree of 29 Jul 42. It is awarded to regimental, battalion, company and platoon commanders who have shown personal courage and daring, combined with able leadership in battle resulting in successful operations by their unit. It is worn on the right breast; the ribbon on the left. Ribbon colours — azure and red.

Right breast

Ribbon on left breast

Orders of the War for the Fatherland

These orders were created in the early stages of the present war. There are two classes. The orders are worn on the right breast, the ribbons on the left breast. Ribbon colours — claret and red.

Right breast

Class I

Class II
Ribbons on left breast

Order of the Red Banner of Labour

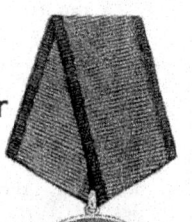

This order is primarily civil. It is worn on the left breast. Ribbon colour — dark blue and blue.

Worn on left breast

Order of the Red Star

This order existed before the present war. It is worn on the right breast, the ribbon on the left breast. Ribbon colour — claret and grey.

Right breast

Ribbon on left breast

Order of the Badge of Honour

Primarily civil award. Worn on the left breast. Ribbon colour — pink and orange.

Worn on left breast

Orders of "Glory"

These orders were created by the decree dated 8 Nov 43, at the same time as the "Victory" Order (i.e., consequent upon the successes of the summer and autumn offensives of the same year). They are the lowest-ranking orders, and are awarded to privates, N.C.Os., and warrant officers, and (in the Air Force) to junior lieutenants. Generally speaking, they are given for deeds of personal valour. There are three classes of this Order.

Class I. — in gold. Awarded only by the Praesidium of the Supreme Soviet. Recipient is entitled to 15 roubles a month for life.

Class II. — in silver with gilt centre. May be awarded by front and army commanders. Recipient is entitled to 10 roubles a month for life.

Class III. — in silver. May be awarded by corps and divisional commanders. Recipient is entitled to 5 roubles a month for life.

The following privileges are also accorded: those holding the rank of private, corporal, or serjeant promotion to serjeant major; those holding the rank of serjeant major promotion to junior lieutenant; those holding the rank of junior lieutenant promotion to lieutenant.

Free education of all children in intermediate and higher educational establishments.

The orders and ribbons are worn on the left breast, to the right of all medals or medal ribbons. Ribbon colours — black and orange.

(Note: The ribbon for the Order of "Glory" is identical with the Tsarist Order of the Cross of St. George, of which the highest class was then the rough equivalent of our V.C.).

left breast

Obverse

Class I

Class II
Silver with gilt centre

Class III
All silver

3. Medals

All worn on left breast

Medal "For Valour"

Awarded to service personnel of all ranks for personal bravery. Recipients receive a pension of 10 roubles a month and have a right of free travel on the tramways. It is worn on the left breast. Ribbon colours — dark blue and grey.

Medal "For Distinguished Services"

Awarded to military or civilian personnel for distinguished services in a war area or in the struggle with Diversionists and spies. Recipients receive a pension of 5 roubles a month and have a right of free travel on the tramways. It is worn on the left breast. Ribbon colours — gold and grey.

Medal "20 years in the Red Army"

This is the Soviet equivalent of the Tsarist decoration of "Vladimir Class III." for length of service. Worn on the left breast. Ribbon colours — red and grey.

Medal "For Valiant Labour"

Primarily a civil award. Worn on the left breast. Ribbon colours — red and lilac.

Medal "For Distinctive Labour"

Primarily a civil award. Worn on the left breast. Ribbon colours — gold and lilac.

Left breast

Medal "To a Partisan of the War for the Fatherland"

Right breast
Class I
Class II ——— Obverse

This medal was created during the present war by a Decree dated 2 Feb 43. It may be awarded by Commanders of the partisan G.H.Q. to members of partisan detachments. There are two classes, Class I. — in silver, Class II. — in bronze. The medals are worn on the right breast, the ribbons on the left breast.
Ribbon colours:
Class I. — light green and red.
Class II.—light green and dark blue.

Left breast
Class I

Left breast
Class II

Medal "For the Defence of Leningrad"

Service medal of this war. Awarded to all participants irrespective of rank. The medal in bronze, is worn on the left breast. Ribbon colours — olive and green.

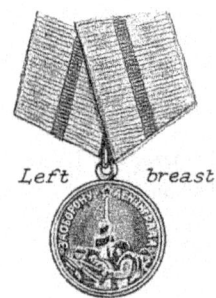
Left breast

Medals *All on this page are worn on the left breast*

"For the Defence of Moscow"

Ribbon colours—
   olive and red.

"For the Defence of Odessa"

Ribbon colours—
   olive and azure.

"For the Defence of Sevastopol"

Ribbon colours—olive and dark blue.

"For the Defence of Stalingrad"

Ribbon colours — olive and red.

"For the Defence of the Caucasus"

Ribbon colours — olive and dark blue.

All the above are service medals of this war. Awarded to all participants irrespective of rank. The medals are in bronze and are worn on the left breast.

Precedence of "Defence" medals is not known.

4. Badges

"Guards" Badge

This badge was instituted in 1941 for units which distinguished themselves in active operations and were then renamed Guards Units (N.B. It is believed that these units receive double pay). The badge

 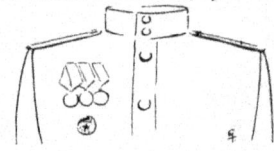

Worn on right breast below other decorations

consists of a metal disc bearing the gilt word ГВАРДИЯ (GUARDS) on the background of a red banner. It is worn by all ranks on all uniforms (including greatcoats on ceremonial occasions), on the right below other decorations.

Wound Badges

Created during the present war. They are classified into "heavy" and "light" wounds — to be determined by Medical Service officers. They are worn on the right breast above other decorations, and consist of coloured strips of material, laid down to be of silk braid, but usually, like the British "flashes" of coloured felt; a gold (yellow) strip signifying a heavy wound and a red strip a light one. When both are worn, the gold strip is sewn above the red.

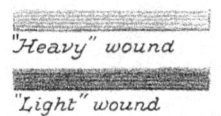

"Heavy" wound

"Light" wound

"Distinguished" Badges

Distinguished Scout

On right breast

These metal badges were instituted during the period Nov 42 — Mar 43, to be worn by NCO's and Ptes. whose work and behaviour is considered to be sufficiently deserving. They are worn on the right breast — below the Guards badge, if the wearer is a Guardsman. There is no ribbon. There are various badges of this sort, such as: ОТЛИЧНЫЙ ПОВАР (DISTINGUISHED COOK), ОТЛИЧНИК САНИТАРНОЙ СЛУЖБЫ (DISTINGUISHED SANITARY MAN) etc. etc. and ОТЛИЧНЫЙ РАЗВЕДЧИК (DISTINGUISHED SCOUT).

Examples of the wearing of Insignia

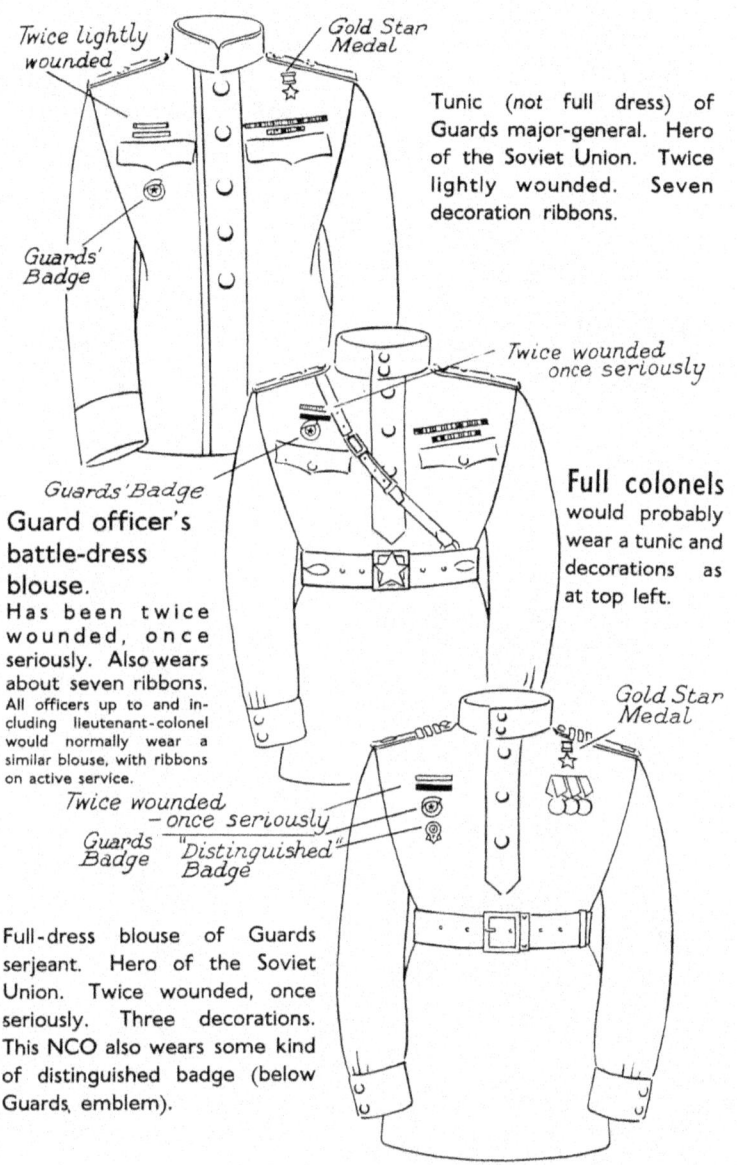

Tunic (*not* full dress) of Guards major-general. Hero of the Soviet Union. Twice lightly wounded. Seven decoration ribbons.

Full colonels would probably wear a tunic and decorations as at top left.

Guard officer's battle-dress blouse.
Has been twice wounded, once seriously. Also wears about seven ribbons. All officers up to and including lieutenant-colonel would normally wear a similar blouse, with ribbons on active service.

Full-dress blouse of Guards serjeant. Hero of the Soviet Union. Twice wounded, once seriously. Three decorations. This NCO also wears some kind of distinguished badge (below Guards, emblem).

Examples of Insignia on greatcoats

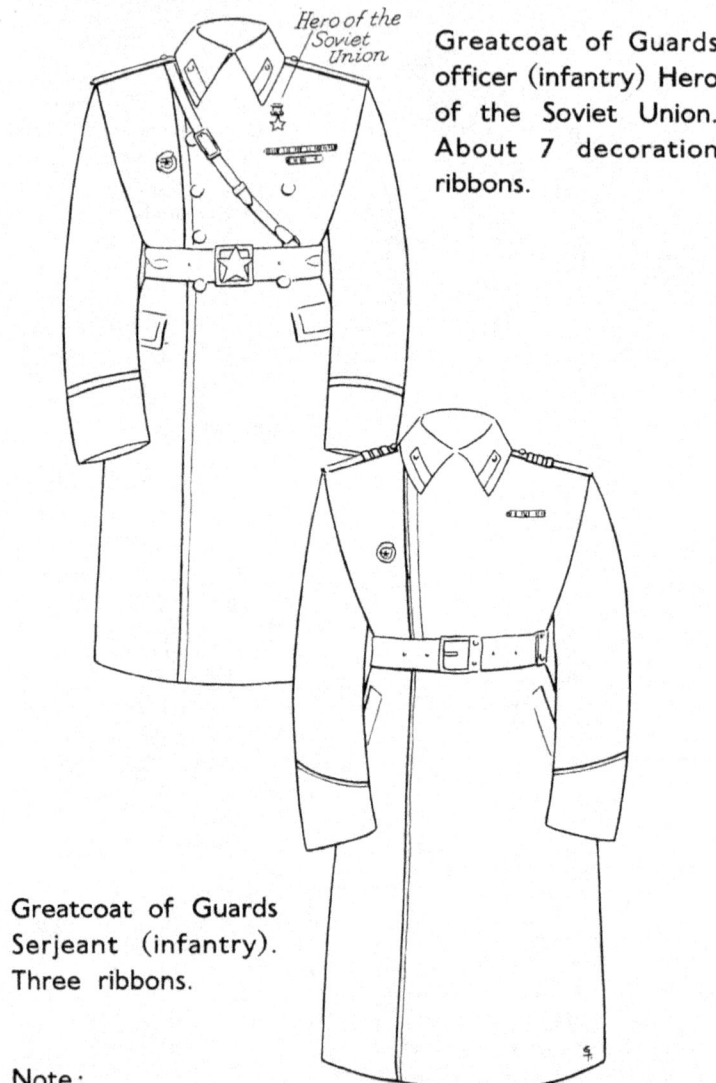

Greatcoat of Guards officer (infantry) Hero of the Soviet Union. About 7 decoration ribbons.

Greatcoat of Guards Serjeant (infantry). Three ribbons.

Note:
Generally speaking, order and medal ribbons are now to be worn by the Red Army in the same way as by the British. The ribbons themselves, however, are shorter and wider than ours.

Standard awarded to 112 Infantry Regiment

5. Honorary Arms and Standards

Honorary standards of red silk and gold embroidery are conferred upon units which have distinguished themselves in the field, usually when they are awarded Guards status or an order. These standards are inscribed with the particulars of the unit, battle honours, etc. Honorary arms are awarded to higher commanders for distinguished military operations.

www.ingramcontent.com/pod-product-compliance
Lightning Source LLC
Chambersburg PA
CBHW070714160426
43192CB00009B/1190